1 MONTH OF
FREE
READING

at

www.ForgottenBooks.com

By purchasing this book you are eligible for one month membership to ForgottenBooks.com, giving you unlimited access to our entire collection of over 1,000,000 titles via our web site and mobile apps.

To claim your free month visit:

www.forgottenbooks.com/free873085

ISBN 978-0-266-59696-7
PIBN 10873085

EVIDENCE

FOR

THE UNITED STATES

IN THE MATTER OF THE CLAIM OF THE

Puget's Sound Agricultural Company,

PENDING BEFORE THE

BRITISH AND AMERICAN JOINT COMMISSION,

FOR THE

FINAL SETTLEMENT OF THE CLAIMS

OF THE

HUDSON'S BAY AND PUGET'S SOUND AGRICULTURAL COMPANIES.

[Papers. v. 10]

———— •••• ————

WASHINGTON CITY:

M'GILL & WITHEROW, PRINTERS AND STEREOTYPERS.

INDEX OF WITNESSES.

	PAGE.
Allen, Edward J	297
Alvord, Benjamin	265
Applegate, Jesse.	11
Bradley, John	140
Burge, Andrew J	104
Carson, John C	44
Casey, Silas.	194
Chambers, Thomas M	127
Chapman, H. L.	96
Chapman, John B	145
Clarke, Frederick A.	89
Davidson, George	269
Dement, John D	3
Denny, Arthur A.	163
Dougherty, William P.	101
Gardner, Charles T	261
Gibbs, George	312
Goldsborough, Hugh A	173
Hewitt, C. C.	69
Hewitt, R. H	93
Hill, Bennett H.	204
Kautz, August V	215
Lane, Daniel E	133
Lee, George W.	287
Light, Erastus A	120
McDonald, J. L	122
McKibbin, David B.	157
McMurtrie, William B	296
Miller, William W.	74
Mogk, Maximilian	271
More, R. S	116
Moses, Simpson P	247
Rinearson, Jacob S	59
Shazer, George W	118
Suckley, George	166, 348
Wilkes, Charles	228
Williamson, James E	110
Wirtz, Horace R	184

ERRATA.

Page 325, Int. 19, for "January" read "February."

Page 334, Ans. to Int. 70, for "the winter of" read "July."

BRITISH AND AMERICAN JOINT COMMISSION

UPON THE CLAIMS OF THE

HUDSON'S BAY AND PUGET'S SOUND AGRICULTURAL COMPANIES' CLAIMS.

––––––– ◆■▶ –––––––

In the matter of the Claim of the Puget's Sound Agricultural Company vs. the United States.

DEPOSITION of a witness [in behalf of the United States] sworn and examined before me, Ralph Wilcox, clerk of the district court of the United States for the district of Oregon, by virtue of a verbal agreement made and entered into between W. C. Johnson, Esq., as counsel for the United States of America, and Amory Holbrook, Esq., as counsel for the Puget's Sound Agricultural Company.

TESTIMONY OF JOHN H. DEMENT.

John H. Dement being first duly sworn, deposes and testifies as follows:

Int. 1.—State your age, residence, and occupation.

Ans.—Age, forty-two; residence, Portland; I am not engaged in business now; I have been engaged in merchandising several years.

Int. 2.—Were you ever in the U. S. Army? If so, in what rank, and how many years?

Ans.—I was eight years in the service, and left it with the rank of first lieutenant.

Int. 3.—During that time, were you stationed on the Puget's Sound Agricultural Company claim at Nisqually? If so, at what time, and how long?

Ans.—I went there in the fall of 1849, and left in the spring of 1853.

Cross-examination by A. Holbrook, Esq.

Int. 1.—Have you seen, or had your attention particularly called to the value and condition of the Puget's Sound Company's property for more than thirteen years?

Ans.—I have not.

Int. 2.—Is not your recollection necessarily indistinct in regard to the condition of the property, so long ago?

Ans.—It may be in regard to the improvements, but not to the quality of the soil.

Int. 3.—Did not that land have an especial value for purposes of pasturage?

Ans.—I never heard of any especial value; it is better adapted to that purpose than any other.

Int. 4.—At the time you were there, did not the Company have several thousand sheep grazing upon it?

Ans.—I think they had.

Int. 5.—Were there not also several thousand horned cattle?

Ans.—I don't know the number they had, but never supposed they had to exceed a thousand, or so.

Int. 6.—Were there not also a thousand horses, or more?

Ans.—I don't know what horses they had—quite a large number.

Int. 7.—Is there any such land, so well situated for stock-raising, on the shores of Puget's Sound?

Ans.—I think that is equal to any, taking into consideration the extent; there were other lands more fertile, and had more grass, but not so extensive.

Int. 8.—Are there any other lands north of it, suitable for pasturage or stock-raising?

Ans.—Very little.

Int. 9.—Is not the land of the Company the proper outlet for the products of the country lying south of it, as well as for stock raised in Washington Territory and Oregon, to be shipped to Victoria and British Columbia?

Ans.—There are other outlets, but I think this is the most convenient.

Int. 10.—Are not these lands of great value for temporary pasturage of stock driven from Oregon and other points south that it may be recruited before being shipped to a market?

Ans.—They are useful for that purpose, but unless the pasturage has improved very much since I saw it last, it would not be very valuable for that purpose.

Int. 11.—Is there any other land which could be used for that purpose?

Ans.—I know of none immediately upon the Sound, but there are lands some few miles back that would answer the purpose.

Int. 12.—In what direction do these lands lie, and how extensive?

Ans.—They lie south, and extensive enough for the purpose mentioned.

Int. 13.—Did not the Company between 1849 and 1853 frequently ship cattle, sheep, and horses to Victoria, by their own and chartered vessels?

Ans.—I believe they did.

Int. 14.—Did not the Company's land in 1849 and 1850 seem to be fully stocked, and even more than fully?

Ans.—I think it was overstocked, taking into consideration the quality of the land.

Int. 15.—Would not the Company's lands, if in their free and undisturbed possession and fully stocked, in view of the population on Puget's Sound, Vancouver's Island, and British Columbia, yearly increasing since 1850, have paid in profits a fair interest on a larger valuation of the land than you have given?

Ans.—Not knowing what the increase of population and demand has been, I cannot say.

Int. 16.—If the Company alone, had had to do with their own cattle, do you think they would have been less wild?

Ans.—I think they were no more wild when I left, than when I went there; I don't remember their being molested by any one except the Company.

Int. 17.—Did you ever know any foot-traveller being disturbed or injured by them?

Ans.—I have no recollection of any foot-traveller being disturbed or injured by them.

Int. 18.—Have you not repeatedly seen cattle lying on the prairie, and remaining in that position without moving, when horsemen rode among them or passed them?

Ans.—I have seen them lying, and have passed them without their getting up.

Int. 19.—Do you remember seeing large cattle corrals in various parts of the land claimed by the Company?

Ans.—I do not; I have seen sheep enclosures.

Int. 20.—Were you in the way of seeing or knowing what settlers in the remote parts of the Company's claim did to the Company's cattle?

Ans.—Nothing except from rumor.

Int. 21.—Were there not in 1849 a large number of tame cattle on the Steilacoom plain, near Fort Steilacoom, belonging to the Company?

Ans.—I remember there were some; but what number, I have no idea.

Int. 22.—State what, in your judgment, was the value of the buildings used as Fort Steilacoom, and of the enclosures around it?

Ans.—In all some seven or eight buildings, including sheds; I suppose they were worth four or five thousand dollars.

Int. 23.—Were there not other buildings on the Company's land, besides those at Nisqually and Steilacoom?

Ans.—There were.

Int. 24.—Please state where and what, as near as you recollect; with their value.

Ans.—There was a house two or three miles from the post, occupied by one of the servants of the Company, two others, also occupied by Company's servants; the value of which I have no idea.

Int. 25.—What quantity of stock could be subsisted on all the pasture lands outside the Company's claim, within forty miles, for the year round?

Ans.—I am unable to say, I never considered it with that view.

Int. 26.—Are there any pasture lands except those, of the Company, nearer than fifteen miles of the place of shipment at Steilacoom?

Ans.—I think there are none except some islands in the Sound.

Int. 27.—During the time you were at Steilacoom, was not the killing of the Company's cattle by unauthorized persons a matter of common and general conversation and joke?

Ans.—I heard something said about it, but I don't know that it was a subject of general talk.

Int. 28.—In making your estimate of the land, did you consider only its condition from 1849 to 1853, or did you have in mind the development of the country, the building of towns, the erection of mills, and other improvements in that section, during the last twelve years?

Ans.—I considered the condition from 1849 to 1853 only.

Direct Examination resumed by W. C. Johnson.

Int. 1.—Whose property were the buildings at Fort Steilacoom, when you first went there, according to your understanding?

Ans.—We rented the buildings from Dr. Tolmie, and supposed they were owned by the Puget's Sound Agricultural Company. I understood, afterwards, that they were erected by a Mr. Heath, who died there, and was not in any way connected with the Company.

Question by Mr. Holbrook.

Int. 1.—Did you not also hear that Mr. Heath was farming on shares for the Company, and that the Company had furnished him means to erect buildings?

Ans.—I may have heard that, but I don't remember now; I have some indistinct recollection of it.

2 P

Int. 2.—Was not the Company in possession of the post when it was leased to the United States Government?

Ans.—I believe it was. This was after Heath's death.

JOHN D. DEMENT.

Portland, July 27, 1866.

UNITED STATES OF AMERICA,
  District of Oregon, ss.

I, Ralph Wilcox, clerk of the district court of the United States for the district of Oregon, do hereby certify that the foregoing deposition, hereto annexed, of John D. Dement, a witness produced by and on behalf of the United States, in the matter of the claim of the Puget's Sound Agricultural Company against the United States, before the British and American Joint Commission for the adjustment of the same, was taken before me, at my office, in the city of Portland, district of Oregon, and reduced to writing by myself, in the presence of W. C. Johnson, Esq., attorney for the United States, and Amory Holbrook, Esq., attorney for the Puget's Sound Agricultural Company, on the 27th day of July, A. D. 1866, according to the date appended to said deposition when the same was signed; and I further certify that to said witness, before examination, I administered the following oath: "You do solemnly swear that the evidence which you shall give in the matter of the claim of the Puget's Sound Agricultural Company against the United States shall be the truth, the whole truth, and nothing but the truth, so help you God;" that after the same was reduced to writing, the deposition was carefully read to said witness, and thereupon signed by him in my presence.

In testimony whereof, I have hereunto set my hand and [L. S.] affixed the seal of said Court, this ninth day of August, A. D. 1866.

RALPH WILCOX, *Clerk.*

BRITISH AND AMERICAN JOINT COMMISSION

UPON THE CLAIMS OF THE

HUDSON'S BAY AND PUGET'S SOUND AGRICULTURAL COMPANIES' CLAIMS.

—◆—

In the matter of the Claim of the Puget's Sound Agricultural Company vs. the United States.

Depositions of witnesses produced in behalf of the United States, taken before me, J. M. Bacon, county clerk of Clackamas county, Oregon, at Oregon City, in said county, in pursuance of a verbal agreement made in my presence by W. C. Johnson, Esq., attorney for the United States, and Frank Clark, Esq., attorney for the Puget's Sound Agricultural Company.

TESTIMONY OF JESSE APPLEGATE.

Jesse Applegate being first duly sworn, deposeth and says :

Int. 1.—State your age, residence, and occupation.

Ans.—Age, fifty-five years ; residence, Yoncalla, Douglas county ; farmer.

Int. 2.—Have you any other profession ? If so, state what it is ?

Ans.—I was in early life a surveyor and civil engineer.

Int. 3.—How long have you resided in Oregon?

Ans.—Twenty-three years next November.

Int. 4.—Have you examined the lands and other property claimed by the Puget's Sound Agricultural Company, north of the Columbia river ? It so, state when, in connection with whom, and under whose instruction? (The last two clauses objected to as irrelevant and immaterial.)

Ans.—I have examined certain property claimed by the

Puget's Sound Agricultural Company, in company with J. S. Rinearson and J. C. Carson, under instructions from W. C. Johnson, attorney on the part of the United States, immediately prior to the 20th day of August, 1866, at which time, in connection with the two gentlemen named, I agreed in the report. (So much of the foregoing answer as follows after 1866, is objected to, because it is not responsive to the question, and because it is immaterial and irrelevant; the agreement of a witness to a report in regard to facts, which must be proved by him, by his testimony, at this time being immaterial and incompetent evidence.)

Int. 5.—Have you made, in connection with the gentlemen named, a statement in writing of your estimate of values resulting from this examination? If so, please now present it, and make it a part of your deposition. (Question objected to by counsel for the Company, as irrelevant and immaterial, and the introduction of the report objected to as incompetent and unauthorized by law. Counsel for the Company also enter their protest and object to this mode of examination of witness, because the same is unauthorized by law, and claim that the witness should be particularly inquired of in reference to all matters testified to by him, so that an opportunity may be given to interpose objections to the questions of counsel, and the answers of the witness so far as the same may be incompetent, irrelevant, and immaterial.)

Ans.—I have, and submit the report marked " G." (Counsel for the United States now tenders to the counsel for the Company the examination of the written statement, referred to in the foregoing answer, so that they may object, if they desire, to anything therein that is illegal or improper.)

(Counsel for the Company insists that if the paper, termed the report, is to be used in any respect as testimony of this witness, it shall be written out in full as his evidence in this deposition, the same being neither an exhibit or a document, capable of being introduced as such, but simply the written statement of the witness and of other parties.)

To Hon. W. C. JOHNSON, *Attorney, &c.:*

SIR: Having inspected the farms and lands now in possession of the Puget's Sound Agricultural Company, in the Territory of Washington, we report upon—

FIRST—"THE COWLITZ FARM."

This possession is on or near the right bank of the Cowlitz river, in Lewis county, Washington Territory. The land in undisputed possession of the Puget's Sound Agricultural Company, and occupied and cultivated by Mr. Roberts, their agent, amounts to about one hundred and sixty six acres; the soil is of good quality, being in most places loam upon a sub-soil of clay; water-polished or rolled stones, everywhere in the middle section of Washington Territory, cropping out only upon points where the winter freshets have removed or prevented the accumulation of soil. Most of the land within the enclosures of the Puget's Sound Agricultural Company, at Cowlitz, seems to have been a long time cultivated, without any attention having been given to the preservation or renovation of the soil, for which reason, the crops upon it are light compared with those upon like soils in the Willamette Valley, and the grazing in the pastures, as well as on the "common," is greatly injured by the growth of sorrel and the untimely and excessive grazing to which it has been subjected. For these and other reasons which temporarily effect the value of real estate in that vicinity, we think the recent sales of real estate on Cowlitz prairie would indicate a lower value to land, exclusive of improvements, than we, in view of its quality and location, would fix upon it. We think the land included by the enclosures of the Puget's Sound Agricultural Company and of the like quality in the vicinity, worth five dollars per acre. The fencing, except a part enclosing a meadow on the west side, is in tolerably good repair; it is of the Virginia, or worm fence description; the rails are mostly old, and around the meadow above referred to, is not in repair. From the price of labor and convenience of material, a worm fence with twenty rails to the rod would cost about eighty cents per rod on Cowlitz prairie. We think the Puget's Sound Agricultural Company's fencing, on an average, worth half as much as a new fence.

The buildings are of the description and values following, to wit:

1st. A dwelling-house 33 by 43 feet, fourteen feet high, in seven rooms, has two fire-places, and Mr. Roberts says was built in 1838; it is in bad order, and the wood exposed to the weather much decayed; value $500.

2d. Kitchen in rear of the house, 16 by 18 feet, and ten feet high, in a state of decay; value $100.

3d. An old store-house 12 by 12 feet, and eight feet high; value, $100. These buildings are of logs, grooved into posts.

4th. A barn 40 by 30 feet, and fourteen feet high, built of squared timber, grooved into posts; there are sheds on three sides of the main building twelve feet wide, roofing of split-boards; value $600.

5th. Stable 25 by 31 feet, and twelve feet high, built and covered similarly to the barn, old and rotten; value $200.

6th. An open cow-shed, roof of split-boards, on posts set in the ground, eight feet high; all new, and worth $150.

7th. Stable 15 by 20 feet, and ten feet high, framed on sills, with walls and roof like the barn; new, and worth $200.

8th. Lodging for servants 14 by 16 feet, and ten feet high, built of round logs, one fire-place, and split board roof; new and in good order; worth $150.

9th. Poultry-house 12 by 12 feet, a pig-sty and well-shed; all valued at $100.

Recapitulation.

Value of Cowlitz Farm, 166 acres of land, at $5 per acre - - - - -	$830 00
1276 rods of fencing at forty cents per rod -	510 40
Nine buildings - - - - - -	2,100 00
Aggregate value - - -	$3,440 40

SECOND—THE PUGET'S SOUND AGRICULTUAL COMPANY'S CLAIM ON
PUGET'S SOUND.

The Company are in undisputed possession of the landing
on the Sound, about one and a-half miles west of their buildings, (Fort Nisqually,) and of a farm of about 847 acres, embracing besides those of the fort, all buildings and appurtenances necessary to a large farm. The farm, except a short
distance bounded by a lake, is enclosed and crossed with
worm fences. Those south of the beautiful little stream
that runs through the premises, are mostly new and in good
repair, and seem to have been made in course of the last
three years; those north of the stream, and the interior lines,
are of old rails and out of repair. For reasons, the same as
considered at Cowlitz, we value the fences here at seventy-
five cents per rod. This valuation does not include yards,
corrals, &c., immediately surrounding buildings, which have
been considered as appurtenances, and valued with the
buildings to which they belonged. The buildings are of the
following description and value, to wit:

1. The warehouse at the landing on the Sound; it is 30 by
61 feet, and 12 feet high, built of squared timber, grooved
into posts, a wooden floor and shingle roof; the sills are beginning to decay; value $500. There is also an old log
building at the landing, but in ruins, and valueless.

2d. A new building, being the southwest in the line, running parallel to the west wall or enclosure of the fort 25½ by
16½ feet, with a shed addition 10 by 16 feet; the main building is twelve feet high, enclosed with unplaned weather-
boards, rough plank floor, and shingle roof; value $250.

3d. A framed house painted white, 20 by 30 feet, and ten
feet high, a hall running through, with two rooms on the
right and one on the left; it is used as a lodging-house, and
worth $400.

4th. An old house of squared timber 32 by 20 feet, and
ten feet high, used as a work-shop, much decayed, worth
$100.

5th. A granary 31 by 20 feet, and ten feet high, built of
squared timber; the roof is bad; value $250.

6th. The "shop" or "store" is built with upright boards, and battens on the joints, is 20 by 30 feet, and two stories (sixteen and a-half feet) high, has an ell [L] shed 10 by 15 feet, in rear, shingle roof; the building new but rough, worth $400.

7th. Two bastions, one at the northwest, the other at the southeast corner of the old enclosure; they are alike in all respects, being built of squared timber let into posts; they are fourteen feet square at base, and about twenty-two feet high; the upper story projects on all sides two feet beyond the lower walls; the northwest is used as a dove-cote, the other seemed to be empty; the two worth $200.

8th. A privy, small houses, and temporary sheds along the west wall, (five in number,) valued at $150.

9th. A hennery, 150 by 92 feet, enclosing an enclosure 44 by 54 feet; the latter enclosure having a hen-house in the middle of it; the whole valued at $250.

10th. Old storehouse 61 by 30 feet, and twelve feet high, built in the usual way with squared timber, and has a first and second floor, roof of split boards, newer than the rest of the building, which is rotting, valued at $500.

11th. Attached to and in rear of the old storehouse, is a packing-house, and a wagon and wood-shed; the house old, the sheds temporary, worth $200.

12th. An old dwelling-house 32 by 18 feet, and ten feet high, of the usual square timber walls, a shed addition of 9 by 18 feet, in rear, old and rotten, worth $200.

13th. A dairy 11 by 16 feet, protected from the sun by a shed covering the building, and extending on all sides six feet beyond it; the whole cheap and temporary; value $100.

14th. Cook-house and wash-house, one 14 by 22, the other 13 by 18, old and temporary; the two worth $300.

15th. The agent's dwelling-house; the body of the building 30 by 50 feet, and twelve feet high, with a porch eight feet wide on both sides, and at one end a bath-house, and bedroom at the other; the walls of the building are of upright planks, weather-boarded and painted white, with plain cornice finish, and shingle roof. The lower floor is divided by a hall, with a flight of stairs running from it to the upper story; there are two fire-places and five rooms below, finished with cloth and paper, ceiled above with plank; this house is in pretty good repair, and worth $3,000.

16th. A paling, the posts of which is now rotting off, separates the mansion from the rest of the buildings, and a new plank fence supplies the place, in part, of the old pickets that once enclosed the quadrangle; we value the whole at $100.

BUILDINGS OUTSIDE THE FORT.

17th. An old stable, but in use, with cart sheds, &c., around it; value $600.

18th. Slaughter-house on the right bank of the stream 32 by 60 feet, and ten feet high, framed, and the walls of round timber let into the posts in the usual way, with its appurtenances; worth $500.

19th. A large old barn north of the stream, its posts rotten and ties giving way, materials worth $150.

20th. A sheep-shed, new and servicable, 70 by 107 feet, roof of split boards, supported by posts in the ground; worth $600.

21st. Six small buildings occupied by farm laborers, the whole worth $350.

22d. Duck and goose house, and appurtenances, worth $150.

23d. Cow-shed and pig-sty, with their appurtenances, worth $250.

Recapitulation and estimate of value of the Nisqually farm.

Land about twenty-seven acres, reclaimed swamp, worth $25 per acre - - - $675.00
820 acres, average land at ninety cents - - 738.00
Buildings - - - - - - - 9,500.00
Fencing, of the value of - - - - 1,500.00

Aggregate value - - - - $12,413.00

To place a just estimate upon the value of unimproved lands in the vicinity of the Puget's Sound Agricultural Com-

3 P

pany's farm at Nisqually, has been the most difficult and delicate duty imposed upon the board of experts; not only from the peculiar character of the natural surface of the country, but its possible and probable development in the future. The surface has evidently been swept by a mighty flood, which has carried away soil and subsoil, if there were any, and left the polished stones, common to the bed of a rapid river, many feet in depth; except upon a narrow beach overlooking the sound at Steilacoom, seventy or one hundred feet below the common surface of the country, we saw no subsoil which would retain the manures necessary to sustain continued cultivation. The shingly plains may once have had a light covering of grass, but now the pernicious sorrel in many places occupies its place. Cultivation is now principally confined to the alluvions along the streams and marshes reclaimed by drainage. These constitute but a small proportion to the whole surface, and from the great labor and expense of removing the heavy growth of timber that covers the bottoms, and ditching and draining marshes to prepare them for the plough, perhaps a moiety of these, the only lands fit for cultivation, remain vacant. By examination of the records at the clerk's office at Steilacoom, it will be found that, except the assessment of the Puget's Sound Agricultural Company's claim, in 1859, land is rated at $1.25 an acre. That in 1859 the Puget's Sound Agricultural Company's claim of 161,000 acres, including improvements, was assessed at $1.00 per acre, and since that time at $1.25 per acre, the levies upon which it has refused to pay.

We do not, therefore, put a higher value upon the land embraced within the claim of the Puget's Sound Agricultural Company, exclusive of improvements, than attaches to vacant land of like character in its vicinity, say one dollar and a quarter currency, or ninety cents gold coin per acre, all which we respectfully submit.

J. L. RINEARSON,
J. C. CARSON,
JESSE APPLEGATE.

Subscribed and sworn to before me this 23d day of August,
A. D. 1866.

J. M. BACON,
County Clerk of Clackamas County, Oregon.

(The foregoing report is objected to, because it is incompetent, immaterial, and irrelevant, and contains statements not pertinent to the issue; it is, therefore, objected to as a whole, because no opportunity has been given to interpose objections to clauses or portions thereof.)

Int. 6.—Was the warehouse at the landing on the Sound, of which you speak in your foregoing statement, occupied or used by the Company, so far as you know?

Ans.—Yes; though I saw nothing in it but hay; but Mr. Huggins in charge of it, told me he used it in receiving goods.

Cross-examination by the Company's Counsel.

Int. 1.—From where did you start to view the lands of the Company in Washington Territory?

Ans.—From Yoncalla, Douglas county, Oregon.

Int. 2.—When did you leave Portland to make this examination, and how did you travel?

Ans.—I left Portland on Saturday, August 11th, I think; I traveled by steam to Monticello, on the Cowlitz, and arrived the same day at Monticello; I left the same evening for, and arrived at Cowlitz farm on the following day, I think, about nine or ten o'clock, a. m.

Int. 3.—What examination did you make at the Cowlitz farm, and what length of time were you making that examination?

Ans.—We were examining the premises from the time we arrived until we left in the evening of Monday; did not make any examination after dinner; what we did at Cowlitz farm, I have already testified to.

Int. 4.—Did you examine any part of the Company's claim called the Cowlitz Farm, except the enclosure in the possession of Geo. B. Roberts? If so, state what part of it was examined by you.

Ans.—The critical examination upon which we report, was the farm claimed by Mr. Roberts as being in the possession of the Puget's Sound Agricultural Company; any further examination was such as was given to lands in its vicinity.

Int. 5.—What lands in the vicinity and upon the claim, except the one referred to, did you examine at all?

Ans.—We passed over nearly all the prairie upon which the farm of the Puget's Sound Agricultural Company is located; we made a regular survey of the farm of 166 acres.

Int. 6.—Did you pass over the prairie to the eastward of Mr. Roberts's possession?

Ans.—I did.

Int. 7.—How far?

Ans.—I am not able to say the exact distance; it was only a short distance.

Int. 8.—Was it a mile?

Ans.—No.

Int. 9.—Did you go half a mile?

Ans.—I went sufficiently far to satisfy myself of the quality of the soil, having no further occasion to go in that direction.

Int. 10.—Was the distance you traveled in that direction a quarter of a mile?

Ans.—I do not think it necessary to make further answer.

Int. 11.—Do you decline to state your opinion of the distance you did travel to the eastward of Mr. Roberts's.

Ans.—I have already declined.

Int. 12.—What examination did you make, if any, of the Company's claim westward of Mr. Roberts's possession?

Ans.—I know of no claim westward, eastward, north, or south, officially.

Int. 13.—What do you mean by stating that you know of no claim in either direction from Mr. Roberts's possessions officially?

Ans.—I only could know of Mr. Roberts's claim from his own showing.

Int. 14.—What do you mean by saying that you know of Mr. Roberts's claim officially?

Ans.—That myself and colleagues were sent to ascertain

the condition and present value of the Puget's Sound Agricultural Company's claim, on Cowlitz, having no authority to examine or report upon anything beyond those actual improvements. Our examinations, outside of those, were made to ascertain or assist us in ascertaining the value of the lands included within or by those improvements.

Int. 15.—Were you instructed by Attorney Johnson to examine and report the value of those improvements and premises only, that at the time of making such examination, were in the actual possession of the Company?

Ans.—I will not say certainly in reference to that special direction from Mr. Johnson, but as the report will show, it refers only to the present time.

Int. 16.—Do you mean to be understood that you were instructed by Attorney Johnson, or that you understood his instructions to be, to examine and report simply upon that part of the Company's claim and improvements, possessed and occupied by them at the time of making the examination?

Ans.—I understood my instructions to be, to examine the property in the possession of the Company; farms, buildings, &c., and make a just estimate of their value; I also understood my instructions to be, by an examination of the soil, the official records in the vicinity, and other legitimate means, to make a just estimate of the value of the farms by reference to the joining country.

Int. 17.—Did Attorney Johnson intimate to you the extent of the Company's claim?

Ans.—I do not think he did.

Int. 18.—Were you instructed to examine and report upon the land and farm at the Cowlitz river, known as the farm, consisting of 3,572 acres, more or less, as claimed in the Company's memorial; or were you instructed to examine and report upon the value of only so much of the claim as was held and occupied by their agent or lessee Roberts?

Ans.—I was furnished with a copy of the Company's memorial by Mr. Johnson, but understood my duty in regard to that to be similar to that required of me in regard to the value of other lands in the vicinity of their actual possessions; I understood we were to examine the actual possessions particularly, and the surrounding country generally.

Int. 19.—Did you understand that you were authorized to select any particular portion of the land claimed by the Company, and confine your examination and report to that alone?

Ans.—I understood we were to examine the actual possessions particularly, and the surrounding country generally.

Int. 20.—Why did you examine and report only upon 166 acres of the land, when the Company claimed in their memorial 3,500 acres and upwards? (Objected to by counsel of the United States, as the witness has already stated in the report, made a part of his deposition, that they did examine the whole prairie, and because the report shows that they have estimated the value of the whole, the question thus assuming to state that which is not the fact.)

Ans.—I understood we were to examine the actual possessions particularly, and the surrounding country generally; by the special examination of the premises, we ascertained the value of the improvements; by the general examination the value of the lands.

Int. 21.—Why did you, in your recapitulation in your report, give the value of only 166 acres, or the value of the Cowlitz Farm, when the Company, in their memorial, claim 3,500 acres and upwards.

Ans.—We found only 166 acres enclosed land; there were other farms adjoining that of Mr. Roberts, of which he did not claim to be in possession.

Int. 22.—Do you not know that these other farms and enclosures are within the limits of the Company's lands as claimed by them in their memorial, and that they were formerly used and occupied by the Company?

Ans.—Mr. Roberts so stated.

Int. 23.—Did you suppose you had any authority in making your estimate of value of the Company's property, to drop from consideration all but the 166 acres specified by you in your report as the Cowlitz Farm? (Objected to, as the report shows that the surrounding lands were not dropped from consideration, but were valued at $5.00 per acre.)

Ans.—I understood we were to examine the actual possessions particularly, and the surrounding country generally, and in reporting the value of that actually enclosed and undisputed, we fix also the value of the land not enclosed or in dispute at the same price.

Int. 24.—If you did not drop all but the 166 acres from consideration, why did you not include in your recapitulation the remainder of the claim, when you testify as to the value of the Cowlitz Farm?

Ans.—We think we did include the value of the whole.

Int. 25.—Please take the report and point out in which item in the recapitulation the value of more land than 166 acres is included?

Ans.—The recapitulation uses the term farm, the Cowlitz Farm; it mentions its area, and the value of that area, and its improvements, fencing, &c.,; beyond this farm, the Company claimed to be in actual possession of no other lands.

Int. 26.—What area does it mention?

Ans.—One hundred and sixty-six acres.

Int. 27.—In the item of $830, stated in the recapitulation as the value of the Cowlitz Farm, is there included the value of more land than the 166 acres?

Ans.—Not if the calculation is right.

Int. 28.—In what item of the recapitulation is the value of more than 166 acres of land contained?

Ans.—The recapitulation does not pretend to give the value, or rather the estimate of it as an item, of more land than the farm contains.

Int. 29.—Do you mean to testify that the Cowlitz Farm only embraces 166 acres?

Ans.—No.

Int. 30.—If the farm embraces more than 166 acres, why was not its value put in the recapitulation?

Ans.—I have not testified that it did contain more.

Int. 31.—If you were sent to estimate the value of the land claimed by the Company, why did you not embrace in your recapitulation the value of the whole amount of land claimed in the memorial?

Ans.—I understood it to be our duty to ascertain the value of lands in actual possession of the Company, not to ascertain the boundaries or extent of their claims; such land as we found in actual possession, included within enclosures, we made an item in estimating the value of that farm or enclosure.

Int. 32.—Was your understanding of your duty derived from the instructions, or your understanding of the instructions given to you by Attorney Johnson, before leaving to make this examination and report?

Ans.—I suppose I did.

Int. 33.—If you were not sent there to ascertain the boundaries of the Company's claim, why did you in your recapitulation cut down the boundaries to 166 acres of land when the Company claimed upwards of 3,500 acres as the amount of their claim?

Ans.—I repeat again we had nothing to do with the boundaries of the claim; we recapitulate the value of the farm as an item of property.

Int. 34.—Would not your recapitulation of the value of the Cowlitz Farm be more fair and correct if there were added thereto seventeen thousand and thirty dollars as the value of thirty-four hundred and six acres, at $5 per acre, claimed by the Company and omitted in the recapitulation?

Ans.—I do not think it would, because that quantity of land is not contained within the enclosures, ascertained by us.

Int. 35.—Was not the true reason why you left out the amount, your belief that the Company had no right to any land, except what they have now enclosed and in their possession?

Ans.—No.

Int. 36.—Have you not testified that the land adjoining the Company's enclosures was estimated by you at $5 per acre?

Ans.—Yes.

Int. 37.—If the Company are entitled to the value of the

land which they claim, and this be admitted by the Commission, should not the amount of $17,030 be added, taking your basis of value?

Ans.—Doubtless, if the calculation is right.

Int. 38.—You have testified to your official knowledge of some lands and your want of official knowledge of other lands of the Company on the Cowlitz Farm, did you regard yourself as being anything more than a messenger, requested by Mr. Johnson to examine the lands and improvements in question, for the purpose of being a witness?

Ans.—What I mean by the term official is simply the observance of instructions given to me by Mr. Johnson. I am here as a witness, and was notified I would be called.

Int. 39.—Having been sent by Mr. Johnson to make this examination for the purpose of testifying in this case, what was your reason for departing from the usual course and submitting a formal report, instead of coming upon the stand and testifying as to your knowledge in the premises, as witnesses ordinarily appear and testify?

Ans.—I was one of three persons sent by Mr. Johnson, and requested to report to him.

Int. 40.—Were you upon the tract of land, situated upon the Company's claim, at present occupied by Jackson Barton, and what examination, if any, did you make of these premises?

Ans.—I did not inquire after the names of the squatters, those, I learned, were mentioned to me incidentally by Mr. Roberts; I know nothing about Mr. Barton.

Int. 41.—Do you know anything about the lands occupied by any of the squatters, situated upon the tract of land called the Cowlitz Farm?

Ans.—If the question refers to the quality of the lands, I answer in the affirmative.

Int. 42.—How many squatters' claims did you walk over and examine?

Ans.—None.

Int. 43.—If you neither walked over or examined any of the squatters' claims, how can you testify as to the quality of their soil?

Ans.—If the question is in relation to the quality of the soil, it has been more than once answered already; if it relates to the squatter's title claim, I again answer in the negative.

Int. 44.—If you made no examination of the soil of the lands occupied by the squatters upon this claim, in what way do you derive information that enables you to testify to the quality of the soil?

Ans.—I have already testified to having made such examination.

Int. 45.—Did you ever see this tract of land before you examined it for the purpose of making this report?

Ans.—I did not.

Int. 46.—Do you know what proportion of the Cowlitz Farm, as claimed by the Company in their memorial, is timber land?

Ans.—I do not know anything about the proportion.

Int. 47.—Did you examine any of the timber land upon the Company's claim?

Ans.—I examined timber land in the vicinity, but do not know whether on the Company's claim or not.

Int. 48.—Do you mean to testify that you went over to examine and report upon the value upon the Company's claim and improvements, called the Cowlitz Farm, and returned without knowing the extent and boundary of their claim or its value, except the 166 acres specified in your recapitulation?

Ans.—I understood it to be our duty to ascertain the value of lands in actual possession of the Company, not to ascertain the boundaries or extent of their claims. . In estimating a farm, such value to the land is made an item in the recapitulation of its value. We were to ascertain, by means we were directed to use, the value of adjoining land or lands in the vicinity, not the names or titles of the occupants.

Int. 49.—Upon your arrival at Cowlitz Farm, did you not meet Edward Huggins, one of the Company's agents, who, by himself or with Mr. Roberts, proposed to show you and the gentlemen accompanying you, over the lands there claimed by the Company in their memorial?

Ans.—I met a gentleman by the name of Huggins there at, the Cowlitz Farm, and I think such a proposition was made by him or Mr. Roberts; I do not remember by which one, perhaps, by both, and declined for the reason already stated in this examination.

Int. 50.—Did you not state to Mr. Huggins that you came there to examine the present possessions of the Company at that place, and that you did not care to be shown or to see the lands formerly claimed or occupied by the Company, or words to that effect?

Ans.—As we did not consider ourselves upon any secret service, and I do not, at the present moment, remember any special time or occasion upon which such conversation was had, I have no doubt myself and companions told Mr. Huggins what we considered our duty to do and not to do, as I have through this blessed day of our Lord attempted to explain to this honorable Commission.

Int. 51.—Is not the land claimed by the Company, called the Cowlitz Farm, of a quality similar to that on which John R. Jackson now resides, situate about six miles north of the Company's land, and on the road leading from Cowlitz Landing to Olympia?

Ans.—That is a question upon which the experts have not consulted, about the relative quality of the two places. My answer must, therefore, be that of an individual; of course of less weight than the concurrent opinion of three. The farm of Mr. Jackson is a very handsome one, in a high state of cultivation; it has upon it a good orchard, a beautiful garden of flowers and shrubbery, excellent water, a capacious if not regular [illegible;] some shade trees, and other ornaments around it; among some other things some grape vines, which in that high northern latitude seem to be more for show than use. His farm seems abundantly stocked with horses, cattle, sheep, and pigs; it has also good barns and other out-buildings; and though further removed from the Cowlitz landing than the land now in possession of the Puget's Sound Agricultural Company, in view of the better condition of the land and its other advantages, being on the public road; I think it would rate with most purchasers, acre for acre, equal to the Cowlitz Farm. I have in my possession an affidavit, duly executed before a notary, of the price paid by Mr. Jackson for a tract of land, partly prairie and partly timber, which he has lately purchased and added to his farm.

Int. 52.—I did not ask you for any conclusions of examinations of experts, neither did I ask you to describe the beauties of John R. Jackson's farm, but I did ask you if the soil of Cowlitz Farm and the farm of John R. Jackson were of similar quality. Will you please to answer whether the soil of these two tracts of land is of similar quality or not?

Ans.—I think the soil of the Cowlitz prairie has been superior in quality to the Jackson farm. I do not think at present the Cowlitz prairie is as productive as the Jackson farm.

Int. 53.—Did you examine any of the springs situated upon or any of the streams running through the Cowlitz Farm?

Ans.—There is no stream that I remember running through the Cowlitz Farm as surveyed by us; I saw no springs.

Int. 54.—Did you examine any of the springs situated upon or streams running through the lands of the Company, as claimed by them in their memorial?

Ans.—I cannot answer as to that fact.

Int. 55.—Did you examine a mill-site or privilege situate upon this claim, upon one of the water-courses running through it, and upon which was a saw-mill, formerly erected by the Company?

Ans.—I cannot answer; I saw some water-courses running through the Cowlitz prairie, and was told a mill had been on one of them; I cannot answer it was on the land claimed by the Company or not, not having ascertained the boundaries.

Int. 56.—State the amount of pasture lands, and land under cultivation, between the mouth of the Cowlitz river and Cowlitz Farm.

Ans.—We landed at a little town or place called Monticello, about four miles, as we were informed, above the mouth of the river. The farms above that point only were seen by us; four or five miles, perhaps, that the road follows the river; the land is mostly in cultivation, either in grass or grain; from that point the road leaves the river, taking up a side stream, upon which there are a few good farms. Mr. Jackson's is the first and Mr. Humphrey's the second stage stations; they are the best, I think. We staid with Mr. Humphrey, and went over and examined his farm and improvements; we examined critically no other points between. I cannot answer as to the number of acres in cultivation.

Int. 57.—Between the two points designated in the last interrogatory, are the lands, suitable for cultivation or valuable for pasturage, generally occupied by settlers?

Ans.—Above the point where the wood leaves the Cowlitz river, but a small proportion of the lands suitable for agricultural purposes are occupied by settlers, for the reason of the great expense and labor necessary to prepare them for agricultural purposes, the best lands being either heavily timbered, or mostly requiring drainage; from the beginning of the open country, known as the Cowlitz prairie, the country is generally in cultivation.

Int. 58.—What distance is it from the mouth of the Cowlitz river to the point where you struck what you term the Cowlitz prairie?

Ans.—The distance is called thirty miles from Monticello; I do not know what point in the prairie is the terminus or place reckoned from.

Int. 59.—Is not the character of the country, and the expense of transportation, such as to render it improbable that any of the products of the cultivated lands lying between the Cowlitz prairie and the mouth of the Cowlitz river would ever be taken in the direction of the Cowlitz Farm for a market?

Ans.—That would depend upon the value of the market, or price paid for the produce of the farms at Cowlitz.

Int. 60.—Is not now, and has not since the settlement

of that section of country referred to in the last interrogation, Monticello and Portland, been the market for products from that portion of the country?

Ans.—I suppose it has.

Int. 61.—Is not the character of the ground and the expense of transportation such as to render it improbable that the products of the lands referred to in the last interrogation will ever seek a market in the direction of the Cowlitz Farm?

Ans.—Upon that question I could only give an opinion; at present the farm productions are most easily transported to the Columbia river.

Int. 62.—What, in your judgment, would be a fair yearly yield of wheat, oats, barley, hay, and potatoes, on the Cowlitz Farm, if properly conducted?

Ans.—I think about twenty bushels of wheat, forty of oats, barley—I never cultivated barley; about one hundred or one hundred and fifty bushels of potatoes; hay would be on an average one and a-half tons.

Int. 63.—Do you know what was the condition of the Company's farm at Cowlitz when you came to Oregon in 1843, and subsequent year?

Ans.—No.

Int. 64.—From the edge of Cowlitz prairie, where you first came out of the timber, in coming from Monticello, through to the end of your journey at Steilacoom on Puget's Sound, did you see a single one hundred pounds of hay of the crop of previous years?

Ans.—No.

Int. 65.—Did all the pasture lands between the same points have the appearance of being stocked and grazed to their full capacity?

Ans.—Yes.

Int. 66.—Does the country between those points present the appearance of being over-stocked, and grazed beyond their capacity?

Ans.—From the appearance of the animals observed, it was not.

Int. 67.—Answer the last interrogatory from your observations of the pasture lands along the line of road traveled by you.

Ans.—It was not.

Int. 68.—How much prairie land, adapted to the purposes of agriculture and valuable for pasturage, lies between the edge of the timber, coming from Monticello, where you struck what you term Cowlitz prairie, and the Company's claim called the Nisqually Farm, in Pierce county?

Ans.—I do not know how much.

Int. 69.—Give your judgment of the amount of the descriptions of lands designated in the last interrogatory, lying between the points designated.

Ans.—From what I saw of the country, I think about one-half of the country is prairie.

Int. 70.—Are you not aware that the lands lying west of the Cascade range of mountains, or the lands generally of Puget's Sound, north of the Company's claim, or Nisqually, are densely timbered lands?

Ans.—No.

Int. 71.—Have you any acquaintance with the lands designated in the last interrogatory?

Ans.—No.

Int. 72.—Are you not aware that the entire amount of agricultural lands and pasture lands lying in Washington Territory, north of the Cowlitz river, are inadequate to supply the demands for pasture lands, and agricultural products of the markets of Puget's Sound, Vancouver's Island, and British Columbia; and do you not know that large amounts of agricultural products and large quantities of live stock have yearly, for a long time, from Oregon, sought a sale in those markets?

Ans.—To the first clause of the question, *No;* to the second, *Yes.* From my observations upon the country, when the lands embraced in the question is put into a proper state of cultivation, it will produce large amounts of agricultural productions; whether enough to supply the demands of the markets named, I cannot say. At present, cattle and sheep dealers for the Victoria markets purchase stock from me, in the Umpqua Valley, southern Oregon; and I also learned from the proprietor of the flouring-mill at Tum-Water, Puget's Sound, that he imports his wheat from California.

Int. 73.—Since the discovery of the mines in British Columbia, in 1858, has there not been large numbers of cattle, horses, sheep, and swine yearly purchased in Oregon, to supply the markets referred to in the last interrogatory?

Ans.—From information, I answer this question in the affirmative, and that the trade is likely to continue.

Int. 74.—How is this stock taken from Oregon to these several markets?

Ans.—From information I answer this question, that the stock designed for Victoria markets are taken by the way of the Cowlitz to Puget's Sound, from there shipped; those for British Columbia, by the way of the Columbia river. By the Victoria markets, I mean to include the other markets in British America, most convenient to that point.

Int. 75.—Is not all that part of British Columbia, lying west of the Cascade Mountains, principally supplied with their meats and live-stock by the way of Puget's Sound and Victoria?

Ans.—I presume, so.

Int. 76.—State, from your knowledge and information, the best point of shipment from Puget's Sound of the live-stock and meats required to supply these markets.

Ans.—I visited but two of the towns on Puget's Sound, Olympia and Steilacoom; my personal impressions accord with the information received from others, that the latter place is best adapted for the carrying on of a large commerce.

Int. 78.—Are not the prairie lands valuable for agricultural purposes and pasturage, in the vicinity and for a long distance around Olympia, occupied by settlers?

Ans.—Yes, so far as my examinations of the country extended.

Int. 84.—Does not all the live-stock driven from Oregon, to supply the markets referred to in the foregoing interrogatory, require rest and pasturage or forage in the vicinity of the point of shipment, on Puget's Sound, before being shipped?

Ans.—I cannot say that *all* live stock requires such rest or forage, but two large enclosures on the prairie, near Steilacoom, were pointed out to me as being used by cattle dealers for those purposes.

Int. 79.—Do you not know that stock dealers, driving stock from Oregon to supply these markets, drive them in large numbers, to make it profitable?

Ans.—Yes.

Int. 80.—Do you not know that only a part of such droves of cattle taken to the vicinity of the point of shipment are shipped at a time to their markets, and that the remainder are left for weeks and months at a time upon the pasture lands in this vicinity before being shipped?

Ans.—I have been so informed by the cattle dealers.

Int. 81.—Did you examine the Company's claim called the Nisqually Farm, lying in Peirce county? If so, state to what extent, and what length of time you were engaged in making such examination; I mean the tract of land at Nisqually, extending along the shores of Puget's Sound from the Nisqually river on the one side, to the Puyallup river on the other, and back to the Coast Range of mountains, containing some 261 square miles, or 167,040 acres?

Ans.—I did not examine a tract of the magnitude named, in your question; with my colleagues, I examined a farm in the possession of Edward Huggins, accredited to us as the agent of the Puget's Sound Agricultural Company, the result of which is contained in the report submitted by us. Our personal examinations were in the vicinity of the farm, extending north no further than the town of Steilacoom.

Int. 82.—What were you sent to Nisqually to examine and report on?

Ans.—I understood we were to examine the actual possessions particularly, and the surrounding country generally.

Int. 83.—How many acres of the Company's claim at Nisqually did you examine?

Ans.—Particularly, about 847 acres.

4 P

Int. 84.—How many acres did you examine generally?

Ans.—As I before said, personally, such only as passed under our own observation in examining the vicinity of the farm, going to and from the town of Steilacoom by different routes, and to and from the farm itself.

Int. 85.—Give your judgment of the number of acres you examined generally.

Ans.—Our examination did not extend to the ascertainment of quantities, but to the general character of the country.

Int. 86.—What was the distance travelled by you in going from Mr. Huggins's to Steilacoom?

Ans.—I think, by the route, seven or eight miles.

Int. 87.—How did you travel, and did you travel rapidly?

Ans.—We travelled in a buggy; in places we travelled rapidly, in others, slowly.

Int. 88.—What length of time did it take you to drive from Mr. Huggins's to Steilacoom?

Ans.—I did not observe the time, but think about two hours.

Int. 89.—From the time you left Steilacoom, until you got to Mr. Huggins's on your return, did you get out of your carriage to make any examination of the soil?

Ans.—No.

Int. 90.—Did you walk over any of the lands of the Company and make any examination of the soil, except the enclosure surveyed by you, and the lands in the immediate vicinity of those enclosures?

Ans.—I walked over and examined some lands in the vicinity of Steilacoom.

Int. 91.—Did you examine any of the lands in the vicinity of Steilacoom, except small quantities upon the town-site?

Ans.—My examination was not extensive; I do not know the limits of the town-site.

Int. 92.—How far back from the waters of Puget's Sound, in the vicinity of Steilacoom, did you examine any lands?

Ans.—About three hundred yards, according to my best information.

Int. 93.—What extent of frontage on the Sound did you examine the land in the vicinity of Steilacoom ?

Ans.—According to my best information, it was about a quarter of a mile.

Int. 94.—Is the land in the vicinity of Steilacoom, examined by you, the only land of the Company at Nisqually that you did examine, except that walked over and surveyed by you and referred to in the 96th [90th] interrogation?

Ans.—We examined the land at Nisqually river, and generally of every part of the country through which we travelled, with sufficient accuracy to determine its quality and character, and in connection with other sources of information, to enable us to form a general estimate of the value of the country. These examinations did not require any particular mode of locomotion.

Int. 95.—What number of acres of land did you walk over at Nisqually river, and examine ?

Ans.—I walked but a short distance at the Nisqually river, and then not specially to examine the land, all the observations necessary to enable us to determine the quality of lands being as easily made from the seat of a carriage as by walking over it, when the quality of like lands, as indicated by the growth of crops, timber, &c., and depth of soil has been ascertained.

Int. 96.—How long a time were you engaged at the Nisqually river in making an examination of the soil?

Ans.—We made no halt at Nisqually, specially, for that purpose.

Int. 97.—How long a time were you at Nisqually river for any purpose ?

Ans.—I cannot say; we made but a short halt going and coming.

Int. 98.—What distance is it from Nisqually river to Mr. Huggins's, and what part of that distance is prairie?

Ans.—About four miles, and about three miles prairie.

Int. 99.—Did you get out of your carriage to make any examination of the soil between Nisqually river and Mr. Huggins's ?

Ans.—No.

Int. 100.—What amount of time were you actually engaged in making your examination of the Company's lands at Nisqually?

Ans.—We were north of the Nisqually river from the 14th day of August, in the evening, until the evening of the 16th, most of the time being spent in the prosecution of our mission.

Int. 101.—How much of the time spent by you north of the Nisqually river, were you engaged in making a survey of the 847 acres, particularly examined by you, and in examining the improvements thereon?

Ans.—A day, except so much of the morning as was necessary to examine the warehouse at the Sound.

Int. 102.—Was not the balance of your time spent north of the Nisqually river taken up in your trip going to Steilacoom, at Steilacoom, and returning?

Ans.—It was so.

Int. 103.—How far back from the shore of the Puget's Sound did your examination of the Company's land extend?

Ans.—About two miles.

Int. 104.—Was not the soil examined by you at Nisqually river fertile, well adapted to the growth of garden and other vegetables, and is it not very valuable for agricultural purposes generally.

Ans.—Yes.

Int. 105.—What is the quality of the soil examined by you at Steilacoom?

Ans.—Land, I think, of great fertility.

Int. 106.—How far back from the shore of the Sound does this description of land extend?

Ans.—My examination extended, according to my best information, about three hundred yards.

Int. 107.—Did you examine the lands of the Muck valley, running through the Company's claim, or the mill-site, situated near the mouth of the Muck stream, where it enters into the Nisqually river?

Ans.—I did not; my information respecting that valley was derived from Mr. Huggins.

Int. 108.—Did you examine the lands or farms lying upon Mourey's Creek, or Talentyre's Creek, situated in the eastern and central portion of the Company's claim at Nisqually?

Ans.—For information respecting other portions of the country not passed over by the Commission, they depended upon information derived from Mr. Huggins and other reliable sources.

Int. 109.—Did you ever see [the] lands of the Company at Nisqually, before you saw them with those other gentlemen, sent by Mr. Johnson to examine them?

Ans.—No.

Int. 110.—Is not the soil of Nisqually Plains a black vegetable mold, mixed in very varying quantities with gravel in some parts, and sand in others, and from one to several feet deep.

Ans.—The lands in the vicinity of the Sound, properly termed plains, have upon them very little soil, not enough except in basins or depressions to support continued cultivation.

Int. 111.—Do you know anything, of your own knowledge, of any part of the Company's lands at Nisqually, except what was passed over and examined by you during the two days thus spent?

Ans.—I do not.

Int. 112.—Did you not observe that the soil of the Second and Third Plains, passed through by you in going from Mr. Huggins's to Nisqually bridge, were composed of a black vegetable mold, mixed with sand, without any gravel?

Ans.—I observed the difference of soil, but cannot say there was no gravel.

Int. 113.—Did Mr. Huggins, the agent of the Company at Nisqually, express a desire to show you over the entire tract of the land claimed by the Company at that place?

Ans.—Yes.

Int. 114.—Why did you not make a further examination of this claim?

Ans.—Because we did not deem a further actual examination of the country necessary to enable us to report the facts we were sent to Nisqually to collect.

Int. 115.—Did you make all the examination of the Company's claim at Nisqually that you were required to make under the instructions of Mr. Johnson?

Ans.—As we understood them, we did.

Int. 116.—What was the condition of the live-stock on the Nisqually Plains?

Ans.—In good condition.

Int. 117.—How can you give a correct valuation of the whole of the Company's claims at Nisqually, from personal knowledge, when you only carefully examined less than the one hundredth and sixtieth part of it, according to your report?

Ans.—We did not claim to do so from personal knowledge.

Int. 118.—Is, then, the valuation placed upon the entire claim, one that should, or of right, ought to have the weight of sworn testimony with those whose province it is to consider the value of the Company's claim?

Ans.—It is not my province to pass upon the value of my own and my colleagues' evidence.

Int. 119.—Do you know what has been the price of beef, mutton, and pork in the markets of Puget's Sound, Victoria, and British Columbia, from 1858, during the different years, up to the present date?

Ans.—I do not.

Int. 120.—Would not the knowledge of the prices of beef cattle, sheep, and other live stock, also of the prices of the agricultural products produced by this tract of land, in the different markets at which they were offered for sale, have enabled you to form a much more correct and satisfactory estimate of the value of these lands, both at Cowlitz and Nisqually, than you now can form?

Ans.—The value of land is everywhere governed by its appreciation in its own locality, and a stranger, by any process of reasoning or calculation, cannot change its money value in the market.

Int. 121.—Has any part of the land, embraced within the limits of the Company's claim at Nisqually, in your opinion, ever been in market, or so situated that any person could get a clear title to land, or can such be the case until the claim of the Puget's Sound Agricultural Company to the same is extinguished?

Ans.—There are a number of deeds of conveyance on record in the clerk's office at Steilacoom, which, Mr. Huggins informed me, were within the limits of the claim of the Company; upon the right of the seller to convey, I cannot answer.

Int. 122.—In your report you state that you made an examination of the records of Pierce county; what length of time were you engaged in making that examination?

Ans.—I did not observe the time, but long enough to make such extracts from the records as were deemed pertinent to the objects of our mission.

Int. 123.—Were you one hour in making the examination?

Ans.—I cannot say, but not exceeding that time.

Int. 124.—Did any of the persons making sales of estate upon this claim, convey any title, or was it simply the right of possession and the improvements, the possession of the person making such conveyance?

Ans.—They were deeds conveying lands, naming the quantities and boundaries of the tracts, in all respects similar to such instruments conveying absolute title, except they were quit-claim deeds, not warrantee deeds.

Int. 125.—Were you the claimant of 161,000 acres of land, and that claim with the value of the lands was left to be determined by referees, would you be willing that the value of such tract of land should be determined by the arbitrators, by the testimony of one or more men, none of whom had seen the hundredth and sixtieth part of the land?

Ans.—My willingness or unwillingness would depend upon the valuation put upon it.

Direct Examination Resumed.

Int. 1.—What did Mr. Huggins tell you had become of the two farms of the Company on the Muck? (Objected to as hearsay, and as immaterial and irrelevant, and also because it is leading.)

Ans.—Mr. Huggins informed me the Muck farms were placed in the hands of servants of the Company, who transferred them to other parties without the Company's authority. One claim transferred for, I believe, $500 for 640 acres. Of the Muck farms there was no records of the transfers.

Int. 2.—When you say in your answer to the 48th [42d] cross-interrogatory that you did not walk over and examine any of the squatters' claims at the Cowlitz Farm, do you mean to say that you did not, in any mode, examine such lands as were there, occupied without the enclosures of the Company? Explain what you did mean by such answer.

Ans.—I make a distinction between the examination of land, and the title or *claim* under which the land is held. I examined none of the claims of any one to land in Cowlitz prairie, but did examine the land.

Int. 3.—Please state what were your instructions as given by the attorney for the United States? (Objected to, as immaterial, incompetent, and irrelevant.)

Ans.—Our instructions were in writing, and were as follows:

" PORTLAND, *August* 9, 1866.

" GENTLEMEN :

" Referring to my former instructions to you, I extend them now to the stations of the Hudson's Bay Company at Vancouver, and of the Puget's Sound Company at Cowlitz and Nisqually. You are furnished with a copy of the Company's memorial, and it is only necessary to say that you are desired to examine the property claimed by them at these points.

"Expressing my great satisfaction with your proceedings thus far,

I am, yours, respectfully,

" WM. CARY JOHNSON,
" *Attorney for the United States.*

" Messrs. JESSE APPLEGATE,
J. S. RINEARSON,
J. C. CARSON."

Int. 4.—What were the former instructions referred to in the foregoing copy? (Objected to the same as before.)
Ans.—They were as follows, to wit:

"BRITISH AND AMERICAN JOINT COMMISSION,
ON H. B. AND P. S. A. Cs'. CLAIMS.
" OREGON CITY, *July* 17, 1866.
" GENTLEMEN :

" You are constituted a Board of Experts for the examination of the lands and buildings at the more important posts claimed by the Hudson's Bay and Puget's Sound Agricultural Companies, and for which they demand compensation. Having accepted this duty, my instructions to you are as follows:

"1st. You will proceed as expeditiously as possible to Fort Colvile, in Washington Territory, and mark out, as nearly as may be, a square mile of land, making the buildings of the Company the middle point on the Company's [? Columbia] river.

" 2d. You will examine the buildings and improvements of the Company at that place, together with the land, with sufficient care to give a just estimate of their actual present value in gold coin, and also, so that you can give a tolerably accurate statement, if I shall hereafter desire, of the manner of their construction, the amount of fencing, &c.

" 3d. You will examine and measure in the same manner what is known as the White Mud Farm, some twelve miles from Fort Colvile, making the ancient improvements of the Company the centre of the square mile of land.

"4th. Observe generally, as you can, the character of the country around Fort Colvile, within four or five miles up and down the river, so as to give some estimate of its value per acre. In this connection, I respectfully suggest the propriety of examining the assessment rolls of the county, which will assist you in estimating the value of property, and you can avail yourselves of all the ordinary modes of acquiring a knowledge of these values, including inquiry from residents at that point.

"5th. Your attention is also called to the grist-mill and water-power, used by the Company, a few miles above the fort.

"6th. On your way down the river you will make a like examination and survey of the Old Fort Walla-Walla, now called Wallula, making the small stream below the fort the lower line of the land. Upon your return as far down the river as Vancouver I will join you, and your proceeding thereafter will be under my verbal instructions, until the completion of the work. Such notes of distances, amounts, nature and character of soil, improvements and buildings &c., as will enable you to make a written report (if called upon) you will see the propriety of preserving. Jesse Applegate, Esq., will be furnished with means to pay the expenses of your transportation and subsistence, of which he will keep an accurate account.

"Wishing you a pleasant and prosperous journey,

"I am, gentlemen, yours, very respectfully,

"W. C. JOHNSON,

"*Attorney and Agent for the United States.*

Messrs. JESSE APPLEGATE,
JACOB S. RINEARSON,
J. C. CARSON."

Cross-examination Resumed.

Int. 1.—What squatters' lands on the Company's claim on the north bank of Cowlitz river did you walk over and examine?

Ans.—I walked over the land on all sides of the farm occupied by Mr. Roberts; I did not inquire who claimed it.

Int. 2.—Did you walk a half a mile in any direction from the enclosure occupied by Mr. Roberts?

Ans.—Yes; I think I did.

Int. 3.—In how many different directions did you walk half a mile from his enclosure?

Ans.—I walked that distance in only one direction.

Int. 4.—Did you walk twenty rods from his enclosure in any other direction than one?

Ans.—No; I do not think I did.

Int. 5.—Did you receive any other or additional instructions, either verbal or written, from Mr. Johnson, than the written instructions which are copied into and made a part of your answer to the 134th and 135th [3d and 4th] interrogation propounded in your re-examination-in-chief?

Ans.—No.

Int. 6.—From these instructions, then, you considered that you had performed your whole duty, when you particularly examined 166 acres of the Company's land at Cowlitz Farm, with their improvements, and the examination of their premises that you have testified to having made at Nisqually?

Ans.—I consider the information contained in the report of the Board of Experts as being a fulfilment of the duties required of them.

Int. 7.—Then, you do not consider your instructions in reference to the Company's claim, called the Cowlitz Farm, did require an examination by you of all of the lands within its boundary lines?

Ans.—Further than to ascertain its quality, no.

Int. 8.—Do you now say that you made all the examination of the Company's claim at Nisqually that by your instructions you were required to make?

Ans.—Yes.

JESSE APPLEGATE.

OREGON CITY, OREGON, *August* 24, 1866.

TESTIMONY OF J. C. CARSON.

J. C. Carson being first duly sworn, deposeth and says:

Int. 1.—State your age, place of residence, and occupation.

Ans.—My age is forty-two; residence, Portland, Oregon; occupation, carpenter and joiner, builder and contractor; I am also engaged in connection with that in the manufacture of windows and sash, doors and blinds, and building materials.

Int. 2.—How long have you resided in Portland?

Ans.—I have resided in Portland since 1853.

Int. 3.—Have you lately examined the lands and improvements of the Puget's Sound Agricultural Company at Cowlitz and Nisqually? If so, in connection with whom, and under whose instructions? (The last two clauses of the interrogation objected to as irrelevant and immaterial.)

Ans.—I have, to some extent, in connection with Jesse Applegate and Major J. S. Rinearson; I left Portland for the Cowlitz Farm on the 11th of August, 1866, completed our examinations and returned to Portland on the 19th of of August, 1866. I was under the instructions of the Hon. W. C. Johnson, the Attorney for the United States.

Int. 4.—Look at the statement or report marked " G," embodied in the deposition of Jesse Applegate, in this case, now shown you, and state what it is, and what you desire to have done with it in connection with your testimony? (Objected to by the counsel for the Company as irrelevant and immaterial.)

Ans.—It is the sworn statement of facts and conclusions, ascertained and arrived at by myself and associates; I wish to adopt it and make it a part of my testimony. (The counsel for the Company objects to the introduction of this report, and to its being made a part of the testimony of the witness, because it is informal, incompetent, and unauthorized by law. Counsel for the Company also enter their protest for this mode of examination of this witness, because unauthorized by law, and claim that the witness should be particularly inquired of in reference to all matters testified to by him, so that an opportunity may be given to interpose objections to the questions, to the questions of counsel and the answers of the witness, so far as the same may be incompetent, irrelevant, or immaterial. Counsel for the United States now tenders to the attorney for the Company the examination of the report, so that he may now, if he desires, object to the whole or any part, for any of the reasons stated in the foregoing objection. Counsel for the Company insists that if the paper termed a report, is to be used in any respect as the testimony of this witness, that it should be written out in full as his evidence in this deposition, the same being neither an exhibit or a document capable of being introduced as such, butsimply the written statement of the witness and of other parties.)

Int. 5.—Do you now so adopt it and make it part of your deposition in this case ?

Ans.—I do. (The counsel for the Company objects to this report being made a part of the testimony of the witness, because it is incompetent, immaterial, and irrelevant, and contains statements not pertinent to the issue; it is also objected to as a whole, because no opportunity has been given to interpose objections to clauses or parts thereof, which are incompetent as hearsay, and for other reasons.)

Cross-examination by Company's Counsel.

Int. 1.—You state in your examination-in-chief that you were one of the parties sent by Mr. Johnson to make examination of the Company's property, at Cowlitz Farm, and at Nisqually, and to report to him the results of your examination. Please state the date of your leaving Portland, the mode of travel, time of your arrival at Cowlitz Farm, what examination you there made, the time of making such examination, when you left Cowlitz Farm, and the time engaged in traveling thence to Nisqually, what examination you there made of the Company's property, and the time employed by you in making such examinations.

Ans.—I left Portland on the 11th of August, 1866, and traveled to Monticello, near the mouth of the Cowlitz river; I arrived there about noon of the same day; from there traveled by land in a two-horse carriage, and arrived at Cowlitz Farm about noon, the 12th, which was on Sunday. In the afternoon of that day we rode over a portion of the farm in a carriage; we made no further examination that day. We commenced our survey of the enclosure about 8 o'clock the next day; I mean the enclosure of 166 acres referred to in the report. We were engaged in making a survey of this enclosure till about the middle of the same afternoon. The balance of that day we were engaged in making a survey and measurement of the buildings upon the tract of 166 acres of land. The next morning we again rode over a portion of the adjoining lands. I should say our examination extended in two directions about a mile, and in the other directions but a very short distance. We started for Nisqually about 10 o'clock the same day, and traveled that day about half way to Olympia, and arrived at Mr. Huggins's house, at Fort Nisqually, about seven o'clock in the evening, where we remained over night. On the morning of the 15th, about nine o'clock, we went from Mr. Huggins's to the warehouse on the beach, a distance of about three quarters of a mile. We there measured and examined the warehouse and another old building, and were engaged during the remainder of that day in surveying the enclosure described in that report of 874 acres, and surveying and measuring the buildings situated thereon. On the morning of the 16th, about eight o'clock, we left Mr. Huggins's in a two-horse carriage, and rode over a portion of the lands outside of the enclosure, and thence to Steilacoom, on about the same route that Mr. Applegate traveled. We were on the road from Mr. Huggins's to Steilacoom, about one and a quarter hours, traveling not to exceed ten miles. We remained at Steilacoom till about three o'clock, p. m., while there, being engaged a portion of the time walking over the town-site, and examining the public records. I was not engaged in looking over the records not to exceed half an hour. I went up to the clerk's office and found Mr. Applegate there; about three o'clock we left Steilacoom for Mr. Huggins's, and arrived there in less than an hour; we left Mr. Huggins's for Olympia about five o'clock, en route for Portland; we left Olympia on the morning of the 17th, and traveled to John R. Jackson's that day; from thence on Saturday morning, the 18th, we went by the Cowlitz landing road through the Cowlitz prairie past L. Dubo's, to Monticello, where we arrived about six o'clock, p. m.; from there we took steamer and arrived at Portland on the 19th, having been absent eight days.

Int. 2.—In returning from John R. Jackson's to Monticello, do you mean to testify that you traveled over any part of the Cowlitz Farm?

Ans.—Not any portion now enclosed; I do not know where the lines of their claim extend.

Int. 3.—Do you mean to swear then that in returning from John R. Jackson's to Monticello, you traveled over any part of the land of the Puget's Sound Agricultural Company, on the north bank of the Cowlitz river, as claimed by them in their memorial?

Ans.—I think I did travel over a portion of the land they claim.

Int. 4.—What part of the claim did you travel over in making this trip from John R. Jackson's to Monticello?

Ans.—If I traveled over any portion of the claim, it was that in the south end of the prairie.

Int. 5.—How near did the road traveled by you go to the enclosure of 166 acres mentioned in your report, and occupied by Geo. B. Roberts?

Ans.—Probably within a half a mile, but I do not know exactly.

Int. 6.—When traveling in the vicinity of the enclosure occupied by Mr. Roberts, did you travel from thence in the direction of the road referred to in the last interrogatory, sufficiently near so that you saw it?

Ans.—I certainly did, but not in a direct line.

Int. 7.—Did you walk or ride on this crooked line described in your last answer?

Ans.—I rode.

Int. 8.—Who accompanied you?

Ans.—Mr. Roberts, Mr. Applegate, and Mr. Rinearson.

Int. 9.—Did you ride from Mr. Roberts's over a public road around the Mission claim, until you came to this road, or did you travel through fields till you came to it?

Ans.—We traveled through a common outside of the enclosure until we came into the road.

Int. 10.—How far did you travel from Roberts's until you came to the road?

Ans.—I do not know the distance we traveled.

Int. 11.—Can you give any idea of the distance you traveled from Roberts's to get to this road?

Ans.—I cannot give a correct idea how far we traveled; as near as I can arrive at the distance, it was from one to three miles in a circuitous route.

Int. 12.—What direction did you travel from Roberts's to get to this road?

Ans.—We traveled in a circuitous route, and I cannot give you the directions.

Int. 13.—Will you swear that you did not travel four miles from Roberts's before you saw the road?

Ans.—I think I did not travel four miles before we came into that road.

Int. 14.—Is your idea of distance from this road to Roberts's enclosure at the nearest point, formed by your observations upon this ride?

Ans.—It is.

Int. 15.—If you cannot tell whether you rode one mile or

three miles, nor in what direction you did ride from Roberts's enclosure, how can you say that the distance from Roberts's enclosure to the road is a half a mile?

Ans.—I rode on the two opposite sides of his enclosure from the road.

Int. 16.—In what direction from Roberts's enclosure do you swear it is but a half a mile to this road?

Ans.—I do not swear to any positive distance; it was on the south or southwest portion.

Int. 17.—If you do not know where the boundaries of the Company's claim called the Cowlitz Farm are, and do not know the distance from Roberts's enclosure to this road, how can you undertake to swear that in passing from John R. Jackson's to Monticello, you passed over any part of the Company's claim?

Ans.—I only swear that from its relative location to the enclosure, that it passes through a portion of their claim, as I suppose.

Int. 18.—You do not mean to swear then that you passed through any of the Company's claim on your road from John R. Jackson's to Monticello, but gave it as a mere guess that you did so?

Ans.—It being outside of the enclosure, I cannot swear that I did.

Int. 19.—Under your instructions from Mr. Johnson, was it, or did you consider it your duty to examine and report upon the value of the farm and improvements belonging to the Company on the north bank of the Cowlitz river, known as the Cowlitz Farm, and consisting of 3,572 acres, more or less, as claimed by the Company in their memorial?

Ans.—I so understood the instructions.

Int. 20.—How many acres of the claim did you ride or walk over and examine, and did you make any examination whatever of the timber land embraced within the boundaries of this claim?

Ans.—I did not examine the timber land on this claim, and probably rode and walked over a portion of two sections of the prairie.

5 P

Int. 21.—What part of the distance did you ride over these lands, and what part did you walk?

Ans.—I walked over that part that we measured and surveyed, and through portions of it, and rode the other part?

Int. 22.—Did you not meet Edward Huggins, one of the agents of the Company, on your arrival at the Cowlitz Farm, and did he not express his willingness and desire to show you over the whole of the Company's claim, so that you might be enabled to form a correct judgment of its value?

Ans.—I did meet Mr. Huggins there at the Cowlitz, and he expressed his willingness to show us over any portion of the farm that we desired to see.

Int. 23.—If then you considered it your duty, from your instructions from Mr. Johnson, to examine the lands of the Company as claimed in their memorial, called the Cowlitz Farm, and the Company's agent was on the ground, and was desirous of your making an examination of the whole claim, why did you not do so? (Objected to, as the witness has already testified in the report that he did do so, sufficiently to determine its value. Answer to the question insisted upon by the counsel for the Company, because, as shown by the Company's memorial, about half of the claim is timbered land, and because the witness has testified in his cross-examination that he made no examination whatever of those timbered lands, also that they made no examination of more than two sections of the prairie land; the memorial showing that upwards of 1,500 acres are claimed as improved and under cultivation for farming and agricultural purposes.)

Ans.—I considered that we had seen enough of the lands in the prairie to arrive at its value, and the timber-lands we did not consider it necessary to examine, because I consider that timber-lands are worth less per acre than the prairie.

Int. 24.—Did you examine any of the springs, watercourses, or the mill-site, upon this claim?

Ans.—I did not.

Int. 25.—Would not the existence of a valuable mill-site, springs of water, and running streams, not subject to overflow, greatly increase the value of this claim, if such are to be found upon it?

Ans.—I should consider that springs and small streams are valuable on this prairie; as to the value of a mill-site, I cannot answer that intelligently, not knowing but that there may be other mill-sites in the same neighborhood.

Int. 26.—If, then, these springs and water-courses, with the mill-site, would add to the value of this claim, how can you testify to the value of lands upon which they are situated, without having examined them, and without having ascertained whether there was any other available mill-site in the vicinity?

Ans.—My experience goes to show that it is often the case, that it is cheaper to use steam-power, than to improve and use water-power; cannot testify as to its worth.

Int. 27.—You state in your cross-examination that you did not examine at all the timber lands upon the claim; state how you can undertake to testify to the value of lands you never saw.

Ans.—I make up my estimate of value from prices asked for other lands fully as favorably situated.

Int. 28.—If you never saw these timbered lands upon the claim, and know nothing of the quality of their soil, or the description and value of timber upon them, state how you can judge of their value by comparison with other lands.

Ans.—I found that the more timber there was on lands, the less it is worth.

Int. 29.—In your recapitulation, contained in your report, why do you estimate and value as Cowlitz Farm, 166 acres of land, at $5 per acre, instead of the Company's claim of 3,500 acres and upwards, as described in their memorial, if it was your duty under your instructions from Mr. Johnson to examine and estimate the value of the whole claim of the Company?

Ans.—I had no boundaries to designate their claim, except that part that I found enclosed and occupied by Mr. Roberts.

Int. 30.—Do you mean to be understood as testifying that

this 166 acres, the value of which is given in your recapitulation, was the Company's claim, called the Cowlitz Farm, that under your instructions from Mr. Johnson, it was your duty to examine and report the value of?

Ans.—I considered that under our instructions we were to report directly upon the improvements and lands that we then found occupied by the Company.

Int. 31.—Do you undertake to swear, that with the examination you made of the Company's claim of 3,500 acres and upwards, you could give a correct and reliable value of this entire tract of land?

Ans.—That is my opinion.

Int. 32.—Had you understood your instructions from Mr. Johnson to report upon the value of the entire claim, instead of the present possessions, which you say consisted of but 166 acres, would you have been satisfied upon your oath with the examination you did make to place a value upon the entire claim?

Ans.—I would.

Int. 33.—Did you consider it your duty, under your instructions from Mr. Johnson, to examine and report upon the land of the Company between Nisqually and Puyallup rivers, as claimed in their memorial, extending along the shores of Puget's Sound from the Nisqually river on the one side, to the Puyallup on the other, and back to the Coast range of mountains, and containing not less than 261 square miles, or 167,040 acres.

Ans.—I did not understand that we were to examine and report upon the whole of that land, but so much thereof as to satisfy us in making up the value of the whole.

Int. 34.—Did you particularly examine the one hundred and sixtieth part of this claim?

Ans.—We rode through the whole or near [the] entire length twice, besides making a more particular examination of that part of the claim now occupied by Mr. Huggins.

Int. 35.—Did you make any examination of this claim whatever, except what you described in your answer to the first cross-interrogatory?

Ans.—We made no other examinations.

Int. 36.—How far back from the shore of the Sound did you examine this claim ?

Ans.—About two miles.

Int. 37.—Did you make any examination whatever, between this point two miles distant from the shore of the Sound, of the lands lying between that and the Sound?

Ans.—None other than as we rode over the land in the carriage.

Int. 38.—How far distant from the shore of the Sound is the eastern boundary of the Company's claims?

Ans.—I do not know.

Int. 39.—Do you know, then, anything about what proportion of the Company's claim at Nisqually you did examine at all?

Ans.—I will answer that by referring to the answer to the first cross-interrogatory.

Int. 40.—In your answer to the first cross-interrogatory, you describe a ride in a wagon at no point, according to your answer to a subsequent interrogatory, not more than two miles distant from the shore of the Sound ; you also state that you made no examination of the ground between that and the Sound, except as you looked around while riding in a wagon ; this, with the description of your particular examination of 847 acres of land occupied by Mr. Huggins, with a portion of the lower site of Steilacoom, is all of the Company's claim that you have testified to having seen in any way, and does not give intelligibly any proportion of the Company's claim at Nisqually ; state, now, the proportions of the Company's claim that you did examine.

Ans.—I cannot state the proportion.

Int. 41.—Did you see 5,000 acres of the Company's claim?

Ans.—No.

Int. 42.—Did you travel over 3,000 acres of the Company's claim ?

Ans.—Taking a mile in width in travelling over the distance, I did, seeing it from the wagon.

Int. 43.—Did you make any examination of any of the

mill-sites improved or unimproved upon the claim, except the one at the mouth of the Segwalitchew?

Ans.—I did not.

Int. 44.—Did you examine any of the prairie lands of the Company's claim northward from the road you came into Steilacoom, when you came from Mr. Huggins's?

Ans.—Only as I could see it from the wagon.

Int. 45.—Did you ever see any of the Company's claim at Nisqually, except as described in your foregoing answers?

Ans.—I did not.

Int. 46.—Did not Mr. Huggins, the agent of the Company at Nisqually, desire you to make an examination of the whole of the Company's claim at that place, and propose to show you over it, and point out its boundaries?

Ans—He proposed to show us over any parts that we desired to see.

Int. 47.—If Mr. Johnson's instructions to you required you to examine and report upon the value of the Company's claim at Nisqually, why did you examine only the small portion of the claim that you testify to having seen?

Ans.—That part of the claim that we did see was so similar, that we considered we had seen sufficient to form our conclusions.

Int. 48.—How can you testify that lands never seen by you were similar to others that you had examined? (Objected to, as the witness has not so testified, but only that the lands he did see were similar to each other. Answer insisted upon, and protest of the counsel for the Company entered against the counsel for the United States entering an objection that simply suggests the answer that the witness shall give.)

Ans.—I have not testified to that; I don't testify to that.

Int. 49.—How, then, can you testify to the value of these lands, not seen by you, being of the same value as lands on the same tract that you did examine?

Ans.—Only upon the similarity of the lands we did see.

Int. 50.—Did you not observe the difference of soil in the several prairies you passed through from Nisqually bridge to Steilacoom?

Ans.—I noticed but very little difference in different prairies.

Int. 51.—About how wide is the belt of timber land between Puget's Sound and the Nisqually plains?

Ans.—I cannot answer that correctly; at the town of Steilacoom. probably half a mile.

Int. 52.—Is not this belt of timbered land, so far as you examined it, of a very fertile quality, and susceptible of a very high state of cultivation?

Ans.—I examined a small portion at the town of Steilacoom that is well adapted to a high state of cultivation, the other portion I did not examine so minutely, and cannot answer.

Int. 53.—Do you mean to swear that the prairies between Nisqually bridge and Mr. Huggins's are a mile wide?

Ans.—I do not.

Int. 54.—Have you any practical knowledge of agriculture, sheep farming, or stock-raising?

Ans.—I was raised on a farm, from my boyhood, until I was seventeen years old, since which time I have not been in the farming business.

Int. 55.—Do you know anything about the price of agricultural products, of live-stock, or of meats in the vicinity of either Cowlitz Farm or Steilacoom?

Ans.—I do know something of the prices of such articles.

Int. 56.—How do they compare with the prices of like articles in the Willamette Valley, are they higher or lower?

Ans.—At Steilacoom they are higher; at Cowlitz, products are lower; as to the price of stock at Cowlitz, I cannot say.

Int. 57.—Are you acquainted with the prices of these different articles, at these different points, during the last eight years?

Ans.—I am not.

Int 58.—What is hay worth per ton at the Cowlitz Farm?

Ans.—I do not know.

Int. 59.—In your recapitulation and estimate of the value

of the Nisqually farm, you designated [it] as consisting of 847 acres. If you were instructed by Mr. Johnson to examine and estimate the value of the lands of the Company at Nisqually, as claimed in their memorial, consisting of upwards of 16,700 acres, why did you give the value in your recapitulation of 847 acres, instead of the value of the whole claim?

Ans.—I understood, from his instructions, that we were to report more directly upon the improvements and the claims enclosed and occupied by them.

Int. 60.—Did not you, or one of the persons with you, say to Mr. Huggins that you did not care to see the whole claim, as you considered that you had nothing to do, except with the grounds and improvements then in possession of the Company, or words to that effect?

Ans.—Not to my knowledge.

Int. 61.—State what personal inspection you made of the records of Peirce county.

Ans.—I made no personal inspection, but was in the office during a part of the time that Mr. Applegate examined.

Int. 62.—How, then, can you, under oath, state that any particular record will be found at the clerk's office at Steilacoom, as you do state in your report, subscribed and sworn to by you, and made a part of your testimony-in-chief in this case?

Ans.—I saw the extract taken by Mr. Applegate, and believe it to be correct.

Int. 63.—What extract did Mr. Applegate make from the records of the county?

Ans.—I have not got that in my possession, and cannot state them properly.

Int. 64.—If you were the owner of 3,572 acres of land on the north bank of the Cowlitz river, valued by you at twenty thousand pounds sterling, and you had made an agreement to dispose of it at a price to be fixed by referees upon testimony as to its value to be submitted to them, would you think it fair, or would you be willing that those referees should determine its value upon the testimony of one or more men who made such examination of it as you made of the Company's claim, called the Cowlitz Farm, and who were unacquainted with the markets for its products, and of any other or different value that it might have, beyond similar lands less favorably located? (Objected to, as it does not appear that the witness and those associated with him were so ignorant.)

Ans.—I would be willing to submit a like claim to one or more ʿpersonsʾ who were old residents of the county, and considered competent judges; I do not admit that I am not acquainted with the market and counties surrounding.

Int. 65.—Were you ever upon or nearer than thirty miles of Cowlitz Farm, until you visited it at this time, and were you ever nearer Nisqually than 130 miles, until this visit?

Ans.—I was never nearer either place than the mouth of the Cowlitz.

Int. 66.—Do you not know that the principal markets for the live-stock of both Cowlitz and Nisqually, and of all the farm products, raised for sale at Nisqually and its vicinity, are the markets of the Lower Puget's Sound country, Victoria, and that part of British Columbia lying west of the Cascade range of mountains?

Ans.—Yes, I do.

Int. 67.—Were you ever in either of these markets, or nearer to them than the mouth of the Cowlitz river, until you made your late visit to Nisqually?

Ans.—I never was.

Int. 68.—Do you know what the prices of agricultural products of meats, or live-stock, have been during the last eight years, or are now in these markets, or either of them? If you do, state them.

Ans.—I do not know the market price.

Int. 69.—If you were the owner of 167,000 acres of land, between the Nisqually and Puyallup rivers, with the improvements thereon, for instance the land claimed by the Puget's Sound Agricultural Company, and its improvements by their memorial to [the] Joint Commission, and valued the same at one hundred and sixty-four thousand pounds sterling, and you had made an agreement to dispose of it at a price to be fixed by referees, upon testimony to be submitted to them as to its value, would you think it fair, or would you be willing that those referees should determine its value upon the testimony of one or more men who made such an examination of it, and only such an examination as you made of the Company's claim at Nisqually?

Ans—I would be willing to submit a like claim upon the testimony of one or more persons who were old residents of the country, and considered competent judges.

Int. 70.—Is this all your answer to the last interrogatory, and the only one you will make?

Ans.—It is.

Int. 71.—What do you mean by saying you are acquainted with the markets of the Cowlitz Farm and the Nisqually sections of country?

Ans.—I am acquainted with those markets chiefly as they are quoted from week to week in the several papers.

Int. 72.—Is there any paper, that you have ever seen, that quotes the market prices of products or live-stock on the lower Puget's Sound or British Columbia markets? If so, state what one.

Ans.—I do not now remember of any papers published on the lower Sound, or at Victoria, or British Columbia.

Int. 73.—Is the judgment you have already passed upon the value of the Cowlitz and Nisqually claims, as correct as a further full and complete examination of those places would enable you to give?

Ans.—I so consider it.

Direct examination resumed.

Int. 1.—In what papers or paper have you seen the market quotations you refer to?

Ans.—I do not remember the names of the papers published at Olympia; it was in those I saw them.

Cross-examination Resumed.

Int. 1.—Did you ever see in any Olympia paper the market prices of the lower Sound, Victoria, or British Columbia markets, or did you ever see the price of live-stock anywhere quoted in either of these papers?

Ans.—I have noticed the sale of live-stock in the Olympia papers of Olympia markets; of the lower markets I have not.

JOHN C. CARSON.

OREGON CITY, OREGON, *August* 25, 1866.

TESTIMONY OF JACOB S. RINEARSON.

Jacob S. Rinearson, being first duly sworn, deposeth and says:

Int. 1.—State your age, place of residence, and occupation.

Ans.—My age is forty-four years; residence, Clackamas county, Oregon, near Oregon City; my occupation is that of a farmer and surveyor; for the last three or four years my business has been that of a soldier, as Major of the first Oregon cavalry.

Int. 2.—How long have you resided in Oregon?

Ans.—Most of the time since 1845?

Int. 3.—Have you lately made an examination of the claims of the Puget's Sound Agricultural Company at Cowlitz prairie and on the Nisqually Plains? If so, state when, in connection with whom, and by whose directions. (The last two clauses of this interrogatory are objected to by counsel for the Company, as irrelevant and immaterial.)

Ans.—I have, within the last two weeks, in connection with Mr. Applegate and Mr. Carson, by direction of Wm. C. Johnson, attorney for the United States in this case.

Int. 4.—Look upon the report marked "G," made part of the deposition of Jesse Applegate in this case now shown you, and state what it is, and what you wish done with it in relation to your evidence now to be given. (Objected to by counsel for the Company, as irrelevant and immaterial.)

Ans.—It is an estimate or valuation of buildings and fencing of the Puget's Sound Agricultural Society, as pointed out by Mr. Roberts and Huggins, and also a valuation of lands claimed by the same Company, which I wish to be part of my evidence in this case. (The counsel for the Company objects to the introduction of this report, and to its being made a part of the testimony of this witness, because it is informal, incompetent, and unauthorized by law. The counsel for the Company also enter a protest against this mode of examination of this witness, because unauthorized by law, and claim that the witness should be particularly inquired of in reference to all matters testified to by him, so that an opportunity may be given to interpose objections to the questions of counsel and the answers of the witness, so far as the same may be incompetent, irrelevant, or immaterial. The counsel for the United States makes the same tender to the counsel for the Company, as noted in the depositions of Jesse Applegate and J. C. Carson. The counsel for the Company insists that if the paper termed a report is to be used in any respect as the testimony of this witness, that it shall be written out in full as his evidence in this deposition, the same being neither an exhibit or a document capable of being introduced as such, but simply the written statement of the witness and of other parties.)

Int. 5.—Do you now adopt that report, and make it part of your deposition?

Ans.—I do. (The counsel for the Company objects to this report being made a part of the testimony of this witness, because it is incompetent, immaterial, and irrelevant, and contains statements not pertinent to the issue; it is also objected to as a whole, because no opportunity has been given to interpose objections to clauses or parts thereof, which are incompetent as hearsay, and for other reasons.)

Int. 6.—Were you ever at either of these places before the time above referred to? If so, state when, and how long you remained in the neighborhood.

Ans.—I was at Nisqually in 1864, and remained in the neighborhood some four or five days. I was at Fort Steilacoom, attending court-martial, and rode around its neighborhood for a mile or so.

Cross-examination by Counsel for Puget's Sound Agricultural Company.

Int. 1.—You state in your examination-in-chief that you were one of the parties sent by Mr. Johnson to make an examination of the Cowlitz Farm, and at Nisqually, and to report to him the result of such examination. Now state the date of your leaving Portland upon this mission, the mode of travel, the time of your arrival at Cowlitz Farm, what examination you there made, the time of making such examination, when you left Cowlitz farm, and the time engaged in traveling thence to Nisqually, what examination you there made of the Company's property, and the time employed by you in making such examination.

Ans.—I left Portland on Saturday, August 11th, 1866, in company with Mr. Applegate and Mr. Carson. I went by steamer to Monticello, and arrived there about noon on the same day. We remained at Monticello not over half an hour, and proceeded by land, in a two-horse carriage. We arrived at the Cowlitz Farm early in the day, on Sunday, the 12th. We spent a few hours at Mr. Roberts's, and then returned to Lucy Debos', and spent the night there. I think we left there about six o'clock in the morning, and returned to Mr. Roberts's and made a survey of the enclosed lands, as pointed out by Mr. Roberts, as the improvements of the Puget's Sound Agricultural Company, then occupied by them. The enclosure amounted to 166 acres. We were engaged in making a survey of the land and measurement of the buildings, I should think six or seven hours. Between two or three o'clock, p. m., on Monday, the 13th, we left Cowlitz Farm, *en route* for Nisqually, and arrived late in the evening at a farm-house near Skookum Chuck, where we spent the night. We left the next morning, and arrived late in the evening of Tuesday, the 14th, at Mr. Huggins's house, at Nisqually. On Wednesday morning after an examination and a walk over the premises of some two or three hours, we returned to Mr. Huggins's, and took breakfast, after which, in company with Mr. Huggins, we visited the warehouse, situated on the beach, about a mile distant from Mr. Huggins's. After examining the warehouse, we returned and spent the remainder of the day in surveying the 847 acres mentioned in the report, and a survey and measurement of the buildings and improvements situated thereon, and remained at Mr. Huggins's the night of the 15th. At about eight o'clock on Thursday morning, the 16th, we drove in a two horse carriage, in an easterly direction, for some miles, making a circuitous route, bearing a northerly direction, to the town of Steilacoom. We drove pretty rapidly, I think we were not more than one and a half hours on the road. We remained in Steilacoom till two or three o'clock, p. m. Whilst in Steilacoom, Mr. Applegate proceeded to the clerk's office and made some extracts from the records of the county. I should think he was engaged in the clerk's office an hour or so, after which, in company with Mr. Frank Clark, we visited various places, including some gardens and other improvements on the town-site. About three o'clock, p. m., the same day, we left for Mr. Huggins's by a different route part of the way. We were not over three quarters of an hour in driving to Mr. Huggins's. We remained at Mr. Huggins's but a short time, and then drove to Olympia, where we arrived about sun-down. We left Olympia on the morning of Friday, the 17th, and arrived at John R. Jackson's late in the evening, where we remained over night. On Saturday morning, the 18th, we proceeded *en route* to Monticello, by way of Cowlitz prairie, and arrived at Monticello in the evening of the same day. Going on board of the steamer, we left that place for Portland, where we arrived about three o'clock, a. m., of Sunday, the 19th.

Int. 2.—Have you described in your foregoing testimony all the examination you ever made, up to this date, of the Company's lands, either at Cowlitz Farm or Nisqually?

Ans.—Yes.

Int. 3.—How many acres of the Company's land, called the Cowlitz Farm, consisting of 3,500 acres and upwards, did you travel over and examine, as claimed in their, memorial?

Ans.—We travelled over what would probably constitute one half the amount, as I understand their boundaries to be.

Int. 4.—What proportion of their, claim of 3,500 acres and upwards, called Cowlitz Farm, is timber land?

Ans.—I understand, from the manner in which it was described, that but a small proportion, but mostly prairie and some brush land.

Int. 5.—Do you know where any of the boundaries of this claim are, by having personally inspected them?

Ans.—I do.

Int. 6.—Which boundaries?

Ans.—The boundary joining the Mission claim; the boundary on the north was pointed out as we were passing over by **Mr. Miles**, stating that this swale is the northern boundary of the Cowlitz Farm; the other boundaries were pointed out to us at **Mr. Roberts's**, upon some maps that were furnished of the surveys of that section of the country, but were not travelled over at that time by either **Mr. Applegate** or myself; **Mr. Roberts**, afterwards, as we were walking over the premises, pointing from the high lands, near where his buildings are, describing to us the boundaries of the Cowlitz Farm.

Int. 7.—Did you examine the northern boundary line, any more than riding across it in a wagon in company with **Mr. Miles**?

Ans.—I made no definite examination of lines beyond merely paying strict attention to the kind of soil over which we were passing, remarking at the time that it was a very large boundary, meaning that if the swale is the northern boundary, that it would be indefinite.

Int. 8.—By the last interrogatory, I did not ask you what remarks you made to **Mr. Miles** on your trip, neither did I ask for your opinion of the definiteness or indefiniteness of the northern boundary line of the Cowlitz Farm, nor whether, what you did see of this line, was consci[ent]ously or carefully observed by you; but I did ask you, and I now repeat the question, which I wish you to answer with Yes, or No; it is as follows: "Did you examine the northern boundary line any more than riding across it in a wagon in company with Mr. Miles? (The foregoing question is objected to by counsel of the United States, as it impertinently undertakes to dictate the answer which the witness shall make, which is not the province of any attorney.)

(The counsel for the Company insists upon a direct answer to the question, and claims that if an impertinence is to be found in the language of either of the attorneys in this case, it is to be found in the last objection of Attorney Johnson.)

Ans.—I have already given all the information that I possess, knowingly, of the northern boundary of the Cowlitz Farm, when your question was first asked me.

Int. 9.—Did you ever see this northern boundary line, except while riding across it and in its vicinity, and while you were sitting in Miles's wagon?

Ans.—I crossed a swale in a wagon, that swale was said to be the northern boundary of the Cowlitz Farm.

Int. 10.—Did you ever see this northern boundary line when you were not in a wagon?

Ans.—I suppose not.

Int. 11.—Do you know that you ever did see it when you were not in a wagon?

Ans.—I do not know that I ever have; we got out of the wagon before we fairly crossed the swale.

Int. 12.—Did you walk any distance from the wagon, on either side of the road?

Ans.—I do not know how many steps I made from the wagon, but was certainly not a great distance from it at any time.

Int. 13.—When you got out of the wagon in the swale, or in its vicinity, were you half a mile from it on either side of the road?

Ans.—No.

Int. 14.—Were you thirty steps from the wagon on either side of the road?

Ans.—No; I think not.

Int. 15.—Did you examine any of the springs, water-courses, or the mill-site upon this claim?

Ans.—I examined no mill-site, but saw a small stream there.

Int. 16.—Did you not meet Edward Huggins, one of the Company's agents, at Cowlitz Farm, and did he not express his willingness and desire to show you over the entire claim, and to point out its boundaries to you?

Ans.—I met Mr. Huggins at the Cowlitz Farm; Mr. Huggins, to my recollection, had but little to say about the Cowlitz Farm; to my best recollection he did not.

Int. 17.—Did Mr. Roberts make this proffer to you?

Ans.—Mr. Roberts did show us over the premises and pointed out his lines. We then got the maps, with a view to ascertain how they laid in reference to the survey, and found by the maps that they closed upon no lines.

Int. 18.—Did, or did not, Mr. Roberts proffer to show you for the Company over the Company's entire claim, and to point out for your personal inspection its boundary lines?

Ans.—Mr. Roberts did show us over the claim, and I have no doubt would, if requested, have gone along and pointed out where their claim run to.

Int. 19.—Did you consider it your duty, under your instructions from Mr. Johnson, to examine the Company's claim, as claimed by them in their memorial, called the Cowlitz Farm?

Ans.—Our instructions were to ascertain the amount of improvements in the way of buildings, fencing, &c.; to ascertain the amount of land enclosed, and the probable value of the same; and to generally so examine the country in the vicinity, so as to be able to judge somewhat as to the value of the lands in the vicinity.

Int. 20.—Are you as competent, in your opinion, to fix a value upon the tract of land claimed by the Company, called the Cowlitz Farm, from an examination particularly made of but 166 acres of it, and a general examination, as you have testified, of not more than half of the claim, as you would be

6 P

if you were to make a full and complete examination of the whole claim?

Ans.—I think not.

Int. 21.—Are you as competent to fix a correct value upon the claim of the Company between the Nisqually and Puyallup rivers, in Pierce county, extending along the shores of Puget's Sound, from the Nisqually river on the one side, to the Puyallup on the other, and back to the coast range of mountains, containing about 261 square miles, or 167,040 acres, with the examination you have made of that tract of land, as you would be were you to make a full and complete examination and survey of the entire claim?

Ans.—I think very probably not.

Int. 22.—Did you discover any difference in the soil of the various prairies passed through by you in traveling from Nisqually bridge to Steilacoom?

Ans.—No great difference.

Int. 23.—What small difference in the soil of these prairies did you discover, if any?

Ans.—There was a great sameness in all the prairies. Excepting the prairie next to Nisqually bridge, there appeared to be more sand and a less amount of gravel on the surface.

Int. 24.—Was the examination you made of the Company's claim at Nisqually made in company with Jesse Applegate and J. C. Carson?

Ans.—Yes; I have traveled over much more of the Nisqually than, perhaps, either Mr. Carson or Applegate did, but was no further back from the Sound than they were.

Int. 25.—Did you make any personal inspection of the records of Pierce county?

Ans.—I did not; I was in the office when Mr. Applegate examined them, and took extracts, and looked over his extracts.

Int. 26.—How, then, can you state under oath that any particular record will be found at the clerk's office in Steilacoom?

Ans.—I was there at the time Mr. Huggins and Mr. Applegate were making the extracts from the records—most of the time.

Int. 27.—If you were the owner of 167,000 acres of land between the Nisqually and Puyallup rivers, with the improvements thereon, for instance the land claimed by the Puget's Sound Agricultural Company, and its improve. ments, by their memorial to the Joint Commission, and valued the same at 164,000 pounds sterling, and you had made an agreement to dispose of it at a price to be fixed by referees, upon testimony to be submitted to them as to its value, would you think it fair, or would you be willing that those referees should determine its value upon the testimony of one or more men who made such an examination of it, and only such an examination as you made of the Company's claim at Nisqually?

Ans.—If I had a claim of that value, and the parties made to examine that claim were men who had had experience in examining, and men who were competent to judge of the value of lands and improvements, and have made sufficient examination to judge correctly of the same, I would be satisfied.

J. S. RINEARSON.

OREGON CITY, *August* 25, 1866.

STATE OF OREGON, } ss.
   Clackamas County. }

I, J. M. Bacon, county clerk of said county, do hereby certify that the foregoing depositions, hereto annexed, of Jesse Applegate, J. C. Carson, and J. S. Rinearson, witnesses produced by and [in] behalf of the United States, in relation to the matter of the claim of the Puget's Sound Agricultural Company, before the British and American Joint Commission for the adjustment of the same, were taken before me, at my office in Oregon City, in said county, and reduced to writing by me, (except the report of the experts,) on the 24th and 25th days of August, A. D. 1866, according to the dates appended to said depositions, when they were signed respectively. I further certify that such depositions were taken before me in pursuance of a verbal agreement made in my presence between W. C. Johnson, Esq., attorney for the United States, and Frank Clark, Esq., attorney for the Puget's Sound Agricultural Company.

I further certify that to each of said witnesses, before his examination, I administered the following oath, to wit:

"You swear that the evidence you may give in the matter of the claim of the Puget's Sound Agricultural Company against the United States shall be the truth, the whole truth, and nothing but the truth, so help you God."

That after the same was reduced to writing, the deposition of each witness was carefully read to and then signed by them.

In witness whereof I have hereunto subscribed my name [L. S.] and affixed the seal of said county this 25th day August, A. D. 1866.

J. M. BACON, *County Clerk.*

BRITISH AND AMERICAN JOINT COMMISSION

UPON THE CLAIMS OF THE

HUDSON'S BAY AND PUGET'S SOUND AGRICULTURAL COMPANIES.

In the matter of the Claim of the Puget's Sound Agricultural Company vs. the United States.

Depositions of witnesses produced and examined in the town of Olympia, in the Territory of Washington, on behalf of the United States, on the 16th day of November, A. D. 1866, and succeeding days, before Andrew J. Moses, a notary public in and for the Territory of Washington, by virtue of a verbal agreement made in my presence by W. Carey Johnson, Esq., on behalf of the United States, and Frank Clark, Esq., on behalf of the said Puget's Sound Agricultural Company.

TESTIMONY OF HON. C. C. HEWITT.

The Hon. C. C. Hewitt being first duly sworn, in answer to interrogatories, deposes as follows:

Int. 1.—State your age, residence, and occupation.

Ans.—Age, fifty-four; residence, Olympia, Washington Territory. I am chief justice of Washington Territory, and also carrying on a farm in Thurston county, Washington Territory.

Int. 2.—How many years have you resided in Washington Territory?

Ans.—Thirteen years.

Int. 3.—What opportunities, if any, have you had to know the market value of agricultural lands in Lewis, Thurston, and Pierce counties, during that period?

Ans.—I have travelled over the settled portions of those counties during that period. I have never dealt in lands, except that I bought a farm four miles from Olympia; I have never heard the price of lands very much discussed among the farmers of those counties.

Int. 4.—Are you acquainted with the tract of land in Pierce county claimed by the Puget's Sound Agricultural Company, known as the Nisqually Plains? If so, state what is the character of the soil, and what, in your opinion, the land is worth per acre, on the average.

Ans.—I have been over the tract of land known in this country as the Nisqually Plains, but do not know the boundary of the Puget's Sound Company's claims, and could not fix an average value. There are several characters of soil included within the claim; the most of the prairie, which includes the greater portion of the claim, I should think is gravelly, and is of but little value except for grazing purposes, and [of] no great value for that. The river bottoms are an alluvial soil, and very rich. There are portions of the timbered lands that are commonly known as the clay loam.

Int. 5.—At about what sum would you fix the average market value of good improved agricultural lands in the counties you have named, in 1863, or at any time since, away from the immediate vicinity of towns?

Ans.—What we know in this country as agricultural prairie lands I should fix at about $5 per acre; timbered land I do not think has any value for agricultural purposes. I would not take it if a man was to give it to me.

Int. 6.—How would the prairie land on the Nisqually Plains compare with what you have described in the preceeding answers as good agricultural land?

Ans.—I would rate it about one to four, or one fourth as much.

Int. 7.—Are the rich lands of the Nisqually claim, which you say are on the river and creek bottoms, timbered or prairie?

Ans.—Most that I am acquainted with are timbered.

Int. 8.—Have you purchased any land in Washington Territory? If so, state the amount, description, nature of the improvements, when the purchase was made, and about the price paid per acre.

Ans.—I have purchased a farm of 320 acres of prairie and timber; about two thirds of it is prairie. The prairie was all under good fence, a very good story-and-a-half frame house, 18 by 40 feet, with an L kitchen and a good well of water; and about 1,200 bearing fruit trees of different kinds, consisting of apples, pears, plums, peaches, and cherries, were on the place. The purchase was made in the fall of 1862; the cost was about $5.30 per acre, including the improvements. I afterwards purchased the improvements on some fractions of Government land, and then entered the land at Government price. (Last question and answer objected to by counsel for the Company as incompetent, irrelevant, and immaterial.)

Cross-examined by Frank Clark, Esq., for the Company.

Int. 1.—Were all the improvements to be removed from the tract of land owned by you and referred to in your examination-in-chief, what would you take for the prairie portion of the same in money?

Ans.—I would charge as much for the prairie land as I would for the whole, and would sell the whole for $5 an acre if the land was in a state of nature.

Int. 2.—Who did you purchase of?

Ans.—John N. Law.

Int. 3.—What was the occasion of his selling?

Ans.—He said he wished to remove to California.

Int. 4.—Was he not in debt and obliged to sell?

Ans.—I cannot say; I know there was a mortgage on the place.

Int. 5.—Was there any sorrel on the place when you perchased it?

Ans.—Yes, plenty of it.

Int. 6.—Is there as much on it now? If not, state the reason.

Ans.—There is not as much. The reason is, the timothy grass has run a portion of it out; and a great portion of the balance has been killed by good cultivation.

Int. 7.—For what purposes is the prairie part of your claim principally valuable?

Ans.—Grain, grass, pasture, fruit, and vegetables.

Int. 8.—When properly cultivated, what quantity of wheat, oats, or barley will it raise to the acre?

Ans.—In my opinion, twenty-five bushels of wheat, forty bushels of oats; barley, I cannot say.

Int. 9.—When properly cultivated, what quantity of timothy will it raise to the acre?

Ans.—One ton and a half, in my opinion; it raised over a ton this summer with ordinary cultivation.

Int. 10.—What quantity of roots will it produce to the acre with proper cultivation?

Ans.—From my experience, I think it would raise three hundred bushels of potatoes, and six hundred bushels of ruta-bagas. For other vegetables, I have not had experience sufficient to form an opinion.

Int. 11.—State the value per bushel of wheat, oats, potatoes and rutabagas.

Ans.—I could not state; I have never raised any for sale.

Int. 12.—What is the value of timothy hay per ton?

Ans.—Timothy hay is worth $10 per ton, in the field, in that neighborhood.

Int. 13.—How do fruit trees thrive there?

Ans.—Nothing extra for most kinds of fruit; cherries and plums thrive extraordinarily well.

Int. 14.—State in detail the portions of Nisqually Plains, or the Company's claim in Pierce county, over which you have traveled, and with which you are familar.

Ans.—I am most familiar with the portion traversed by the road from Olympia to Steilacoom, and the military post back of the town. I have traveled the road several times from Fort Steilacoom to the crossing of the Puyallup, at Carson's; twice about 1859 or 1860, once in 1858, and at other times, the dates of which I do not remember. I have traveled the road once from Fort Steilacoom to Montgomery's, in 1856 or 1857. I have travelled the road once from Fort Steilacoom to Yelm Prairie, I think in the spring of 1854. I have also been on the Nisqually Indian Reservation, and four miles above it on the river.

Int. 15.—Are you acquainted with Dominick's prairie?

Ans.—No.

Int. 16.—Are you acquainted with the land known as Thomas Tallantyre's claim, situate on the Company's claim, in Pierce county, containing about 320 acres of rich soil, composed of black mould and gravel? (Objected [to] by Counsel for the United States, as there is no evidence showing that the soil of this particular claim is of the description named.)

Ans.—No.

Int. 17.—Are you acquainted with the claims of any of the squatters on the Company's lands in Pierce county? If yea, designate and describe them.

Ans.—I can only designate the claim of John Montgomery, but cannot describe it.

Int. 18.—Can you describe the tracts on the Company's claim, consisting of gravelly soil, and those consisting of sandy and other descriptions of soil?

Ans.—I cannot particularly describe them.

Int. 19.—Please describe, if you can, the soil on and around the Indian reservation, situate upon this claim.

Ans.—The most that I have seen of it is gravelly; I do not know where the lines of the reservation are.

Questioned by W. C. Johnson, Esq.

Int. 1.—Is the soil of your claim what would be called sandy?

Ans.—No, sir.

Int. 2.—How far is it from Olympia?

Ans.—About four miles.

Cross-examination Resumed.

Int. 1.—If the soil of your claim is not sandy, what is it?
Ans.—It is a vegetable mould, mixed with sand and loam.

C. C. HEWITT.

[L. S.]   Subscribed and sworn to before me this 19th day of
November, A. D. 1866.

ANDREW J. MOSES,
Notary Public, W. T.

TESTIMONY OF GEN. WILLIAM W. MILLER.

General William W. Miller being first duly sworn, in answer
to interrogatories, deposes as follows:

Int. 1.—State your age, residence, and occupation.

Ans.—I am forty-one years old; reside at Olympia, Washington Territory; by occupation a broker and money-lender.

Int. 2.—When did you first come to Washington Territory?

Ans.—About August, 1851.

Int. 3.—At what points have you resided since that time?

Ans.—I first came to the Territory as surveyor of customs and trading office at Nisqually landing, until I was removed in the summer of 1853; during this time I have spent most of my time at Olympia; since the summer of 1853 I have resided altogether at Olympia.

Int. 4.—What official positions have you held in Washington Territory since 1853?

Ans.—I was clerk of the United States district court, deputy collector of customs, quartermaster and commissary general of volunteers during the Indian war of 1855 and 1856, member of both branches of the Territorial Legislature, and superintendent of Indian affairs.

Int. 5.—In loaning money, what kind of security do you ordinarily take in this Territory? (Objected to by counsel for the Company, as irrelevant and immaterial.)

Ans.—Personal security and real estate.

Int. 6.—What kind of real estate have you most frequently loaned money on? (Objected to by counsel for the Company, for the same reasons as before.)

Ans.—Donation land claims, town property, and mill property.

Int. 7.—What other facilities and opportunities, if any, have you enjoyed for obtaining a knowledge of the value of land in Washington Territory?

Ans.—I know of no other facilities than those afforded by my business.

Int. 8.—State whether or not you have had conversations with farmers and other owners of lands about their value, and whether or not you have known of purchases and sales; if yea, state whether frequently or otherwise. (Objected to by counsel for the Company as incompetent, and as hearsay.)

Ans.—Of course, in pursuit of my business, I have had many conversations with divers persons, with regard to the value of lands and other property; of course I have had much to do with the purchase and sale of lands; probably more than any other man in this part of the country.

Int. 9.—Into what counties has your business principally extended?

Ans.—Principally in Thurston, Lewis, Mason, and Chehalis; and to a limited extent, to all the counties on the Sound.

Int. 10.—About what was the market value per acre of good farming land in Lewis, Thurston, and Pierce counties, in 1863, without including the value of improvements away from the immediate vicinity of towns?

Ans.—It is a hard question to answer. This portion of Washington Territory is composed of some excellent lands, but much the larger portion is very poor. I have known some small tracts of very rich land, that were surrounded by grazing land of a poorer kind, to sell for from ten to twenty dollars per acre; but these were extreme cases. I have known other tracts of the best quality of prairie land, free from gravel, to sell for from a dollar and a-half to four dollars per acre, not including the improvements; gravelly prairie land is generally worth about Government entrance price, and sometimes a shade higher.

Int. 11.—Are you acquainted with the tract of land in Lewis county, of something less than 4,000 acres, known as the Cowlitz farm, claimed by the Puget's Sound Agricultural Company?

Ans.—I am not well acquainted with its metes and bounds, though I own two or three thousand acres in the immediate vicinity; with that portion of the Cowlitz prairie claimed by the Puget's Sound Company I am not very familiar. Several years ago I rode over that portion of the prairie which I supposed belonged to the Puget's Sound Company.

Int. 12.—Have you lately passed through the Cowlitz prairie, and in the vicinity of the land occupied by Mr. Roberts, as lessee of the Puget's Sound Agricultural Company?

Ans.—I don't know precisely where Mr. Roberts lives, and I imagine I was not nearer his residence than the mission claim, which is on the Cowlitz prairie.

Int. 13.—Taking the tract of land claimed by the Company above the mission claim on that prairie, including the heavy timber next to the river, and running back across the prairie, so as to include the ash swale, at what price per acre would you fix its value in gold, without any improvement?

Ans.—The prairie portion of the land, without the improvements, I would value at from three to five dollars per acre in gold coin. The timbered portion of the land would have no market value at present; or at any rate, it would be very small.

Int. 14.—Are you acquainted with the tract of land between the Nisqually and Puyallup rivers, in Pierce county, known as the Nisqually Plains, and claimed by the Puget's Sound Company?

Ans.—I am very well acquainted with the tract of country known as the Nisqually Plains, though I do not know what are the exact metes and bounds of the claims of the Puget's Sound Agricultural Company.

Int. 15.—Taking a tract lying between the two rivers named, and extending from Puget's Sound back to the timber, near to the Cascade Mountains, so as to include (160,000) acres, at what price per acre would you fix its value, in gold coin, excluding the improvements?

Ans.—The prairie portion I would value at about $1.25 per acre. That portion of the timber lying east of the Nisqually Plains I consider has little or no market value. That portion of the timber immediately on Puget's Sound I am not sufficiently well acquainted with it to fix a value on it.

Int. 16.—Describe the soil of the prairie portion.

Ans.—It is almost entirely gravelly prairie, only fit for pasturage, though there are here and there small tracts large enough for gardens, or small fields of very rich lands.

Int. 17.—Is there any material difference between the character of the prairie lands lying within three miles of Puget's Sound and those extending further to the eastward?

Ans.—The nature seems to me to be pretty much the same all over the plains, though the best grass grows on the eastern portion.

Int. 18.—Would men passing along the road from the Nisqually river to Fort Nisqually, where Mr. Huggins resides, thence around by Lake Sequalitchew, down to Steilacoom, and then back to Mr. Huggins's, by the road leading from Steilacoom to Olympia, pass over, and be able to see an average quality of these plains?

Ans.—I think he would be able to see nearly, though not quite an average quality of the land. But from the fact of the land being more closely pastured on this portion of the claim, a stranger would be more unfavorably impressed than he would be with that portion lying to the eastward.

Int. 19.—State, if you know, whether the Company's cattle on the Nisqually Plains were tame, or otherwise, in 1851, 1852, and 1853?

Ans.—I never knew much about the Company's cattle; I saw some cattle on the plains, which I understood to be the Company's cattle, which were wild; I saw others about the fort that were tame.

Int. 20.—Do you know whether or not these wild cattle were considered dangerous to travelers on foot by people living in the vicinity? (Objected to by counsel for the Company as irrelevant and immaterial.)

Ans.—I did not consider them dangerous, having had some experience with Spanish cattle in Oregon; I do not think the people living on the plains considered them dangerous.

Cross-examined by Frank Clark, Esq., for the Company.

Int. 1.—Have you a general acquaintance with the country lying between Monticello, near the mouth of the Cowlitz river, and Olympia, at the head of Puget's Sound?

Ans.—I have, especially with that portion lying along the public road.

Int. 2.—Is there any prairie or grazing land, of any extent, between the points designated in the first interrogatory, except that lying along the present public highway or line of travel between them?

Ans.—The different highways between the two points designated touch nearly all of the large prairies or grazing land; there are smaller prairies not far remote from those different highways.

Int. 3.—Designate the different highways, with the amount of agricultural and grazing lands lying along and in the immediate vicinity of each.

Ans.—Over that portion of the country lying and being in Thurston county, there are three highways all of which run, to a great extent, through open grazing country. [In] that portion of the country lying and being in Lewis county there are two main highways; one of which is known as a military road, runs mostly through a timbered country, the other, known as the old highway or Hudson's Bay road, runs, to a great extent, through a prairie country, one of those prairies being the large prairie known as the Cowlitz prairie. That portion of the country lying in Cowlitz county has only one main highway at present; formerly, there was a Hudson's Bay trail on the east or left bank of the Cowlitz river, both of which run through a timbered country, running through Thurston county. Three-fourths of the country on the stage road is prairie; two-thirds of the country on the middle road is prairie, and about one-half of the country on the Black river road is prairie, as near as I can approximate. I suppose there are from twenty-two thousand to twenty-six thousand acres of prairie land lying along these roads. On the old highway, or Hudson's Bay road, in Lewis county, I suppose there are from eight thousand to eleven thousand acres of rich prairie land. On the Military road there are about five thousand acres of rich prairie land. On the right bank of the Cowlitz river, at Monticello, in Cowlitz county, there may be six or seven hundred acres of prairie land; though immediately in that vicinity there is a larger extent of open bottom land that overflows.

Int. 4.—What amount of prairie land, adapted to the growth of grain and timothy, or clover, and valuable for grazing, in your judgment, is there in the counties of Cowlitz, Lewis, and Thurston, all told?

Ans.—I do not know of there being more than six or eight hundred acres of any prairie land, all of which is of the best quality, in Lewis county; I suppose there are from fourteen thousand to seventeen thousand acres of clear prairie land, nearly all of which is free from gravel, and the best quality prairie land known to this country; in Thurston county there are from twenty-two thousand to twenty-six thousand acres of open prairie land, nearly all of which is of the poorer gravelly kind known to this country.

Int. 5.—Are not all the lands suitable for agriculture and valuable for pasturage in these counties now fully occupied by settlers and are not all the pasture lands fully, if not overstocked?

Ans.—The open prairie lands in Thurston county are nearly all owned by individuals, and pretty much fully stocked. In Lewis county a large portion of the prairie land is owned by individuals, but is not stocked to its fullest capacity. All of the dry prairie lands in Cowlitz county, known to me, are owned by individuals, and are fully stocked.

Int. 6.—Do not British Columbia, Vancouver's Island, and dependencies, and the various Government and other vessels visiting the respective localities and the waters of Puget depend, to a great extent, for supplies of fresh butter, eggs, poultry, vegetables, and other like necessaries upon that part, of Washington Territory lying north of the Cowlitz river?

Ans.—The western portion of British Columbia, Vancouver's Island, and the vessels trading to those countries and to Puget's Sound, afford a very good market for the articles named in the question.

Int. 7.—Are these different articles, referred to in the last interrogatory, produced by this section of country in sufficient quantities to supply the local markets and these other demands for the same?

Ans.—This section of country is capable of producing a full supply of articles mentioned to meet the demands of our local market; but, for want of enterprise in our people, a full supply is not produced, although good prices are always offered.

Int. 8.—Do not British Columbia, Vancouver's Island, and those various vessels depend almost solely upon Washington Territory and Oregon for their supplies of fresh meats?

Ans.—They do.

Int. 9.—Does the amount of beef, mutton, and pork raised in that portion of Washington Territory lying north of the Cowlitz river, after supplying the local demands, have a surplus that can be stated as more than one-third of the amount to supply these other markets?

Ans.—I am not able to answer the question.

Int. 10.—State what, in your judgment, the proportion of surplus beef, mutton, and pork, raised in this country after supplying the local demands, is, of the whole amount shipped from the different points of shipment on Puget's Sound, to supply these other markets.

Ans.—I am unable to answer the question.

Int. 11.—Are the lands referred to in the last two interrogatories that are available for agriculture or for stock-raising, if well cultivated and fully stocked, capable of producing such supplies as are hereinbefore enumerated, in sufficient quantities to supply the local and these other markets for the same?

Ans.—I believe they are.

Int. 12.—Are not large quantities of beef cattle, sheep, and hogs, yearly driven from the State of Oregon to supply a demand of British Columbia, Vancouver's Island, and these vessels, with meats, which this country has failed to produce?

Ans.—Yes.

Int. 13.—How is stock generally taken from Oregon to the respective markets?

Ans.—For Western British Columbia and the other markets named in the question, the cattle are driven from Oregon overland to Puget's Sound, and thence taken by water to Victoria and other places where wanted. Stock, here mentioned, is driven over the highways in Cowlitz, Lewis, and Thurston counties mentioned and described in my former answer.

Int. 14.—Commencing with the year 1858, please give me your judgment on the amount of stock so annually brought from the State of Oregon to Puget's Sound for shipment to these respective markets?

Ans.—I am not able to fix upon the exact number furnished by this route, though I am of the opinion the markets mentioned were almost entirely supplied by means of this route.

Int. 15.—What length of time does it take to drive stock from Monticello to the vicinity of points of shipment on Puget's Sound?

Ans.—I would say from seven to ten days.

Int. 16.—Is it not a matter of necessity to pasture or feed said stock in the vicinity of points of shipment, for a considerable length of time, before the same is slaughtered and shipped, or shipped alive to supply the various markets referred to in former interrogatories?

Ans.—Yes; cattle dealers while driving their cattle over

7 P

said route, and whilst waiting to ship them to the various markets, are necessarily compelled to feed or graze them. I believe that some of the large cattle dealers always keep some such stock on hand, in readiness to be shipped as the demand in the various markets require.

Int. 17.—Are not a large proportion of these cattle unfit for immediate butchering when brought to the immediate point of shipment, and do not cattle dealers generally there graze or feed them for a considerable length of time to prepare them for market?

Ans.—Yes; I believe that such is the case.

Int. 18.—Since the year 1858, has there not been a demand for all or more pasture lands than are to be found in the vicinity of these several points of shipment on Puget's Sound?

Ans.—I believe that often, if not generally, there has been such demand.

Int. 19.—Have not the pasture lands referred to in the last interrogatory, together with the stock of the residents and settlers, and these stock dealers, been fully, if not over-stocked since 1858?

Ans.—I believe that the pasture lands, lying in the vicinity of the shipping ports on Puget's Sound, have been stocked to their full capacity since the year 1858.

Int. 20.—Has there not been, since 1858, a local demand in this section of country for much more hay and grain than is produced in it?

Ans.—I think there has been a fair demand for what hay and grain that has been produced in the country.

Int. 21.—Are not large amounts of hay, chopped, and other feed, annually shipped from California to Vancouver's Island, British Columbia, and Puget's Sound, to supply the demand for the same, over and above the amount produced in this country?

Ans.—I am not well informed as to what importations Vancouver's Island and British Columbia makes from California; but I believe the large milling companies on Puget's Sound import most of their supplies of the kind mentioned from California.

Int. 22.—Whence is the greater part of the wheat obtained that is ground at the Port Gamble, Seattle and Tum-Water grist-mills?

Ans.—I believe a large portion is brought from California.

Int. 23.—What is the price of freight on hay, feed and grain, from San Francisco to these points?

Ans.—I do not know; I have heard the merchants say that they paid from six to eight dollars per ton for bringing them goods.

Int. 24.—Since 1858, what has been the price of pasturage, in this vicinity, per week, for sheep, horned cattle and horses?

Ans.—I do not know as to the exact price per week; I rented one pasture myself, of about two hundred acres, I think, for $200 in coin, for the season; the summer had partially gone. This was the ordinary gravelly prairie of the country, and was somewhat set in sorrel. This, I think, was during the summer and fall of 1863.

Int. 25.—Is the prairie part of the Company's claim called Cowlitz Farm well adapted to the production of grain and the various grasses?

Ans.—As I understand it, the prairie portion of that claim consists of the very best quality of upland prairie land known to this country, and will produce good crops of the kind mentioned in the question.

Int. 26.—What amount [of] timothy hay, if properly cu'tivated, will the prairie part of the land called the Cowlitz Farm annually yield per acre?

Ans.—I could not say as to the exact amount, but I believe it will produce equally as fine crops of hay as the richest upland prairies of Illinois, where I resided before coming here.

Int. 27.—Since 1858, what has been the average price of good timothy hay per ton in Lewis County?

Ans.—I am not well informed as to the price of hay during the whole time mentioned; last year my agent sold a small quantity, for myself, at $10 per ton, and this year he writes me that he can sell some sixty tons, that I have there, at $8 per ton.

Int. 28.—Since that time, what has been the average price per bushel for wheat, oats, and barley?

Ans.—I do not know.

Int. 29.—Since the same time, what has been the average price per pound of beef, pork, and mutton?

Ans.—I do not know.

Int. 30.—What quantity of sheep, cattle, and horses will the Puget's Sound Agricultural Company's claim, consisting of the prairie land lying between the Puyallup and Nisqually rivers in Pierce county, annually afford pasturage for?

Ans.—I do not know the precise number.

Int. 31.—Is it necessary to give salt to stock pasturing upon this tract of land, having access, as they do, to the salt marshes and salt water?

Ans.—I think it is necessary for cattle to have salt; and this tract being a large one, the most of it would be so remote from salt water that, in my opinion, it would be necessary to salt them.

Int. 32.—What number of horned cattle would the 200 acres of land, rented by you during the year 1863, annually afford good pasturage for?

Ans.—Mr. Coulter, who rented the field, told me [he] would put about eighty head of beef cattle in it, and that they would consume all the grass therein for that season in about six weeks or two months.

Int. 33.—Did this pasture, rented by you for $200 in gold coin, for the year 1863, contain only the natural grasses of the country, and was there the necessary supply of water in it for the stock?

Ans.—It contained only the natural grasses of the country, and was well supplied with water.

Int. 34.—Would the stock pasturing upon the lands of the Company in Pierce county, lying next to the salt marshes, or shores of the Sound, require to be given any salt from one year's end to the other?

Ans.—The shore of the Sound being skirted with timber,

I think it would be necessary to salt the cattle, though on this subject I am not well informed.

Int. 35.—Are not the timber lands upon this tract necessary for shelter for stock during the storms of fall and winter seasons, and do they not afford valuable pasturage during the same period, and are they not also valuable as a summer range, being covered, as they are, with pea-vine rushes and the coarse grasses?

Ans.—I have noticed on the Nisqually Plains scattering timber, which I think is very useful in protecting stock pasturing on those plains. I do not know as to the value of the pea-vine pasturage in the densely timbered tracts surrounding the plains. I believe that at certain seasons of the year, in this country, stock running at large leave the open country and seek the timber to get forage; and I presume that stock running on Nisqually Plains do the same.

Int. 36.—During your residence in this country, has not this tract of land, belonging to the Company in Pierce County, afforded such pasturage for stock as to render it unnecessary to feed them from one year's end to another?

Ans.—I have resided in this country some fifteen years, and during that time there have been many winters when it would not be necessary to feed stock running on those plains.

Int. 37.—Since the year 1856, what has been the average of sheep per head in this vicinity?

Ans.—I do not know precisely; I have heard of sheep selling for as high as six dollars per head, by the wholesale, and I have known one drove sold for two dollars per head; I think that about $5 per head would be the average price up to 1863; they have fallen a little since.

Int. 38.—From 1856 to 1863, what has been the average price per head of good milch cows, yearlings, two, three, and four-year old heifers and steers, that were fit for beef, and what has been the average value of good work oxen during the same period?

Ans.—I cannot say as to the average price of stock cattle;

work oxen have nearly always sold readily for from one hundred dollars to two hundred and fifty dollars per yoke.

Int. 39.—What proportion of the stock shipped to supply the different markets in the foregoing interrogatories referred to, has been shipped from Steilacoom, a town-site on the Company's claim in Pierce county?

Ans.—I do not know precisely, but I think that nearly all have been shipped from the two ports of Steilacoom and Olympia.

Int. 40.—Is not the frontage, or points of the frontage of this claim, very valuable as a point or points for such and other shipments?

Ans.—I think Steilacoom is probably the most convenient point to ship stock from on the Sound; how valuable it is I do not know.

Int. 41.—Are not the timber lands on the Company's claim, called the Cowlitz Farm, of great value to a person or company owning the same, for fencing, fire-wood, and building purposes, and as affording winter and summer range, and shelter for stock?

Ans.—In that portion of the country there is such an over supply of timber, that I do not consider it very valuable as timber, and I consider it rather as a nuisance, as a general thing; I am not well acquainted with the timbered portion of the Company's Cowlitz claim.

Int. 42.—While you were at Nisqually, have you not frequently seen the Company's men driving cattle in large quantities into a corral on the beach, near where you had your office, that were shipped to Victoria and other places?

Ans.—I have.

Int. 43.—What is the extent of Dominick prairie, situate on the Company's claim, in Pierce county, and what is the description of its soil?

Ans.—At a rough guess, I would say it consists of 1,000 acres and over; the soil is of a sandy nature, and much better for pasturage than the average of the plains, in my opinion.

Int. 44.—Is it not also valuable for purposes of general agriculture, when properly cultivated?

Ans.—As to that, I am not well informed.

Int. 45.—Are there not large tracts, consisting of thousands of acres, in different localities on the Nisqually Plains, of a mixture, in varying proportions, of black vegetable mould and sand, all of which, by skillful cultivation, could be made to yield fair grain crops, in rotation with root crops and grasses?

Ans.—As to the question, generally, I am not well informed, and cannot answer; but I do know of one tract of land of the description mentioned in the question, consisting of some two or three hundred acres, known as the Gravelle claim, which produces good crops of wheat and other grain.

Int. 46.—Do you not know that a large quantity of land, on and surrounding the Indian reservation, upon the Company's claim in Pierce county, is to be found of like quality to that of Dominick prairie?

Ans.—I think that portion of the reservation lying on what is known as Douglas river, and in that vicinity, is of a sandy nature, and much like the soil of Dominick prairie.

Int. 47.—Do you not know that there is a notable proportion of gravel in the richest tracts of land at Muck and other points on the Nisqually Plains, and that there is great diversity in the quality of the gravelly soils, there being some in the low, moist basins, susceptible of the highest cultivation?

Ans.—I have at Muck and Tlitlow, and other points on the plains, seen very good crops growing in a rich black soil, very much mixed with gravel.

Int. 48.—Are you acquainted with the claim or tract of land at present occupied by Chief Justice C. C. Hewitt?

Ans.—I am.

Int. 49.—How does the soil of his place compare with the soil of Dominick prairie?

Ans.—Judge Hewitt's prairie land is of a sandy nature, and for pasturage about of an equal value with Dominick prairie, in my opinion.

Int. 50—Are the soils of these two localities, in your opinion, of like value for agricultural purposes?

Ans.—I presume they are, though I do not deem either of them valuable for that purpose.

Int. 51.—Do you not know that there are on the Nisqually Plains many valuable swamp lands, several of which have been drained, and now annually produce large crops of timothy hay?

Ans.—Of my personal knowledge, I do not know that such is the case, though I have heard of several of the swamps being drained, and fine crops being obtained therefrom. I have a personal knowledge of two swamp farms that produce good crops of hay and roots.

Int. 52.—Is not the Company's entire claim in Pierce County well watered; and does it not, on this account, have a greater value for stock-raising than it otherwise would possess?

Ans—Said claim is remarkably well watered, and, as stock drink water, it is for that reason more valuable.

Int. 53.—Have not this Company and their agents, since you have known them, been very obliging to emigrants, and supplied them with necessaries generally when required; and did they not, during the Indian war, furnish all such supplies as they had that were needed and called for by the public authorities?

Ans—I have always found the agents of the Company kind, gentlemany men; and I believe they dealt with settlers and others on as liberal terms as the American merchants. As quartermaster and commissary of the volunteers, myself and agents had many dealings with Dr. Tolmie, the agent of the Company, and we always found him willing to sell such supplies as he had.

Int. 54.—When you came to the country, were not the different Indian tribes of this vicinity greatly under the influence and control of the agents of this Company?

Ans.—From my observation at Nisqually, I am of the opinion that Dr. Tolmie had great influence with the Indians; and he is the only one of the agents with whom I had much to do.

Int. 55.—In your opinion, did not the agents of this Company afford a great protection to the first settlers of this section of country, by the exercise of their influence over the different Indian tribes?

Ans.—In my opinion, the officers of the Company, being educated gentlemen, have always exerted whatever influence they might have had with the Indians to protect the whites of all nations in the early settlement of the country.

W. W. MILLER.

OLYMPIA, *November* 20, 1866.

TESTIMONY OF FREDERICK A. CLARKE.

Frederick A. Clarke, being first duly sworn, in answer to interrogatories, deposes as follows:

Int. 1.—State your age, residence, and occupation.

Ans.—I am thirty-eight years old; residence in Pierce County, Washington Territory; by occupation, I am a farmer.

Int. 2.—What is your present official position?

Ans.—I am one of the county commissioners of Pierce County, and a representative elect to the Legislature.

Int. 3.—How long, and at what place, have you resided in Washington Territory?

Ans.—I have resided in Washington Territory since 1852, at the Cowlitz; in Lewis county, from 1852 to 1862; and since 1863, in Pierce County, at Muck, on the Nisqually Plains.

Int. 4.—What have been your opportunities for knowing the market value of land at Cowlitz and its neighborhood, and in Pierce county?

Ans.—They have been good. I have purchased and sold more land in Lewis county than any one else I know of.

Int. 5.—Are you acquainted with the Puget's Sound Agricultural Company's claim, known as the Cowlitz Farm, in Lewis county? If so, state when you first saw it.

Ans.—I first saw it January, 1852, and have known it ever since.

Int. 6.—Who was the Company's agent in charge at that place in 1852?

Ans.—H. N. Peers.

Int. 7.—How long did he remain, and who succeeded him?

Ans.—He remained, I think, until 1856, and was succeeded by William Sinclair.

Int. 8.—How long did Sinclair remain, and who succeeded him?

Ans.—He remained until 1859; and by Mr. Huggins taking charge of the place and putting Mr. Roberts on it.

Int. 9.—In what condition were the buildings and fencing on the place when you first saw it in 1852?

Ans.—Generally bad; some of the fields were kept up; one on the eastern portion of the claim, and one below the house to the southwest; also one north of the house; most of it, however, was thrown open to the common pasturage. The shed barns that were around the place had all rotted down but one in the eastern field. The hewed log barn near the house was also still standing. The log storehouse near, and east of the dwelling, was also standing, as well as a hewed log stable. The dwelling was a hewed log building, as Mr. Peers told me, weather-boarded on the outside, and ceiled and painted, or papered on the inside. Mr. Peers told me the under-pinning, or under-logs, were decaying, so as to effect the shape of the fire-place and doors. He said he would not make any expensive repairs, because the Yankees were going to get it so soon. The reason why he said that, I understood to be that they were jumping every part of the claim at the time.

Int. 10.—What became of the Company's live-stock and trading goods which were at Cowlitz Farm?

Ans.—Sinclair turned them over to Mr. Huggins, who removed them to Nisqually.

Int. 11.—How much farming was done by the Company's agents after 1852, at Cowlitz?

Ans.—I suppose when I first went to the Cowlitz, perhaps there were from 100 to 150 acres in grain; one field of 100 acres or upwards—might be two hundred—was kept for meadow, about half of which, or a little more, would pay for cutting. From 1852 to the time of Sinclair leaving, in 1859, the farming grew less and less every year. I don't suppose there were over twenty-five or thirty acres in grain in 1859. In 1858 Sinclair mowed very little meadow; most of it had been turned out to pasture.

Int. 12.—Do you know of any encouragement being given by the Company's agents to settlers on the Cowlitz Farm? If so, state when it was, and by whom.

Ans.—I do not know that their agents ever encouraged any one, except from hearsay.

Int. 13.—What did the Company's agents do with the rails surrounding the fields which were thrown out to common pasture in 1852, and afterwards?

Ans.—They did nothing with them, but let them lie there; after that time they used some of them to repair the other fences.

Int. 14.—What, according to your best information and knowledge, was the market value of good prairie land at Cowlitz Farm and vicinity, in 1862, when you left there?

Ans.—At no time, that I know of, has land sold for more than five dollars an acre on Cowlitz Prairie or vicinity; I mean by the vicinity Jackson's Prairie, Drew's Prairie, La Kamass, and Grand Prairie. I have bought and sold land on La Kamass and Cowlitz Prairie, and Grand Prairie, for five dollars and less. I have sold land here, within the last few days, on the Cowlitz Prairie, 115 acres on the prairie, and adjoining, for $500 in greenbacks. This piece of land is fenced, and has about 500 bearing apple trees. This land has a good title, and is not on the Company's claim.

Int. 15.—About what portion of the whole Cowlitz Prairie is covered by the Company's claim of 3,500 acres?

Ans.—Something near half, I should think.

Int. 16.—Are you well acquainted with the Company's claim on the Nisqually Plains, in Pierce County?

Ans.—I am.

Int. 17—What, in your opinion, is that land worth per acre, averaging it together?

Ans.—Not to exceed one dollar or one dollar and a quarter per acre.

Int. 18.—About what is the present population of Steila-coom ?

Ans.—I should not think there would be over 150 to 200, including men, women, and children.

Int. 19.—About what is the present population of Pierce County ?

Ans.—I should say from 1,500 to 2,000.

Int. 20·—Has there been any material variation in the market value of land in Washington Territory in the last five years; if so, has the tendency been downward or upward ?

Ans.—I don't think there has been any material variation, so far as my knowledge goes.

Cross-examination by Frank Clark, Esq., for the Company.

Int. 1.—Was not the land recently sold by you encumbered by mortgage or other lien ? If yea, state the amount, the length of time it had been so encumbered, and to whom the land was sold.

Ans.—It was encumbered by a judgment amounting to about $4,100, and was sold to Gen. W. W. Miller, the judgment creditor. There were about three and one half sections of other land encumbered by the same judgment.

Int. 2.—Could you have spared the money to relieve the land sold by you from the lien of this judgment, would you have sold the same at the prices realized as stated in your examination-in-chief?

Ans.—I would not have sold it for that price, had they not been otherwise encumbered; I bought it for a home; I was compelled to sell it, or have it sold by the sheriff; and preferred to do that rather than to take the chances of a forced sale.

Int. 3.—Do you not think the property so sold of greater value than the amount realized by you for it ?

Ans.—I would not have sold the property for the money, if it was not encumbered, and I could have kept it as a home.

Int. 4.—Before you did, consent to sell it for that price, did not the purchaser agree within a time stated to re-deed the property to you, or your order, upon the payment to him of the amount of your indebtedness, with interest?

Ans.—No; he made no promises previous to the sale.

Int. 5.—Do you own any land in Washington Territory?

Ans.—No.

FRED. A. CLARKE.

OLYMPIA, *November* 20, 1866.

TESTIMONY OF R. H. HEWITT.

R. H. Hewitt, being first duly sworn, deposeth, in answer to interrogatories, as follows:

Int. 1.—State your age, residence, and occupation.

Ans.—My age is about twenty-seven years; my residence is Olympia, Washington Territory; by occupation, I am a printer and editor, and publisher of the Pacific Tribune newspaper.

Int. 2.—Were you ever offered any money, or other valuable consideration, by any one connected with the prosecution of this claim, to affect the course of your newspaper, in commenting upon such claims? If so, state how much, when it was, and by whom. (Objected to by counsel for the Company as incompetent, irrelevant, and immaterial.)

Ans.—I was offered a consideration, but I cannot say that it was by a counsel for the Company; it was in June or July, 1865; the sum was one hundred dollars, and was by Mr. Frank Clark.

Int. 3.—Is he the same gentleman who now sits in this room, acting as the attorney for the Company?

Ans.—Yes, sir.

Cross-examined by Frank Clark, Esq., for the Company.

Int. 1.—Did not Judge Lander and myself state to you before, or about the time you took the hundred dollars, that we only wanted your paper to remain silent upon the subject, and not to publish inflammatory articles, that would have a tendency to prevent men from coming forward and stating such facts as were within their knowledge, relating to this claim of the Company?

Ans.—I had a conversation with Mr. Clark on the subject; I had no conversation on the subject with Mr. Lander. I had previously published the memorials of the Hudson's Bay and Puget's Sound Agricultural Companies; also a short article, calling the attention of the public to their gigantic demands. Mr. Clark expressed himself as being afraid that the papers of the Territory would take a wrong course in this matter, and the tender of money was made to keep the paper silent from prejudicing the public mind.

Direct Examination Resumed.

Int. 1.—Did you accept and keep the money?
Ans.—I accepted it, but did not keep it.

Cross-examination Resumed.

Int. 1.—Did you not afterwards justify the fears expressed to you by publishing articles in your paper, either contributed by others, or written by yourself, based upon rumor, and not upon testimony, as to the merits of this claim?
Ans.—I did publish a series of articles on this subject, but not to justify any fears of prejudice. The articles, as I believe, were a true history, founded upon fact and evidence, and not on rumor.

Int. 2.—How long have you resided in this country?
Ans.—Since the fall of 1862.

Int. 3.—Had you any acquaintance, previous to your coming here, with your contributor or contributors, or with the affairs of the Companies?
Ans.—I had no previous acquaintance with the contributors of the articles. I had read numerous newspaper articles with reference to the Companies. These were about the time it was understood the Government of Great Britain refused to renew the charter of the Hudson's Bay Company.

Int. 4.—Prior to the publication of these several articles, have you ever heard or read a single word of sworn testimony affecting the merits of either of these claims, and have you since, except detached parts furnished by the counsel of the United States conducting this examination, on this coast, in behalf of the Government, to different newspapers for publication?

Ans.—I had, previous to publishing the articles, read testimony elicited either before a committee of Parliament, or Parliament itself. The Counsel for the United States, conducting this examination, has never submitted to me any fact or evidence on this subject.

Int. 5.—How long a time did you keep this "*filthy lucre*" in your possession?

Ans.—This " root of all evil" was in my hands about forty-eight hours.

Int. 6.—What was the reason assigned in the letter accompanying the return of the money for its being returned?

Ans.—I kept no copy of the letter; I think it contained two reasons: first, a change in sentiment; second, a change in the proprietorship of the establishment.

Int. 7.—Did it not state, as the reason for its return, the numerous objections made by partisan friends and would-be contributors to your paper of articles urging reasons against the favorable consideration of these claims of these companies?

Ans.—I think I made use of no such terms.

Int. 8.—Were not such reasons among those that influenced you in making such return?

Ans.—If they were not expressed in the letter, they would be of no value in this case, and cannot be admitted.

Int. 9.—Has the Hon. Carey Johnson, the attorney now present on the part of the United States, conducting this examination, recently conversed with you in reference to the testimony you would give if examined on this subject?

Ans.—No, he has not; Mr. Johnson simply informed me that he wanted me as a witness.

Int. 10.—To what person or persons, before this examination of to-day, have you communicated the facts, or any of them, hereinbefore stated?

Ans.—I cannot say.

Int. 11.—Is it usual for you to communicate generally to persons the business transactions of your office?

Ans.—Not to persons unconcerned.

R. H. HEWITT.

TESTIMONY OF H. L. CHAPMAN.

H. L. Chapman being first duly sworn, deposeth, in answer to interrogatories, as follows :

Int. 1.—State your age, residence, and occupation.

Ans.—I am thirty-five years old; my residence is Olympia, W. T.; my occupation is teaming.

Int. 2.—How long have you resided in Washington Territory?

Ans.—Since the fall of 1852.

Int. 3.—Have you ever resided on or near the Company's claim known as the Nisqually Plains? If so, state during what years.

Ans.—The first claim I located was in Pierce county, on Nisqually claim, in January, 1853, where I resided about two months. While there, I was served with a written notice by Mr. Huggins to abandon the claim.

Int. 4.—Where then did you remove?

Ans.—I removed from this claim to near Steilacoom, where I remained two or three months, engaged at Mr. Chambers's saw-mill. Thence I removed to the Segualichew Mill, where I remained, perhaps, four months. Then I located another claim, near the mouth of the Nisqually river, on the right bank, where I remained about one year. From thence I removed to Thurston county, where I have since resided.

Int. 5.—Did you, at any time, have any agreement with Dr. W. F. Tolmie, agent of the Puget Sound Company, about the killing of the Company's cattle on the Nisqually Plains? If so, state where it was, and the terms of the agreement.

Ans.—I made arrangements with the Doctor to kill some cattle for my own use in the summer of 1854, I think, for which I was to pay six dollars per head. He said I could kill for my own use, but ńot abuse.

Int. 6.—What other agreement, if any, did you make with any other agent or employé of the Company about beel or beef cattle?

Ans.—When I went on to the first claim, I cõntracted for my beef of one the employés, Mr. Dean, at seven cents per pound.

Int. 7.—Were the Company's cattle tame or wild during your residence in Pierce county?

Ans.—They were wild.

Int. 8.—Was any objection made by the Company's agents to your holding the claim taken by you near the mouth of the Nisqually river?

Ans.—There was none.

Int. 9.—Were you living on this claim when you effected the arrangement with Dr. Tolmie, before spoken of?

Ans.—I was.

Int. 10.—Did the Company keep up their various enclosures on the Nisqually Plains after 1852? If not, state what they did with all, or any of them.

Ans.—I have known a good many pieces of ground, the cultivation of which was abandoned, and the fencing removed to other tracts of land.

Cross-examination by Frank Clark, Esq., for the Company.

Int. 1.—When you first came to the country, how much of a family did you have dependent upon you?

Ans.—A wife.

Int. 2.—Had you not, before you located on the last-named place, in Pierce county, received a notice not to settle upon their claim?

8 P

Ans.—I never received but one notice, and I think that that was a notice to abandon the claim I was then occupying, only.

Int. 3.—Did you not see a notice in a newspaper, in the year 1853 or 1854, describing the boundaries of the Company's claim in Pierce county, and warning persons against settling upon the same?

Ans.—I could not say that the boundaries were described, but am sure I saw a notice warning persons against settling on the Company's claim.

Int. 4.—In how large numbers, during the year 1854, did the Company's cattle come around your house and door?

Ans.—I have seen them in companies of from ten to fifty. They came by my place going to a salt marsh or tide prairie.

Question by W. C. Johnson, Esq.

Int. 1.—How near were you able to get to the wild cattle of the Company, when they saw you, say as early as the spring of 1853?

Ans.—The cattle would come out of the timber to feed on the prairie. When any person would approach them, especially on foot, before he would get within gun-shot of them, they would seem as if they were going to run at him, and after standing and looking at him for a time, they would run for the woods.

Int. 2.—Were you ever attacked by any of these cattle? If so, state what you did, and who were with you.

Ans.—There were two gentlemen with me. Once in summer of 1854, after night, we were travelling on the plains from the Ségualichew Mill to my land claim, near the mouth of the Nisqually river. There was a band of cattle surrounded us, bellowed considerable, and closed in the circle, and we went up a tree. We were kept up the tree about an hour, I should think, having no dog or fire-arms.

Cross-examination Resumed.

Int. 1.—Did this band of cattle close in upon your party in good military order, and with military precision, and when you descended the tree and left, was any flank move· ment attempted by them ?

Ans.—I do not think there were any military tactics exhibited in their approach, and we retired in good order, they having changed their base first.

H. L. CHAPMAN.

OLYMPIA, W. T., *November* 20, 1866.

————

TERRITORY OF WASHINGTON, ⎱ *ss.*
   County of Thurston. ⎰

I, Andrew J. Moses, a notary public in and for said Territory, residing in said county, do hereby certify that the foregoing depositions of C. C. Hewitt, W. W. Miller, Fred. A. Clark, R. H. Hewitt, and H. L. Chapman, were taken before me at my office in Olympia, in said county, on the 16th, 17th, 19th, and 20th days of November, A. D. 1866, in pursuance of a verbal agreement made in my presence by W. Carey Johnson, Esq., in behalf of the United States, and Frank Clark, Esq., in behalf of the Puget's Sound Agricultural Company, and reduced to writing by me, or in my presence and under my direction, by persons agreed upon between the parties.

I further certify that to each of said witnesses, before his examination, I administered the following oath:

" You do solemnly swear that the evidence you shall give in the matter of the claim of the Puget's Sound Agricultural Company against the United States shall be the truth, the whole truth, and nothing but the truth, so help you God."

I further certify that said depositions were each carefully

read to or by said witnesses, after the same were reduced to writing, and then signed by them respectively.

In witness whereof I have hereto set my hand and affixed [L. S.] my notarial seal, at my office in Olympia, the twentieth day of November, A. D. 1866.

ANDREW J. MOSES,
Notary Public, Washington Territory.

BRITISH AND AMERICAN JOINT COMMISSION

ON THE

HUDSON'S BAY AND PUGET'S SOUND AGRICULTURAL COMPANIES CLAIMS.

————————•◦•————————

In the matter of the Claim of the Puget's Sound Agricultural Company vs. the United States.

Depositions of witnesses taken in behalf of the United States.

TESTIMONY OF WILLIAM P. DOUGHERTY.

William P. Dougherty being first duly sworn, deposeth, in answer to interrogatories, as follows:

Int. 1.—What is your age, residence, and occupation?

Ans.—My age is about fifty years; I reside in Pierce county, Washington Territory; I am a farmer by profession.

Int. 2.—How long have you resided in Pierce county?

Ans.—Since 1851.

Int. 3.—Do you reside upon the land claimed by the Puget's Sound Agricultural Company, known as the Nisqually Plains?

Ans.—I presume I do.

Int. 4.—What official position do you hold in Pierce county?

Ans.—Probate Judge.

Int. 5.—Are you well acquainted with the Nisqually Plains, generally?

Ans.—I am not generally; I have passed from Nisqually bridge to Fort Steilacoom; I have passed from my house to

Andrew Burge's; I have been from Andrew Burge's to Van-
buren's claim; I have been from my house, by the way of
Gravelly Lake, to Fort Nisqually.

Int. 6.—On what part of the plains is your residence?

Ans.—I live about three miles east of Fort Steilacoom, between that and the Puyallup river.

Int. 7.—On what part of the plains does Andrew Burge
reside?

Ans.—He lives at the place known as Muck, about ten or
twelve miles from Steilacoom.

Int. 8.—Describe the soil of the Nisqually Plains, so far
as you are acquainted with them.

Ans.—They are inclined to be gravelly, sandy, rocky in
some parts; some small isolated valleys are inclined to be
black loamy soil.

Int. 9.—Taking the whole tract together, at what price per
acre would you fix the value of this land, so far as you are
acquainted with it, without regard to improvements?

Ans.—Seventy-five cents an acre in coin.

Int. 10.—About what proportion, in your judgment, is at
all suited to purposes of general agriculture?

Ans.—Some lands become exhausted in one year's cultivation; two-thirds are fit for general agriculture.

Int. 11.—Does this two-thirds include the land which you
say is exhausted by one year's cultivation?

Ans.—No, sir.

Int. 12.—In what condition were the Company's cattle, as
to tameness or wildness, when you came here, in 1851?

Ans.—They were very wild when I first came to the
country.

Cross-examination by Frank Clark, Esq., for the Company.

Int. 1.—Describe the prairie, and the extent of the prairie
where you live?

Ans.—I live on what is called the Round Prairie; some
portion of it is sandy, some gravelly, and some rocky, surrounded with timber; a large swamp on one side of it. I sup-

pose there must be at least three or four hundred acres of land in the prairie.

Int. 2.—How many settlers are there on Round Prairie?

Ans.—There are three, at present.

Int. 3.—Is there any valuable swamp land surrounding this prairie?

Ans.—I suppose about four hundred and sixty acres in a body, that might be made valuable by a large outlay in draining and cleaning and ditching and ploughing in proper time, which is the fall of the year; there is about twenty acres of this swamp partly improved at present.

Int. 4.—What would it cost to properly drain and fit this body of swamp land for cultivation?

Ans.—About twenty dollars per acre?

Int. 5.—How much prairie land have you enclosed?

Ans.—About one hundred acres, I think.

Int. 6.—How much of this hundred acres have you under cultivation?

Ans.—Seventeen acres in wheat, two acres in an orchard.

Int. 7.—When you first came to the country, what number of cattle and sheep were occasionally grazed upon this prairie by the Company?

Ans.—They were remarkably wild, and it was almost impossible for any one to count them; I don't remember of seeing any sheep there when I first came to that place, or afterwards.

Int. 8.—Did John Bradley settle upon this prairie, and if yea, when and how long did he reside there?

Ans.—He did; came there the same time that I did, and remained there six or seven years, or longer.

Int. 9.—Do you not know that the Company complained of John Bradley on account of his taking rails used by the Company for sheep folds, and taken by him to fence lands for his own use, without their permission?

Ans.—I don't know of any complaint, of my own knowledge.

Int. 10.—Do you not know that Bradley enclosed and cultivated lands upon this prairie that had been richly manured by folding of the Company's sheep thereupon?

Ans.—I do not know of my own knowledge, but I do know that he enclosed lands and cultivated them.

Int. 11.—Do you not know that he used old rails, found there, belonging to the Company, for enclosing these lands?

Ans.—I do not know.

Int. 12.—When you first came to the country, were there not often five hundred and more head of cattle on the Round Prairie, and did they not often trouble your enclosures?

Ans.—There were apparently large droves of cattle passing through and feeding upon this prairie; I do not recollect distinctly about their bothering us.

Int. 13.—Had you lived in Oregon previous to settling upon this prairie?

Ans.—I lived in Oregon, having emigrated there in 1843, where I lived until I came here, with the exception of five or six months that I was absent in California.

Int. 14.—Were there not, during your residence in Oregon, large herds of Spanish cattle scattered over different sections of the country?

Ans.—I don't know.

Int. 15.—Is not all of Round Prairie enclosed, and are not the lands between this and your residence so enclosed and fenced as to render the travel a much longer distance than formerly, and are there not many thousand acres of prairie enclosed between your residence and that of A. J. Burge?

Ans.—Yes.

W. P. DOUGHERTY.

STEILACOOM, W. T., *November* 22, 1866.

TESTIMONY OF A. J. BURGE.

A. J. Burge being first duly sworn, deposeth, in answer to interrogatories, as follows:

Int. 1.—How old are you, where do you live, and what do you do for a living?

Ans.—I am thirty-seven years old; I live at Muck, in Pierce county, Washington Territory; I farm and raise stock for a living.

Int. 2.—How long have you lived at Muck?

Ans.—Since November, 1854.

Int. 3.—Do you know of any contract between Dr. Tolmie, agent of the Puget's Sound Company, and any other person about the killing of the Company's cattle, on the Nisqually Plains? If so, state all you know about it, and the price agreed upon per head.

Ans.—I belive I do. In 1853 I worked on the Cascade road, under E. J. Allen. Mr. Allen sent me to kill a wild bullock. He told me he had arrangements with Dr. Tolmie. He told me to kill a fat one, not larger than two mules could pack. He said he was to pay $5 per head. I came into the plains according to Allen's order. I found a band of cattle in the oak grubs. I selected such an one as I thought would be a load for the two mules, and shot it down. About two weeks afterwards I killed another; I also killed for the same purpose in 1854. In conversation with Dr. Tolmie, afterwards, he told me, yes, he had authorized Mr. Allen to kill what he wanted for use on the road, at $5 per head.

Int. 4.—Did Dr. Tolmie, at that time, or at any other time, say anything to you about emigrants having leave to kill cattle? If so, state what he said.

Ans.—At the same time of the conversation about Allen, Dr. Tolmie said some of the emigrants were coming in poor and needy, and if they would pay $5 per head in advance, they could kill a few for their own use.

Int. 5.—Did Dr. Tolmie, at any time, make you any offer of the privilege of killing cattle? If so, state when and what it was.

Ans.—In the winter of 1854, Dr. Tolmie overtook me as I was coming into Steilacoom, and joked me about my having bought a long rifle gun. He said he had given Andrew Byrd permission to kill cattle for his own use, at $5 per head, and it would look more respectable if I would do the same.

Int. 6.—Did he tell you of any other persons, than those you have named, that he had made such an arrangement with?

Ans.—Not at that, or any time, that I remember.

Int. 7.—Did Dr. Tolmie ever tell you of any arrangement he had made with persons to kill wild cattle for him on the shares? If so, state who the persons were, and the nature of the arrangement.

Ans.—He told me he had made a bargain with George Shazer and MacAlister, to kill cattle for the Company at a stated price per pound; I think at four cents per pound delivered, but not on shares.

Int. 8.—Are you well acquainted with the lands generally on the Nisqually Plains?

Ans.—I am.

Int. 9.—Taking them together, at what price per acre, in gold coin, would you fix their value, without the improvements?

Ans.—I don't believe, on a twelve month's notice, they could be sold for Government price.

Int. 10.—So far as you know about the killing of the Company's cattle, was it done principally by American settlers, or by the Company's servants discharged, or otherwise?

Ans.—The greater number of cattle that were killed, to my knowledge, were killed by persons who were or had been in the Company's service.

Cross-examination by Frank Clark, Counsel for the Company.

Int. 1.—When did you first come to Pierce county?

Ans.—In June, 1852.

Int. 2.—Where had you resided immediately previous to coming here?

Ans.—In Yamhill county, Oregon.

Int. 3.—State the length of time you resided in Oregon, and the parts of country therein with which you were acquainted?

Ans.—I resided in Oregon between three and four years; I had a general acquaintance with the Willamette Valley, but resided principally at Portland and in Yamhill county.

Int. 4.—What extent of prairie lands were there in Yamhill county fit for purposes of general agriculture?

Ans.—I think between a half and two-thirds; I do not know the number of acres in the county.

Int. 5.—In your judgment, is there 80,000 acres of such land in Yamhill county; I mean by that prairie land, fit for agricultural purposes?

Ans.—I would suppose there was.

Int. 6.—What quantity of land, of the description referred to in the last interrogatory, in your opinion, was there in Yamhill county unoccupied when you left there?

Ans.—All of a third.

Int. 7.—Were there not large quantities of land, of the description last mentioned, then unoccupied in different parts of the Willamette Valley?

Ans.—Yes.

Int. 8.—Were not some herds of stock-cattle of the Spanish breed in Yamhill county—not the offspring of milch cows—and running on the western hills of the county, wild, and difficult to drive in 1849, 1850, and 1851?

Ans.—I never struck a band that three men, on horseback, could not drive from there to Portland; my answer refers to 1850 and 1851.

Int. 9.—Were not bands of cattle, of the Spanish breed, grazed in different parts of the Willamette Valley, difficult to drive?

Ans.—I helped to drive some of the worst bands there, and found them difficult to start.

Int. 10.—Were any of the bands of cattle referred to in the last two interrogatories drivable by persons on foot?

Ans.—I never saw it tried.

Int. 11.—How large a piece of ground have you enclosed on the Company's claim, and now used by you for grazing and other purposes?

Ans.—I don't give the Company credit for having any

claim; I have from 800 to 1,000 acres under fence, perhaps more.

Int. 12.—Are you acquainted with Isaac Carson, a settler upon the Company's claim in Pierce county, Washington Territory?

Ans.—I know Isaac Carson, of Pierce county, Washington Territory.

Int. 13.—What amount of lands has he enclosed for grazing, and other purposes, on the Nisqually Plains?

Ans.—Two thousand acres or more.

Int. 14.—What amount of horned cattle would Mr. Carson's enclosed lands annually afford good pasturage for?

Ans.—Two hundred and fifty head the year round; I mean grown cattle.

Int. 15.—What kind of beef and mutton do the pasture lands of Nisqually Plain at present produce for market?

Ans.—Before the plains were over grazed, good quality; but now they are over grazed so that we can't get good beef but eight months in the year.

Int. 16.—What proportion of the Nisqually Plains are at present enclosed?

Ans.—About one-fourth, in my opinion.

Int. 17.—In your judgment, what number of horned cattle, what number of sheep, and what number of horses are at present grazed upon or fed from the product of the Nisqually Plains?

Ans.—In all I should think about 12,000 head.

Int. 18.—What proportion of this number would you say were cattle and horses?

Ans.—About one-fourth.

Int. 19.—What is it worth per week to pasture grown cattle and horses per head within the enclosures situate upon the Nisqually Plains?

Ans.—One dollar per head per month the year round.

Int. 20.—In your examination-in-chief you have stated that the large portion of Company's cattle killed, to your knowledge, were killed by Company's servants, or persons formerly in the Company's employ. What proportion of these cattle so killed were killed by the Company's servants, and for whom were they killed?

Ans.—The Company's servants, then in their employ, killed about the one-twentieth.

Int. 21.—Had not these persons, mentioned by you as former employés of the Company, at the time they killed the cattle referred to by you in your former answer, left the Company's employment and squatted on claims; were they not American citizens, or declared their intention to become such?

Ans.—They were not at the time in the Company's employment, and resided upon claims on the Nisqually Plains; I cannot state as to their citizenship.

Int. 22.—State the names of all the persons who, to your knowledge, killed Company's cattle that had, prior to such killing, been in the Company's employ?

Ans.—Francis Gavelle, Xavier Latour, Richard Fiander, William Young, George Dean, William Northover, Charles Wren.

Int. 23.—At the time MacAlister and Shazer were killing cattle for the company, what was the price per head of good milch cows and beef cattle?

Ans.—A good American milch cow was worth from seventy-five to eighty dollars. A good Spanish milch cow was worth about fifty dollars. Beef was worth fourteen and fifteen cents per pound dressed.

Int. 24.—How will the beef and mutton raised on the Nisqually Plains compare with that raised in the Willamette Valley?

Ans.—I do not know of any material difference.

Int. 25.—Have you accumulated means, besides supporting yourself and family, by farming and stock-raising where you now reside?

Ans.—No; I have gone down hill.

Int. 26.—Does this result, in a greater or less degree, from the fact that the price of stock has fallen, and from the fact that you lost a considerable amount by the felonious taking of bad neighbors?

Ans.—That includes a part of the causes, but not all; the hard winter was a dead stroke on me.

Int. 27.—Did you ever kill any cattle of the Company, under an agreement with any of its agents, for your own use or for sale?

Ans.—No, sir.

A. J. BURGE.

STEILACOOM, *November* 22, 1866.

TESTIMONY OF JAMES E. WILLIAMSON.

James E. Williamson, being duly sworn, deposeth, in answer to interrogatories, as follows:

Int. 1.—Please state your age, residence, and occupation.

Ans.—I am thirty-six years of age; I reside in Steilacoom, Washington Territory; I am a butcher by trade; at present I am a teamster.

Int. 2.—When did you first come to Pierce county?

Ans.—I came here in October, 1849.

Int. 3.—Were you ever attacked by any of the Company's cattle on the Nisqually Plains? If so, state when it was, and the circumstances.

Ans.—I was attacked only once by a bull, between where the garrison is and Byrd's Mill. I had a Government musket; went out fowling to shoot ducks and pheasants. I had killed some game, and was returning back to the garrison, when a bull came after me, and I got out of his way up a tree. The bull started off a short distance, when I fired at him with duck shot, hitting him on the hips. After he had gotten off some distance, I came down from the tree, and made some haste toward the garrison, in the meantime loading my musket with ball-cartridge. When I had gone some distance, and come near to a field, I found the animal was again coming after me. I sprang over the fence, and as he charged up, I fired, and gave him, as I suppose, a death wound.

Cross-examination by Frank Clark, for the Company.

Int. 1.—How were you dressed at this time, when the bull pursued you?

Ans.—I had on fatigue dress of an artillery soldier; I had a red silk handerchief tied across my shoulders, and some game tied to the end of it.

Int. 2.—When you came to the county in 1849, did not the Company have large numbers of cattle upon the Nisqually Plains, and were they not as tame as stock cattle usually are, running in so large a tract of country, in such large numbers?

Ans.—Yes; there were large numbers of cattle in every direction, no matter which way you started; from the garrison you would see cattle. They were sufficiently tame to drive into a corral and yoke up and work them. They were large, stout oxen, six or seven years of age, and it took considerable help to drive them in and yoke them. Cattle, then, were seldom driven into a corral, except for the purpose of branding and marking, and that made them more afraid of being corralled than they otherwise would have been.

Int. 3.—At this time, was there any difficulty in getting sufficiently near them on foot, while feeding on the range, to shoot them?

Ans.—When I first came here, the cattle were as tame as some of Isaac Carson's cattle, now running on the prairie. If you were to go among them with a gun, they were frightened, and would run off a short distance from you; they had evidently been shot at enough to be skittish of a gun. If you went among them with a handfull of salt, they would follow after you, and lick the salt scattered on the ground, at no great distance off. When Christopher Mahon and Joseph Larey settled on the Company's claim, about ten miles east of Fort Steilacoom, they built a fence around the house, partly to keep the Company's cattle from annoying them that came around the door licking the slops for salt.

Int. 4.—You say you were attacked only once by the Company's cattle, by a bull, between the garrison and where Byrd's Mill now stands. Will you please to state how many times after this attack of the bull you attacked other cattle of the Company, and with what results?

Ans.—The only one that I killed, that I was certain belonged to the Company, was the one Mr. Huggins caught me with on the prairie, and that was killed on the order of Mr. Burge for Allen's road work. The other cattle that I killed were as wild as March hares. I can't tell how many I attacked; but I hunted them daily for between two or three months. Sometimes for a week I killed none. One day, another man and myself killed nine. In the fall of 1853 the cattle began to be killed; that fall I came into the prairie where Minson, Larmain and Harrison lived, about four miles east of Fort Steilacoom; saw beef hanging round the house, and more salted in barrels. I afterwards killed a hundred cattle, more or less, myself. The cattle that I killed long after were as wild as the deer, and required an expert hunter to kill them.

Int. 5.—Did not all the settlers of this vicinity, and many persons from adjoining counties, during and after the fall of 1853, as long as the Company's cattle were to be found on Nisqually Plains and adjacent timber lands, make a practice of killing them in such numbers as they could find and wanted?

Ans.—Yes, sir; they did, and came from other counties to hunt them.

Int. 6.—Are not the timber lands surrounding and near Nisqually Plains useful and necessary for pasturage at most seasons of the year, but especially in the droughts of summer, during the winter season, for bands of cattle grazing on the Nisqually Plains? (Counsel for the United States objects to all the foregoing cross-examination, except what relates to the subject matter of the examination-in-chief, and he protests that if the Company's counsel thus makes the witness his own, he will be cross-examined as a witness of the Company.)

(Counsel for the Company insists that all the foregoing interrogatories propounded by him are within the legitimate range of a cross-examination, and protests against any cross-examination of this witness by Counsel for the United States.)

Ans.—Yes.

Int. 7.—Were not many of the Company's cattle killed by some men wantonly, and the carcasses left where they fell?

Ans.—I don't know; I never left any.

Direct-examination resumed, and Cross-examination with reference to New Matter.

Int. 1.—Give the names of all the men who came from other counties to kill cattle, whom you saw kill them.

Ans.—James Riley was one; Allen Porter was another.

Int. 2.—How many did you see Riley kill?

Ans.—I saw him shoot one, and kill it.

Int. 3.—How many did you see Porter kill?

Ans.—I saw Porter kill one.

Int. 4.—How far did Riley live from the Nisqually Plains where he killed the animal?

Ans.—From fifteen to twenty miles.

Int. 5.—How far did Porter live from the Nisqually Plains?

Ans.—A mile or two nearer than Riley.

Int. 6.—Give the names of the residents of Pierce County that you saw kill cattle, that you know belonged to the Company.

Ans.—I don't know of any one that killed cattle that I knew belonged to the Company; I never saw any killed until they were perfectly wild in the woods.

Int. 7.—In what years were these wild cattle shot of which you have been speaking?

Ans.—In part of 1853, all of 1854, and part of 1855.

Int. 8.—What became of the principal portion of the large number of cattle you say you saw in 1849 and 1850?

Ans.—In the spring of 1852, on the 29th day of February, there was a deep snow; it lay on the ground until the first days of April. I saw some ten or fifteen heads of, I suppose, Company's cattle, lying dead near the garrison of cold and hunger. The settlers had but very few cattle then. Judge Chambers occasionally sold a cow to the garrison.

9 P

Int. 9.—Did not this snow extend all over the Nisqually Plains?

Ans.—Yes.

Int. 10.—Would it not produce the same results elsewhere, as it did near the military post where you saw the cattle dead? (Objected to by counsel for the Company, because it is leading, and because the answer must be an opinion simply, and not a statement of facts.)

Ans.—I should think there would not be much difference.

Int. 11.—Have you not seen the Company's servants shoot cattle running the range?

Ans.—I won't be certain, but I think I once saw an Indian named Wyamoch and a man named Legg, who belonged to Fort Nisqually, dressing the carcass of an ox on the prairie; the Company's cart was there to carry the meat away.

Int. 12.—Was not a large portion of the killing of wild cattle, after 1853, done by discharged servants of the Company? (Objected to as leading by counsel for the Company.)

Ans.—Yes; I think there was a large portion killed by discharged servants.

Int. 13.—Were not a great many more also killed by Indians? (Objected to by counsel for the Company, for like reasons as the last.)

Ans.—Yes, sir.

Int. 14.—Was it not generally understood that the hostile Indians, in the war of 1855 and 1856, procured much of their subsistence by killing these wild cattle? (Objected to by counsel for the Company because leading, and the answer can be but mere hearsay.)

Ans.—I don't think they killed a great many of them during the war. They subsisted partly on them and partly on tame cattle. Their best hunters were fighting, and could not hunt as they had before. They could not hunt and fight too, particularly when the volunteers were after them.

Int. 15.—During these years, was not the Company killing cattle, and having them killed, for the purpose of supplying beef to the garrison, to citizens, to emigrants, and for the supply of Victoria market?

Ans.—I don't know of my own knowledge; I heard they were.

Cross-examination Resumed.

Int. 1.—Were the animals killed by you, and others that you have stated were wild, marked and branded, or either, with the mark or brand, or both, of the Puget's Sound Agricultural Company?

Ans.—I don't know what the Company's mark was.

Int. 2.—Had not the steers that were killed an ear mark?

Ans.—Some of them probably had, but I don't remember what it was.

Int. 3·—Do you not know that the cattle so killed were the property of the Company, and were they not generally so considered?

Ans.—No, sir; I did not consider that they belonged to the Company after they became wild.

Int. 4.—What Indians did you ever see kill cattle?

Ans.—I saw an Indian named Pistichin kill three or four out at Mahon's; I saw one other Indian bringing beef out of the woods on his horse; but it was so common to have plenty of fresh beef in those days, that I thought nothing of it. I think I saw other Indians, but I cannot name them.

Int. 5.—At the time Pistichin killed these cattle referred to by you, with whom was he living; and state, if you know, for whom he killed them.

Ans.—He was living with his wife. I am pretty confident that two of those carcasses went up to Mahon's; I suppose he took a portion of it himself.

Int. 6.—Was this Mr. Mahon, to whose house this beef was taken, an American settler?

Ans.—He was an Irishman, and a discharged soldier; I suppose he was naturalized; he settled and claimed land on the Company's land under the United States donation law.

Int. 7.—Did you ever know of any other settlers, either upon these lands of the Company, or upon the public lands of the vicinity, getting Indians to kill and bring them beef?

Ans.—Yes; I have employed Indians to kill beef for me.

Int. 8.—Did you ever see but two cattle killed by the Company's servants?

Ans.—I think not.

Int. 9.—How many cattle did you see killed by others, that you know of?

Ans.—I remember none, except those I have already mentioned.

Int. 10.—How many men that you have not named as killing cattle have you heard from themselves or others did kill them? (Objected to as incompetent.)

Ans.—I have heard of a great many that have killed cattle here in the county, but can't tell the number; there were but two or three in the county that were not said to kill cattle, and they were very poor shots.

Int. 11.—Did not nearly all the settlers on the Nisqually Plains, and many living in the adjoining counties of Thurston and King, to the best of your judgment, principally supply themselves with meat, from the time that the cattle were commenced to be killed in the fall of 1853, until these cattle were all gone, or nearly? (Objected to as incompetent.)

Ans.—On Nisqually Plains, yes; as to the other counties I do not know.

JAMES E. WILLIAMSON.

STEILACOOM, *November* 22, 1866.

TESTIMONY OF R. S. MORE.

R. S. More, being duly sworn, deposeth, in answer to interrogatories, as follows:

Int. 1.—State your age, residence, and occupation?

Ans.—My age is thirty-eight; residence in Pierce County, Washington Territory; I am a farmer.

Int. 2.—How long have you resided in Pierce County?

Ans.—Since April, 1853.

Int. 3.—What official positions have you held in Pierce County?

Ans.—I have been county commissioner two terms; once a member of the Legislature.

Int. 4.—Were you one of the county commissioners about 1854?

Ans.—I think I was elected in 1854.

Int. 5.—Did Dr. Tolmie, about that time, make an application to the commissioners for the reduction of the tax against the Puget's Sound Company assessed on cattle? (Objected to by counsel for the Company, because, if made, the same is a matter of record, and the record is the best evidence.)

Ans.—He made application to have the assessment reduced.

Int. 6.—What reasons did he urge for this reduction? (Objected to by counsel for the Company for like reason as above, also because it is incompetent, irrelevant, and immaterial.)

Ans.—He urged several reasons: 1st, he said the cattle were wild, and he could not get hold of them; 2d, that he could not find but few of them; 3d was, that the Company did not claim only either 150 or 250 head that were tame and running about the fort; he called them milch cows and work cattle. The Commissioners informed Mr. Tolmie that he must either renounce all claim to the wild cattle, or be assessed for them, and he renounced claim to them.

Int. 7.—Was the tax then reduced?

Ans.—It was reduced on between two and three thousand head of cattle.

Int. 8.—Was this application in writing?

Ans.—It was made orally, and then spread upon the records and sworn to.

Int. 9.—Have the records of Pierce County been burned; if so, when? (Objected to by counsel for the Company, because the inquiry does not go to the record of the statement made by the agent of the Company, and is therefore incompetent.)

Ans.—They were burned several years after that; the exact date I do not remember.

Int. 10.—How many head of cattle remained assessed to the Company after this reduction?

Ans.—My impression is there were 150 or 250 head.

Int. 11.—Are you generally acquainted with the Nisqually Plains claimed by the Company?

Ans.—Yes, sir, I believe I am; I have been over them a great deal.

Int. 12—At how much per acre, in gold coin, would you value these lands, taking them as a body together, and averaging the whole?

Ans.—About Government price, or $1.25 in greenbacks. The value in coin would depend on the price of greenbacks.

Cross-examination by Frank Clark, Esq., Counsel for the Company.

Int. 1.—Were you ever elected county commissioner for Pierce county, before the annual election in 1854?

Ans.—I think not.

Int. 2.—Was there any correction of the assessment rate for 1854, by the Board of County Commissioners after your election?

Ans.—No; I think it was corrected for the year 1855.

Int. 3.—The application for reduction of assessment then by Dr. Tolmie referred to in your examination-in-chief, was for the assessment made in the year 1855?

Ans.—I think so.

R. S. MORE.

STEILACOOM, W. T., *November* 22, 1866.

Geo. W. Shazer, being first duly sworn, deposeth, in answer to interrogatories, as follows:

Int. 1.—State your age, residence, and occupation.

Ans.—I am forty-eight years of age; I reside in Thurston county; I am a farmer by occupation.

Int. 2.—Did you ever reside in Pierce County? If so, when?

Ans.—I resided in Pierce County the latter part of 1855, and the first part of 1856, for nine mouths.

Int. 3.—How far is your residence from the Nisqually Plains?

Ans.—About one mile, just across the river.

Int. 4.—Did you ever have any arrangement with Dr. Tolmie, agent of the Company, about killing cattle? If so, state when, and what it was,

Ans.—Yes; I had in 1851. There was a beef in Thurston County with my cattle, belonging to the Company. I notified Dr. Tolmie that I did not want it with my cattle. He told me if it was a big one, I could have it for $10, and kill it myself. In 1852 I got five more, two cows, two calves, and one yearling, running in the same place, at $5 per head. In 1855 I had another arrangement to kill cattle for the Company. The first contract was at five cents per pound for killing and delivery to Fort Nisqually. This lasted but a short time, and we afterwards had four cents per pound.

Int. 5.—How did you kill these cattle?

Ans.—I shot them out on the plains, and in the range, wherever I could find them.

Int. 6.—Did the Company pay you anything for delivering the hides? If so, how much?

Ans.—Thirty-seven and a-half cents each.

Cross-examination by Frank Clark, Esq., Counsel for the Company.

Int. 1.—While killing cattle under the last arrangement with the Company, did you kill any cattle by mistake not belonging to the Company? If so, state their size and description, who they belonged to, and what you had to pay the owner for the same.

Ans.—I killed two; the beef weighed about fifteen hundred pounds; the beef was good; I delivered it to the Company. One belonged to Charles Wren, and the other to

Sandy Smith. We had to pay them $100 a piece for them. The Company allowed me eight cents a pound for this beef.

his

GEORGE W. SHAZER. ⋈

mark.

STEILACOOM, *November* 23, 1866.

Attest to signature:

GEORGE W. SLOAN.

TESTIMONY OF E. A. LIGHT.

E. A. Light being duly sworn, deposeth, in answer to interrogatories, as follows:

Int. 1.—State your age, residence, and occupation.

Ans.—I am forty-four years old; I reside in Steilacoom, Pierce County, Washington Territory; I am a merchant.

Int. 2.—How long have you resided in Pierce County?

Ans.—Since the fall of 1853; I came in with the emigration of that year, by Nachess Pass.

Int. 3.—Did Dr. Tolmie ever make you the offer of the privilege of killing cattle belonging to the Puget's Sound Company? If so, state when it was, and the terms of the offer.

Ans.—He did in the fall of 1853. He told me I could have them for five dollars a head, small ones for my own use.

Int. 4.—Have you ever farmed any on the Nisqually Plains or near to the same?

Ans.—I have on the Nisqually's river bottom.

Int. 5.—Are you acquainted with the Nisqually Plains, claimed by the Puget's Sound Company?

Ans.—Yes, sir.

Int. 6.—At how much per acre, in gold coin, would you fix their value, averaging the whole tract claimed by the Company together?

Ans.—Fifty cents per acre; it is a matter I have thought

a good deal about, and talked about considerably, and that is my opinion.

Cross-examination by Frank [Clark,] Counsel for the Company.

Int. 1.—Is the town of Steilacoom, where you reside, within the limits of the Company's claim in this county?
Ans.—It is.
Int. 2.—What is the size of the town-lots, where you reside?
Ans.—Sixty feet, by one hundred and twenty feet.
Int. 3.—Did you not purchase an unimproved lot, some distance back from the shore of the Sound, within the last two or three years, and pay therefor in coin, or its equivalent, the sum of $100?
Ans.—I did purchase such a lot, and gave $100 for it; it was unfenced, stumps remaining, and timber taken away.

Direct Examination Resumed.

Int. 1.—Has property in the town of Steilacoom increased, or decreased in value since you purchased that lot?
Ans.—I think it has decreased.
Int. 2.—Was there anything specially desirable about the particular lot in question which caused you to pay so large a price? If so, state what it was. (Objected to by Counsel for the Company, because it assumes what is not stated in testimony, that a large price was paid for the lot.)
Ans.—It was a corner lot, and the last one of four comprising a half block, of which I owned the other three; I supposed at the time my barn was partly on this lot.

Cross-Examination Resumed.

Int. 1.—What improvements have you made upon that lot since you purchased it?
Ans.—I have taken the roots and stumps out, enclosed it with a picket fence, and set it out with fruit trees.

Int. 2.—What was the cost of the improvements you have placed upon it?

Ans.—About $50, I think.

Int. 3.—What will you take for that lot and improvements to-day?

Ans.—I would not sell it, under the circumstances as it is situated, for less than $400; I don't want to sell it all.

ERASTUS A. LIGHT.

STEILACOOM, *November* 23, 1866.

TESTIMONY OF J. L. McDONALD.

J. L. McDonald being duly sworn, deposeth, in answer to interrogatories, as follows:

Int. 1.—State your age, residence, and occupation.

Ans.—I am forty-six years old; I reside in Steilacoom, Washington Territory, for the last two years; I have been a sea-faring man since 1835, with slight variations on shore; I have no particular occupation at present.

Int. 2.—Have you ever been a ship master?

Ans.—Yes.

Int. 3.—Have you, at any time in this Territory, engaged in ship building?

Ans.—Not much; I have built a sloop here, or had her built here; I worked on her myself too, under the supervision of the builder.

Int. 4.—Have you, at any time, examined the oak timber on the Nisqually Plains, with reference to its adaptation to the purposes of ship-building? If so, state when it was, the circumstances, and what is your opinion of the timber.

Ans.—I have examined it on three different occasions, in three different years, on three different routes. I will first state what it is not adapted to, and then state what it is adapted to. It is not adapted to the building of A-1 ship, for the reason that the trunks of the trees are too short for the keel, the kelsons, the bends, the lower-deck beams, the floor timbers, the futtock timbers, hood planks, and railing. The trunks averaging not over twelve feet in length. Without those elements of oak timber in a ship, she is not A 1 ship. It would be difficult to find stem, stern, or rudder posts of twenty feet length in those trunks. The trunks are adapted to the purposes of hatch combing, stanchions, windlass bodies, pall bits, timber heads, cleats, jaws for gaffs and booms, belaying pins, tree nails, and the smaller work in the finish in the upper part of a ship. The branches of the trees are susceptible of being used in the floor timbers of small vessels, scows, or boats of fifty tons or under. They are also susceptible of being used as cat-heads, stern davits, and knees of six inches clear or under. As to the knees under those trees, I am not a judge of them, having never seen any such on the Sound. I may mention that those oaks partake of the nature of New England pasture oak.

Int. 5.—What is the nature of this oak timber as to toughness or brittleness?

Ans.—I don't know.

Int. 6.—To what extent is the fir timber of this country adapted to the purposes you have said the oak is fit for?

Ans.—I would prefer the oak for the purposes for which I have stated it is adapted all the time?

Int. 7.—Knowing what you do of this oak timber, and of the other timbers of this country, what importance do you attach to the oak of the Nisqually Plains for ship-building purposes?

Ans.—I attach little or no importance to them in the construction of large sailing ships or steamships; but in the construction of a fishing fleet of superior vessels, those oaks will furnish important materials in the construction and finish of fishing vessels of one hundred tons or under.

Cross-examination by Frank Clark, Counsel for the Company.

Int. 1.—You state in your examination-in-chief that you made in three different years, each one trip, by different routes, please to describe the part of Nisqually Plains at these times, or any other you have examined the oak trees upon, with a view to convince yourself as to their value for ship-building purposes.

Ans.—I traveled out here in 1863, with Mr. Lane and lady in his wagon, by Byrd's mill to Dr. Spurning's farm, from thence we crossed over to the Tallantyre farm, and joined the military road at Montgomery's. In 1864, I took a Sabbath journey with the late George Gallagher in a wagon out to Mr. Cawley's farm, six miles east of Steilacoom. The last three miles of which was in a more southerly [course] than the former trip. I performed a circuit there, or a radius of three miles beyond Mr. Cawley's farm, and examined all the timber growing within the purview of my observation; returned same evening by same route. Third and last trip, I left the hospitable roof of Edward Huggins, Esq., and performed a circuit by the way of Captain Berry's house, with whom I tarried for twenty-four hours, when I journeyed along east of the Legelechechew [? Segualichew] and American Lakes, and pursued my way then to Isaac Carson's, with whom I tarried some twenty hours; from whence I came into town, journeying slowly on the way, the distance being about seven miles from Carson's to town.

Int. 2.—Have you visited the following named plains, many of them containing from 3,000 to 6,000 acres and upwards each, and all of which contain large groves of good oak trees, namely: Spanoway, Elk, North High Muck, Low Muck, South Muck, French Prairie, Dominick Prairie, Lastin Plain, Indian Reservation Prairie, Squally Plain, Red Pine Plain, Sandhill Prairie, Back Squally Plain, Red House Plain, Judson's and Boatman's Prairies?

Ans.—I cannot answer those questions, without those prairies and plains are depicted to me on the map.

Int. 3.—If the trunks of oak trees could be found on the Nisqually Plains of sufficient length to answer the purposes, those you say you have seen not adapted for, would not this section of country afford facilities for obtaining ship-building material not presented by any other portion of this coast?

Ans.—To a certain extent, it would.

Int. 4.—Is not the prairie country nearly all under fence

on the different routes you traveled; and how often, in your examination, did you cross fences into enclosures to examine groves of oak, or to look for the tall scattered oaks growing in the skirts of the pine timber?

Ans.—No; not one-quarter is fenced; I crossed but one fence in my travels from Captain Berry's to Mr. Carson's gate. The oaks are not generally in the enclosures, but principally on the margin of the lakes.

Int. 5.—How many lakes, in your travels through Nisqually Plains, have you ever seen, and what are their names?

Ans.—If I remember right, I saw four; I do not know their names.

Int. 6.—How far distant from the shores of Puget's Sound in a straight line to the nearest point, in your judgment, are either of the lakes seen by you?

Ans.—I have taken no means to ascertain.

Int. 7.—Are either one of them five miles from the shore of the Sound?

Ans.—I could not say.

Int. 8.—Were not all the lakes seen by you between Mr. Huggins's house and the present site of Byrd's mill?

Ans.—I cannot say, sir; I have been in the habit of dealing with fine instruments, and not jumping at conclusions.

Int. 9.—In your different trips hereinbefore described, did you not see the stumps and remains of large quantities of oak trees?

Ans.—Yes; within a radius of two miles of the garrison.

Int. 10.—Did you ever cut down, dig up, or use a single oak tree grown upon the Nisqually Plains for ship-building purposes?

Ans.—I did not.

Int. 11.—Are not all the *varieties* of timber growing between the Nisqually and Puyallup rivers in Pierce county, that are required in the construction of a first-class ship?

Ans.—I have not seen it. Nothing but oak and teak, that I have any knowledge of, will make a first-class ship.

Int. 12.—Is there any place known to you on this coast furnishing like quantities of the different varieties of timber required in the construction of a first-class ship, that is to be found growing on the claim of the Puget's Sound Company in Pierce county?

Ans.—There is not; I have already stated that a first-class ship is not built out of such timber at all.

Int. 13.—Did you ever work at ship-building at all, except the labor performed by you in the construction of the sloop referred to in your examination-in-chief?

Ans.—I did; I assisted in planking the "Massachusetts" in 1845, in East Boston, Massachusetts. I immediately had a new schooner built in Truro, Massachusetts, named "Alleghany;" I worked on her. All that I have got to say about that is, that there has not been a year since, excepting such years as I have been to sea, but what I have either been building up or tearing down vessels.

Int. 14.—How many years have you been at sea since 1845?

Ans.—I have been on the deep sea twelve years, and three years on Puget's Sound.

Int. 15.—Did you ever take charge of the building of a first-class ship?

Ans.—I did not.

Int. 16.—Do you consider yourself a master-shipwright?

Ans.—I do not.

Int. 17.—What was the tonnage and denomination of the vessel built for you on Puget's Sound, and mentioned in your examination-in-chief?

Ans.—Seven tons, and sloop rigged.

Int. 18.—Is this the vessel you went to sea in during your three years you went to sea on Puget's Sound?

Ans.—She was.

Int. 19.—What number of seamen was needed and did you carry to sail her?

Ans.—I carried no seamen; I carried all dead heads; I could sail her myself; she was a trading sloop.

Direct Examination Resumed.

Int. 1.—Where did you build your sloop?

Ans.—At Seattle.

J. L. McDONALD.

STEILACOOM, *November* 23, 1866.

TESTIMONY OF THOMAS M. CHAMBERS.

Thomas M. Chambers, being first duly sworn, deposeth, to interrogatories, as follows:

Int. 1.—State your age, residence, and occupation.

Ans.—I am seventy-one years old; I reside in Pierce county, Washington Territory; my present occupation is a miller; formerly I was a farmer.

Int. 2.—How long have you lived in what is now Washington Territory?

Ans.—Since 1847.

Int. 3.—How long have you resided at your present location near Steilacoom?

Ans.—I commenced improvements in 1849, but moved my family on, I think, in 1851.

Int. 4.—At what place did you reside in Washington Territory before moving to Steilacoom Bay?

Ans.—In Chamber's Prairie, in Thurston county, about seven or eight miles south of Nisqually river.

Int. 5.—From your earliest knowledge of the Company's cattle on the Nisqually Plains, were the cattle killed or tame?

Ans.—There was some part of the cattle that Dr. Tolmie used for milch cows and for oxen that might be called tame cattle; the balance that was not accustomed to that, I would rather call them wild.

Int. 6.—Are you well acquainted with the Company's claim, known as the Nisqually Plains generally?

Ans.—Yes, sir; I have been all over it a great many times.

Int. 7.—What, in your judgment, is the value per acre of this land for agricultural and grazing purposes, taking it as a body together, without regard to improvements?

Ans.—I would not put it at more than fifty cents an acre, in gold.

Int. 8.—Describe the soil of these plains generally.

Ans.—Some portions are sandy; the greater body gravelly; there is good soil in the swamps, but it costs a good deal of money to drain them to get the soil.

Int. 9.—What official positions have you held in Pierce county?

Ans.—I have been county commissioner several times.

Int. 10.—Did Dr. Tolmie, agent of the Puget's Sound Company, ever object to paying taxes on the Company's claim? If so, state the reasons he gave to the county commissioners. (Objected to by counsel for the Company as leading, and because the answer, if responsive to the question, must be incompetent and immaterial.)

Ans.—I don't recollect the reasons he gave at the time, or whether he gave any reasons at all or not; he did object.

Int. 11.—State the circumstances as near as you can remember. (Objected to by counsel for the Company, because the only competent evidence of the subject-matter referred to is the record of the transaction, which the witness states is now to be found on file in the office of the auditor of of Pierce county.)

Ans.—The reason why we knew it was there, was because he paid it under protest.

Int. 12.—In what year was this?

Ans.—I do not recollect, for I have not been a commissioner for six years or more.

Int. 13.—Have the records of Pierce county, including those of the commissioner's court, been burned since that date?

Ans.—No; it was previous to that; I think in 1859.

Cross-examination by Frank Clark, Esq., for the Company.

Int. 1.—Where had you resided for the two years previous to coming to what is now Washington Territory?

Ans.—Near Oregon City, Oregon.

Int. 2.—Were you well acquainted with the lands of the Willamette Valley before coming here?

Ans.—I was acquainted with a portion of it; I traveled up as far as the Santiam and over the Tualatin Plains.

Int. 3.—When you came over here from Oregon, were there not in the Willamette Valley and its vicinity, with which you were acquainted, large quantities of unoccupied lands valuable for purposes of general agriculture and stock-raising?

Ans.—Yes.

Int. 4.—Commencing with the point of the northern boundary of your donation claim in Pierce County, and taking one mile and a half in width of the frontage of the lands lying on Puget's Sound to Segualichew Creek, at what price per acre would you place their value for milling, town-site, timber, and other purposes?

Ans.—Take the improvements off, and I would not value it at scarcely anything at all.

Int. 5.—What value would you place on the balance of the frontage lands, say a mile and a half in width, between the mouth of the Puyallup and Nisqually rivers?

Ans.—It is not very valuable, so far as I know.

Int. 6.—From a point on Puget's Sound, running due South, so as to include your claim, and making a frontage one mile and a half in depth, to Segualichew Creek, is the land referred to in the last interrogatory for any purpose of greater or less value, in your opinion, than this tract would be?

Ans.—The land between the northern boundary of my claim and Segualichew Creek is the most valuable.

Int. 7.—How much prairie land would a line drawn from near the mouth of the Puyallup to a point near the mouth of the Nisqually, so as to embrace a frontage of one mile and a half in width from the shores of the Sound, include?

Ans.—I think over half prairie land.

Int. 8.—Have you recently sold the poorer half of your claim, consisting of 320 acres?

Ans.—I have been compelled to sell half of my claim, consisting of 320 acres?

Int. 9.—Did you esteem that of equal value, if unimproved, to the half of the claim still retained by you, if unimproved also?

10

Ans.—I do; there is the best water-privilege on it.

Int. 10.—What did you sell that half of your claim for?

Ans.—It was all a forced arrangement; it was for a debt of between three and four thousand dollars.

Int. 11.—What do you consider the value of the water-power on the half of the claim you still retain?

Ans.—I can't fix a value.

Int. 12.—Have you ever owned any lots in the present town-site of Steilacoom?

Ans.—Yes, sir; I have. They were donated to me by the proprietor to get me to take an interest in the place. At that time the town-site was not considered a part of the Company's claim.

Int. 13.—From the time you first came to the county, have you ever thought the Company had any claim here, or elsewhere in this Territory? If so, describe the amount that you thought belonged to them?

Ans.—I don't know the number of acres they had enclosed at that time; but it was not a large amount, not to exceed two hundred acres. I considered they had no rights outside of their enclosures.

Int. 14.—What proportion of the half of your claim, still retained and occupied by you, is prairie land, and what number of acres upon it have you improved at present?

Ans.—There is about five acres of prairie on it; I have about four acres of this half of the claim improved.

Int. 15.—Excluding the four acres you have improved from this half of the claim, and reserving the use of the water-power, what will you take per acre in cash for the remaining part of the claim?

Ans.—I does not belong to me; I cannot sell it.

Int. 16.—If it did, and you had a clear title to the same and wished to dispose of it, what value in money would you place upon it per acre?

Ans.—If I had a title, and there was a buyer, I would think about [it;] I would not sell it on credit.

Int. 17—Do you consider the frontage of a mile and a half in width on the Puget's Sound, between the mouths of the

Nisqually and Puyallup rivers, with its water-powers, its advantages as affording points of shipment, its value for townsite purposes, dry-docks, and timber, of greater value than any tract of like extent lying between it and the eastern or southern boundaries of the Company's claim in Pierce County?

Ans.—It is of more value.

Int. 18.—Do you know of any frontage on Puget's Sound, of like extent, that you consider of greater value than the one last referred to?

Ans.—I do not.

Int. 19.—Did you ever sell any of the lots given to you by the town-proprietor of the town of Steilacoom to Philip Keach?

Ans.—I did. The house that I built on it cost me about as much as I got for it.

Int. 20.—Did you not sell unimproved town-lots to Philip Keach?

Ans.—I did not.

Int. 21.—Did you not sell unimproved lots in the town of Steilacoom to men by the name of Maher?

Ans.—Yes; four; a number.

Int. 22.—What price did you sell them for per lot?

Ans.—I sold the four lots for $500.

Int. 23.—From the time you first settled on the place where you at present reside, have you not frequently been consulted by persons desirous of settling on Nisqually Plains as to their right to do so, notwithstanding the claims of the Puget's Sound Agricultural Company to the same, and have you not invariably advised them to settle and pay no attention to the claims of the Company?

Ans.—I have, excepting the lands they occupied; I would do it over again; I did not consider they had any rights.

Int. 24.—Is the exception referred to in your last answer confined to the 200 acres that you have hereinbefore stated you believed comprised the whole amount of land to which the Company had any right?

Ans.—Yes.

Int. 25.—Did you not, without permission, in 1849, 1850, 1851, or later, remove to your own claim some thousands of rails from the Puget's Sound Agricultural Company's enclosure, at and around the present site of Fort Steilacoom

Ans.—I did not; the soldiers moved them.

Int. 26.—Did you use any rails in making any enclosures upon your donation claim, at, or subsequent to the time of its location, that you found thereupon or in its vicinity ?

Ans.—There were no rails there, except what was on Mr. Heath's claim, which I occupied after he died. These I took and used.

Int. 27.—Did you, before taking and using them, first have the permission of Mr. Heath, his heirs, or legal representatives, and were they accounted for to the person or estate to whom they belonged ?

Ans.—They were on my claim. He was dead. I had as good a right to them as any one. I was his legal representative in his will.

Direct Examination Resumed.

Int. 1.—What amount of money had you expended in improving the half of your claim, which you sold to pay your debt of less than $4,000 in greenbacks ?

Ans.—It cost me upwards of $15,000; I paid $5 a day for common labor a part of the time.

Cross-examination Resumed.

Int. I.—What would be the coin value of all the improvements on the half of the claim you sold that you stated in your last answer cost you $15,000; I mean the value at the time you sold it last summer ?

Ans.—I could not say what it is worth; they are old and dilapidated now.

Int. 2.—Were all the improvements on the place, at the time you sold them, of the coin value of $250 ?

Ans.—I don't know their value; I won't say a word about it.

Int. 3.—Will you swear that the improvements on the claim at the time you sold them were of the coin value of $250?

Ans.—I do not know whether they were or not.

Int. 4.—Has there not been a large amount of valuable oak timber, also saw logs, removed from this part of the claim, between the time that you settled upon it and the time you sold it in summer 1866?

Ans.—Dr. Tolmie rented a part of my claim to the soldiers, and I want him to pay me for it now. Dr. Tolmie has been receiving rent from the Government yearly. The most of the oak timber on that part has been cut off by soldiers and others.

Int. 5.—Is not that part of the claim, stated by you as rented to the soldiers by Dr. Tolmie, and upon which he has yearly received rent, included within the limits of the Military reservation commonly known as Fort Steilacoom?

Ans.—Yes.

Int. 6.—Does not the Military reservation at Fort Steilacoom include the site of the buildings and most part of the farm formerly occupied by J. T. Heath?

Ans.—Yes.

Int. 7.—Was not Dr. Tolmie appointed with yourself, by the will of J. T. Heath, executors of his estate?

Ans.—Yes.

THOS. M. CHAMBERS.

STEILACOOM, *November* 23, 1866.

TESTIMONY OF DANIEL E. LANE.

Daniel E. Lane being first duly sworn, deposeth, in answer to interrogatories, as follows:

Int. 1.—State your age, residence, and occupation.

Ans.—I am fifty-five years of age; I reside in Pierce County; I am a farmer by occupation.

Int. 2.—How far from Steilacoom is your present residence?

Ans.—Twenty-five miles.

Int. 3.—Did you ever reside on any part of the Nisqually Plains? If so, state when it was that you settled there.

Ans.—I did; I settled there in the fall of 1853.

Int. 4.—Was any notice served on you by the agents of the Puget's Sound Company to leave this place?

Ans.—There was a notice in this way, that I was trespassing on the Puget's Sound Company's land; it was to show me that I had no lawful right; that I was trespassing on their land.

Int. 5.—Did you afterwards have any conversation with Dr. Tolmie about the intention of this notice? If so, state the substance of what he said.

Ans.—Dr. Tolmie told me, if I recollect right, and I think I do, that he did not care particularly about my settling on the land; was willing I should settle there. This notice was merely to show that they maintain their claim to the land. This conversation took place in Dr. Tolmie's house; my son William was with me at the time.

Int. 6.—Are you well acquainted with the claim of the Puget's Sound Company, known as the Nisqually Plains?

Ans.—Yes; with the greater portion of it.

Int. 7.—At what price per acre would you fix the value of these lands, averaging them together?

Ans.—It is a pretty hard question for me to answer. A small proportion of it is good land; but the remainder is almost worthless. To estimate the value of the whole, I would not put it above Government price; I would not be bound to pay that much for it myself; I consider it poor farming land; I consider it just as Dr. Tolmie told me he considered it.

Int. 8.—What do you refer to when you say Dr. Tolmie considered this land? State the substance of any conversation you had with him about its value.

Ans.—At the time that Mr. Dean had a trial with Mr. Huggins and Mr. Greig for trespass, I was then living on George Gibbs' farm. Dr. Tolmie asked me if I still held my claim at the Puyallup. I told him I did. He told me I was wise, and stated that Mr. Dean was very foolish for contending for that place, out on the gravelly plains, for it was worth but a trifle for farming purposes. All the land was of value was for grazing, and their stock had eat it so out that it was not worth much for that. That is about all that I recollect.

Int. 9.—Was your claim on the Puyallup within the Company's claim?

Ans.—Dr. Tolmie told me it was not; that they did not claim that land down there.

Int. 10.—On what part of the Nisqually Plains did you settle in 1853?

Ans.—About two miles from Mr. Dean's place.

Int. 11.—When did you leave there to go over to the Puyallup?

Ans.—In the fall of 1854.

Int. 12.—Did you then take the claim on which you now reside?

Ans.—Yes, sir.

Int. 13.—How did you come to be living on the Gibbs place, which is on the Company's claim, at the time of the Dean suit?

Ans.—In the fall of 1855, I came out on the account of Indian difficulties; lived out on the plains until 1859, I think.

Int. 14.—Did you then move back to your present place, on the Puyallup bottom?

Ans.—Yes, sir.

Cross-examination by Frank Clark, Esq., Counsel for the Company.

Int. 1.—Previous to emigrating to this Territory, where had you resided?

Ans.—In Laporte County, Indiana.

Int. 2.—How long had you resided there?

Ans.—Nine years.

Int. 3.—Where had you resided previous to that?

Ans.—In Elkhart County, Indiana; Noble County, Indiana; Paulding County, Ohio, and in New York city before that, and on Long Island, where I commenced life.

Int. 4.—What was your age when you went to New York city ?

Ans.—Nineteen years.

Int. 5.—How long did you reside there.

Ans.—Seven years.

Int. 6.—What was your business while there ?

Ans.—Cartman.

Int. 7.—How long did you reside in Paulding County, Ohio ?

Ans.—About two years.

Int. 8.—What was your business there?

Ans.—Principal business, fever and ague and farming.

Int. 9.—Which was the principal branch of your business there ?

Ans.—I was not able to work at farming but a small proportion of the time; almost everybody was sick on the Maumee river.

Int. 10.—Where did you move from this place to ?

Ans.—Noble County, Indiana.

Int. 11.—How long did you remain there ?

Ans.—I do not exactly recollect; I think it was six years.

Int. 12.—What was your business while there ?

Ans.—Farming.

Int. 13.—Where did you go to next?

Ans.—Elkhart County, Indiana.

Int. 14.—How long did you remain there?

Ans.—I can't recollect; I think it was somewhere about five or six years.

Int. 15.—What was your business while there ?

Ans.—Farming.

Int. 16.—Where did you go next?

Ans.—Laporte County, Indiana.

Int. 17.—How long did you reside there ?

Ans.—Nine years.

Int. 18.—What was your business while there?

Ans.—Farming.

Int. 19—.Where did you move to from there ?

Ans.—To Washington Territory, Pierce County.

Int. 20.—At what time, in what year did you leave Laporte County, Indiana, for Washington Territory?

Ans.—About the 1st of March, 1853.

Int. 21.—When did you arrive in Pierce County, Washington Territory?

Ans.—About the middle of October, 1853.

Int. 22.—What is your age?

Ans.—Fifty-five last month, October.

Int. 23.—Are you as certain that you were nineteen years of age when you went to New York and of all the facts detailed subsequent to the statement of that fact in your cross-examination, as you are of any statement that you have made upon your examination-in-chief?

Ans.—I might be mistaken in the time; I have kept no exact record of the time.

Int. 24.—Could you be mistaken in the time to the extent of six or seven years?

Ans.—It is possible I might be; it is something that I have not thought of; a great part of it is mere guess work in regard to the time.

Int. 25.—Is it not possible that you might have made a like mistake in the statement you made in your examination-in-chief?

Ans.—I have made no mistake, unless it be in regard to the price of land; that is my opinion; people differ in opinion.

Int. 26.—Designate that part of your testimony, in answer to cross-interrogatories, in which it is possible for you to have made a mistake of either six or seven years.

Ans.—I am not positive of my exact age when I went to New York city; I am not positive of the exact time that I lived in Paulding County, Ohio; Noble County, Indiana; Elkhart County, Indiana; it was mere guess work.

Int. 27.—Is the part of your testimony, referred to in your last answer, all that you are now willing to swear was mere guess work when given?

Ans.—What I stated for facts, are facts.

Int. 28.—Did you not, in your first answer, state as a fact that you were nineteen years of age when you went to New York city?

Ans.—I made the statement. When I came to think further, I had lived in New York some time before I was nineteen, on the account of some business that was transacted when I was nineteen, that I did not think of when the question was first asked me; and that is the reason why I was mistaken.

Int. 29.—How long had you resided in New York when you were nineteen years old?

Ans.—I don't recollect exactly.

Int. 30.—Had you lived there a year?

Ans.—Very likely I had, and perhaps more. That is just as near as I can come at it.

Int. 31.—Had you lived there two years?

Ans.—I don't know whether I lived there two years, or more, or less; don't know, can't tell, don't remember.

Int. 32.—Had you lived there three years?

Ans.—Well, I do not think I had, but still I am not positive.

Int. 33.—Had you lived there four years?

Ans.—No, sir.

Int. 34.—Is the George Gibbs referred to in your examination in chief, the same George Gibbs that is now acting as one of the secretaries, on the part of the United States, to the British and American Joint Commission appointed to adjust and determine the H. B. and P. S. A. Companies claims against the United States?

Ans.—It is the same George Gibbs that has been in that Commission, but whether he is in it now I do not know.

Int. 35.—Did you state as a fact, in your cross-examination, that you resided two years in Paulding county, Ohio, and was principally engaged with fever and ague and farming?

Ans.—My business was farming when I was able to work; the exact time I have stated before I could not tell.

Int. 36.—Did George Gibbs squat upon, and to some extent improve, a piece of land upon the Company's claim in this county?

Ans.—George Gibbs took under the donation act, as I understood it, on land the Company claimed, and he improved a part of it himself.

Int. 37.—How long did Gibbs reside upon this claim?

Ans.—He lived there, personally, over a year; and I think two years, if I am not mistaken.

Int. 38.—Have not you lived on his place, more or less, with his assent, or at his request, since he left it?

Ans.—I have lived on it by agreement between him and me. He never left the place, that is to forsake it, and always had some property there, and made it his home until he went away on the boundary line business.

Int. 39.—Does he still claim it under the donation law?

Ans.—He has sold it to John Flett.

Int. 40.—How recently was that sale made?

Ans.—Some time last winter.

Int. 41.—Have you had any communications by letter, message, or otherwise, from this Mr. George Gibbs, regarding your giving evidence in this matter?

Ans.—No, sir.

Int. 42.—Can you pretend to swear particularly as to conversations you took part in twelve or thirteen years ago?

Ans.—Some conversations I had, I can; and some conversations I have had with different individuals, I cannot.

Int. 43.—What year were you born in?

Ans.—In 1811, October 24.

Int. 44.—In what year was this conversation between Dr. Tolmie and yourself had about your Puyallup claim, and the propriety of Mr. Dean's leaving that of the Company and taking one along side of you?

Ans.—In regard to the time of the conversation you allude to, was the time that Mr. Dean had the trial with Huggins and Mr. Craig; I don't recollect the year, but the time can be ascertained by going to the probate records; I was on the jury.

Int. 45.—When Dr. Tolmie was talking to you, do you not think he was very much pleased with your leaving the Company's claim, and very anxious that the balance of the squatters thereupon should follow your example, but more especially Mr. Dean, who was then prosecuting frivolous complaints against the employés of the Company?

Ans.—Well, every person has their thoughts, and can't help their thoughts, and I thought of course Dr. Tolmie thought the gravelly plains were frivolous, and the land in the Puyallup bottom was valuable, and by talking so to me would please me, and he would get a sort of an understanding how the case was going.

Int. 46.—Is this last answer of yours stated as a fact, or do you wish to modify it, and have it considered like the answer as to your age, when you went to New York city, mere guess work?

Ans.—I answered it exactly agreeably to my thoughts.

Int. 47.—Was this Mr. Dean referred to a squatter upon the Company's claim?

Ans.—He was an employé of the Puget's Sound Company, under Dr. Tolmie.

Int. 48.—Was this Mr. Dean referred to a squatter upon the Company's claim?

Ans.—He was an employé of the Company, and when his time was out, he jumped the place he occupied.

Int. 49.—At the time this suit of which you speak was pending, had he not left the service of the Company, and jumped this claim?

Ans.—I understood that his time was out, and he did not choose to remain longer in the Company, and quit and jumped the claim.

DANIEL E. LANE.

STEILACOOM, *November* 23, 1866.

––––––

TESTIMONY OF JOHN BRADLEY.

John Bradley, being first duly sworn, deposeth, in answer to interrogatories, as follows:

Int. 1.—State your age, residence, and occupation.

Ans.—I have to give my age as my mother gave it to me.

I was born 11th of March, 1819; I reside on the Elk Plain, Pierce county; I am a farmer.

Int. 4.—When did you first come to Pierce county?

Ans.—In the spring of 1847.

Int. 3.—Have you resided here ever since?

Ans.—I have resided here all the time, till the 19th day of November, 1849, I left for California mines; I returned the following June.

Int. 4.—Did you ever have any conversation with Dr. Tolmie, the agent of the Company, about a notice served on Sidney Smith? If so, state when it was, and the substance of the conversation.

Ans.—In 1847, I came over here with L. E. Smith; I went up to Muck with him; he went to Mr. Heath and got the lent of a plough. At the time that he and I was ploughing, to put in a spring crop, Dr. Tolmie and several of his servants came along and warned him off the place. I asked Dr. Tolmie what was the reason that he warned him off? Says I, did you not bring him here from the Willamette and show him this claim, and now you are warning him off. He told me, no; that he did not show him that claim, but that he sent some of his men to show him. I asked him what was the reason that he warned him off; he said there was a treaty made, and that the Government was so good as to reserve some for them, for they did not claim any before. I told him then, if there was a good claim there, that I fancied I would take it, and if it belonged to the American Government, I would hold it; and if it did not, I did not want it.

JOHN BRADLEY.

STEILACOOM, *November 23, 1866.*

TERRITORY OF WASHINGTON, }
    County of Pierce. } *ss.*

I, George Washington Sloan, county auditor in and for said county and Territory, residing in said county, do hereby

certify that the foregoing depositions of Wm. P. Dougherty,
A. J. Burge, James E. Williamson, R. S. Moore, George
W. Shazer, E. A. Light, J. L. McDonald, Thomas M. Chambers, Dan'l E. Lane, and John Bradley, were taken before
me, at my office in Steilacoom, in said county, on the 22d
and 23d days of November, A. D. 1866, in pursuance of a
verbal agreement made in my presence by W. Carey Johnson, Esq., on behalf of the United States, and Frank Clark,
Esq., on behalf of the Puget's Sound Agricultural Company,
and reduced to writing by me, or in my presence and under
my direction, by persons agreed upon between the parties.

I further certify that to each of said witnesses, before his
examination, I administered the following oath:

" You do solemnly swear that the evidence you shall give
in the matter of the claim of the Puget's Sound Agricultural Company against the United States shall be the truth,
the whole truth, and nothing but the truth, so help you
God."

I further certify that said depositions were each carefully
read to or by said witnesses, after the same were reduced to
writing, and then signed by them respectively.

In witness whereof I have hereunto set my hand and affixed
the county commissioner's seal, this twenty-third
[L. S.]   day of November, A. D. 1866.

GEORGE W. SLOAN,
Auditor Pierce County, W. T.

BRITISH AND AMERICAN JOINT COMMISSION

ON THE

HUDSON'S BAY AND PUGET'S SOUND AGRICULTURAL COMPANIES' CLAIMS.

—————•◦•—————

In the matter of the Claim of the Puget's Sound Agricultural Company against the United States of America.

Deposition of witnesses sworn and examined in the city of Washington, District of Columbia, by virtue of an agreement between Eben F. Stone, Agent and Attorney for the United States of America, and Edward Lander, Esq., Agent and Attorney for the Puget's Sound Agricultural Company, before me, Nicholas Callan, a Notary Public in and for the County of Washington, and District of Columbia, on the part of the United States.

TESTIMONY OF JOHN B. CHAPMAN.

John B. Chapman, being duly sworn, deposeth and saith:

Int. 1.—What is your name, age, place of residence, and occupation?

Ans.—My name is John Butler Chapman, aged 68 years, residence Washington, D. C., and I am a clerk in the Treasury Department.

Int. 2.—Have you ever been in Washington Territory, if so, when? and are you acquainted with any of the lands there which are claimed by the Puget's Sound Agricultural Company. If you say that you are, please to describe as fully as you can the extent and character of the lands so claimed by them.

Ans.—I have been there. Was there in 1851 and 1852. I know all the lands there, and I know of their claiming it. (*See note, infra.*) It is difficult for me describe these lands, unless I have a map of the United States, as I had out there.

11 P

The Company, called the Puget's Sound Agricultural Company, was on the Sound and what is now Washington Territory, lying, as it was represented to me, between the Nisqually and the Puyallup rivers. I made a survey between those rivers.

Int. 3.—Who employed you to make this survey?

Ans.—Mr. Tolmie, the factor or head of the Puget's Sound Agricultural Company.

Int. 4.—What directions or orders, if any, did you receive from him in regard to the making of this survey? State as particularly as you can.

Ans.—I was to go according to the direction of one of his employés, Mr. Montgomery. Dr. Tolmie stated he wished to run around as much of the land as his cattle, sheep, and horses roamed over. One of his employés was ordered to direct around the land where they ran, to show their range. I was also ordered to run into this plain, so as to take the position of the improvements. This was all done for the purpose of mapping the land where the cattle roamed over.

Int. 5.—Did Dr. Tolmie appoint some one to accompany you in making the survey? If so, who?

Ans.—He did. He appointed Mr. Montgomery, an employé of the Company, who was employed for the purpose of watching the cattle. Montgomery knew where the cattle roamed, and went with me to show it. I followed the directions of Mr. Montgomery.

Int. 6.—Did you complete the survey, and make a plan of the land? If so, what did you do with the plan?

Ans.—I did not complete the survey; I made a plan of [it] as far as we got. We commenced (*see note, infra,*) at the mouth of the Nisqually, and run up some distance, and on the bank of the Nisqually made a corner, and then started across the country, to comprise the bottom lands and ravines, as they came down the mountains. After running through some desperate swamps, up to our waists, we got to a plain. We then stopped on that line, and from a designated place, run into the plain to take observations where there were settlements. We took observations of the houses and sheep-pens, and what improvements were made. Then went back to the original line, at the place where we left it, and pursued our course. We then ran in that zigzag course for two or three days. We kept on this line until we were near the Puyallup. Left our camp at the corner. We came in again to the prairie for the purpose of taking observations, according to the custom of surveys. While we were in the plain, the reason we did not complete it was, some of the inhabitants that lived there, after I had been to all their houses, supposed it would be dangerous to them if Tolmie continued his surveys, and they could not get their land. Before we went back to the course, to start again to run to the Puyallup, the inhabitants got alarmed, and came and stopped us; they were the former employés of the Company; they threatened to break my compass and other instruments; then I quit until he got authority to continue. Then he, Dr. Tolmie, took me over here, to the mouth of the Nisqually, and I began to plat the notes I had already taken. He told me to begin near the mouth of the Nisqually, and I meandered around the Sound, and don't know whether I ran to the Puyallup or Steilacoom, it's been so long ago. We intended to run to the Puyallup. I was directed not to include a man on the Sound, near the mouth of the Puyallup, because he was a friend. In running the outer line, I occasionally left the line and run in for the purpose of determining the position of interior objects.

There was no line of any former survey to guide us.

Int. 7.—Were there any land-marks, or fences, or spotted trees, or monuments of any kind to indicate where the line was, which you ran out at this time; and did you, while running the line, see anything to indicate that you were running out an old line, or were you, in your judgment, running out a proposed line for the first time?

(Objected to as leading and directing the witness as to his answer, and asking the opinion of the witness as to what he was doing.)

Ans.—There were no monuments or marks of any description, or marks of trees indicating surveys on the line. There was nothing of the kind sought for. There were no monu-

ments or marks sought for or referred to by the guide or Mr.
Tolmie. It was only to run, according to Montgomery's
judgment, the line for the pasturage for cattle. I supposed
I was running out a line for the first time. There were no
monuments to show a previous line, nothing; only the man
was influenced by where the grass grew.

Int. 8.—What did you do with the plan which you made,
and do you know where it is now?

Ans.—I don't know where it is now; I gave it to Mr. Tolmie, the superintendent, who employed me.

Int. 9.—Is your name attached to the plan which you gave
to Mr. Tolmie?

Ans.—I think it is; I drew off the notes from my field-
book, and I gave him, Tolmie, a copy of my notes.

Int. 10.—Please to describe, as minutely as you can, the
condition which this land was in at the time you surveyed it,
its quality and character, the extent and nature of the improvements of the Puget's Sound Agricultural Company, the
proportion of cultivated land, if any, to that which was wild
or unimproved.

Ans.—The whole flat land is barren, and gravelly; if stirred
up, remains gravelly. There is nothing in the whole area that
will produce anything, except the alluvial in the depressions.
There is a fine, light grassgr ows over this gravelly soil. If
disturbed and ploughed it looks like a creek bottom. It looks
like Pennsylvania avenue well paved. Where there are prairie
swamps, there is grass that can be mowed. Wherever there
are depressions by washings, potatoes, &c., can be cultivated,
and for that reason they are sought. The alluvial spots are
very limited. They appear to be subsided lakes; those that
are on the plains. It will be very hard for me to tell the
proportion of that country. I shouldn't think the one-twentieth part of the land could be tilled, or would afford a grass.
It is a very rough guess. Englishmen have come over,
ploughed up the ground, and built up houses, but abandoned
them. There was not any land around Fort Nisqually cultivated. The Indians were fencing in a piece at the time I was
there, before I surveyed it; but whether they cultivated it or

not I don't know. There were very few improvements claimed by the Company. When I surveyed it, Mr. Montgomery had a house, and piece of land fenced in, but these other improvements of which I have spoken were those of the persons who stopped me by force of arms, who ignored having anything to do with the Puget's Sound Agricultural Company, denying the Company had any right to survey it at all. There were a few little sheep pens which were scattered over the plains. They were built in a circle, with snake fence about four feet high, for the purpose of folding sheep. Some were as large as a house, and some as high as two acres. I saw a great many sheep on the plain.

Int. 11.—What use, if any, was made of this land at the time you surveyed it, by the Puget's Sound Agricultural Company?

Ans.—The cattle run over a great deal of it up in the heads of the ravines. I couldn't see them down in the plains. The only use the Company ever had, judging from what they said, and from what I saw, was for the cattle to run over it in a state of nature.

Int. 12.—Did you see any cattle, sheep, and horses there? If any, how many, and in what condition were they, tame or wild?

Ans.—I saw sheep and horses and cattle stock. I can't tell how many. There were a great many sheep. The sheep were tame, and herded by Indians. The cattle were wild as deer; there were more than a thousand. They were taken as deer, except when driven into the corral by a particular mode to take them off.

Int. 13.—Did you have any conversation with Mr. Roberts in regard to this survey at the time you made it or before? If yea, please to state what it was.

Ans.—I had none with him at the time of the survey or before, concerning the survey I made.

Int. 14.—How long did you reside in Washington Territory, and when did you leave there?

Ans.—I went there in March, 1850, but did not settle then

to make any improvement until February, 1851, and left
there in June, 1852.

Int. 15.—Have you heretofore had considerable experience
as a surveyor of land, and are you well acquainted with the
marks which surveyors generally use to designate a line?

Ans.—I am well acquainted with the marks which surveyors use. I have never made public surveys, but I have surveyed a great deal.

Int. 16.—Did you not say incidentally, in reply to a former
question, that the men who interrupted you in making the
survey were formerly the employés of the Hudson's Bay or
Puget's Sound Agricultural Company?

Ans.—Most of them were; they went there with the Company and left it, and had filed their claims for land with the
United States. (*See note, infra.*)

Cross-Examination.

Int. 1.—Have you not been troubled with deafness for some
time, and has not the counsel been compelled to repeat frequently through your ear-trumpet portions of the questions
put to you, in order to explain them?

Ans.—I am very deaf; Mr. Stone has repeated the questions; it was through the mystification of the question that
he repeated it; I heard him distinctly through the trumpet;
I thought it was through the misapprehension of the clerks
to understand me. (*See note, infra.*)

Int. 2.—Did you have many conversations with Dr. Tolmie
about the land you were about to survey?

Ans.—I had a great many.

Int. 3.—Did he not, in most of these conversations, speak
of this land you were about to survey as the Company's, and
being held by them for some time?

Ans.—That is what he claimed.

(Objected to as leading.)

Int. 4.—In making this survey, was or was not the line run
in some instances through the woods, so as to enclose some
wood land?

Ans.—It was; a great deal of the line run through the woods.

Int. 5.—Did not Mr. Huggins accompany you in this survey, or in some portions of it?

Ans.—I had forgot his name entirely; but a clerk and two other white employés were along and a corps of Indians carrying the chain.

Int. 6.—You have stated that the alluvial soil was about one-twentieth of the whole; are you certain about this?

Ans.—Not at all; only a guess.

Int. 7.—Did you not take a donation claim in the timber on the shores of the Sound, and lay out a town-site and sell lots, and make a clearing; this on the land of the Company?

Ans.—I did; I laid out the town-site, sold lots, and made a clearing; all this on the land of the Company. They gave me notice to quit before I surveyed the Company's claim. I took my claim under the donation laws of 1850. (*See note, infra.*)

Int. 8.—Did you consider this a good place for a town? If so, for what reasons?

Ans.—I considered it was a good location for a town, for the reason that it was a very prominent place for a landing place; bluff bank, very deep water, sheltered by an island immediately opposite to it. There were fine level banks from the tide-water. It was covered with a dense growth of timber, which no cattle had roamed through. This about four miles of Nisqually.

Int. 9.—Where was the back country to support this town?

Ans.—If it depended upon the fertility of the country to support the town, it was not there as we then saw it. We knew it would be valuable for the exportation of the timber there; that it was valuable for the facility of navigation, the fine harbors, the fisheries there, and the anticipation we had of manufactures in connection with the navigation of the sea to China and the Hawaiian Islands. I don't know that we had any other views; I believe that is as far as we thought it would be of any advantage.

Int. 10.—Do you recollect the low ground south of the fort at Nisqually, the Muck Prairie, and the bottoms of the rivers and swales on this tract of land?

Ans.—I do not recollect any low ground until we got to the Nisqually. I don't know the Muck Prairie. There were a great many low swales. There was no improvement when I went there. (*See note, infra.*)

Int. 11.—Was not this fine light grass you have spoken of good for pasturage?

Ans.—It was first rate. (*See note, infra.*)

Int. 12.—Do you mean to say, seriously, that when this land was ploughed it looked like Pennsylvania avenue well paved, or was it a figure of speech?

Ans.—I meant they might as well try to cultivate Pennsylvania avenue as places and fields I have seen ploughed up and laid bare after two or three years' tending. It was right in the open prairie, at Steilacoom; I mean where the soldiers were quartered.

Int. 13.—Were not these people who stopped your survey settlers on the Company's claim under the donation laws?

Ans.—They quit the Company and went to themselves and made little farms; they intended to secure their claims in that way. They had settled on this land, and were living there as servants to the Company, and when the donation law was passed they declared their intention to become citizens of the United States.

Int. 14.—Do you not know that where this very land is unploughed it is excellent pasturage?

Ans.—It does. (*See note, infra.*)

Int. 15.—Did you survey some of these claims for the settlers under the donation law?

Ans.—Yes, a great many.

Int. 16.—Did you pay much attention to the quality of land when you settled there, and did you not settle there to bring on the question of the title of the Puget's Sound Agricultural Company to these lands?

Ans.—I did pay much attention to the quality of land. I did not settle there for the purpose of bringing up the question; I settled there for the advantages of the location, not believing that the Company, after mature deliberation and investigation as a lawyer, had any claim to that vacant land. I had understood all about it before I went there. I travelled over it and looked into it. I don't think any man took more notice of the quality of land than I did. I observed very particularly the timber and land in Oregon and Washington Territory; I have travelled over the whole of them. The agricultural properties of all the land were particularly observed by me. (*See note, infra.*)

Examination-in-Chief Resumed.

Int. 1.—Describe particularly the condition of the section of six hundred and forty acres on the Sound at the time you entered and claimed it; and state what you did when you commenced to clear it—the nature and difficulties of the undertaking.

Ans.—It was a dense forest of timber and chapparal. The undergrowth of the chapparal was over my head; I was lost in it, and could not get out for a day; it was so densely covered with forest that I commenced down at tide-water of the beach on the Sound. I lay at the edge of tide-water for several days and cut the brush until I got a foothold on the land; I then would cut away the brush sufficiently large to build a house. As soon as I got a place large enough for a house I built a log cabin. There was no outlet from there, where I could get to a road, except by the beach; no improvement made on it. It was such an impenetrable forest that no one appeared ever to have gone there, and when I cut a road out, the settlers in the neighborhood were astonished to see the development of the point. The cause of its being impenetrable was not only the thick growth of chapparal, but the immense amount of fallen timber. The fallen timber lay in such a manner, that in its natural state no horses or cattle could pass through. This forest continued up to within half or a mile of Nisqually. I took particular notice that there was no trace of an Indian or white man had ever been there, for I thought that would be made evidence of occupation, except a point where the Indians always camped on the tide-water line, which was in the middle of my claim, and where I lived. This tract, and forest, and chapparàl, as I have described, was about three miles south, about three miles on the high land beyond my claim. Then toward Fort Steilacoom it was about one and a half mile. I run it, but don't recollect the length. I cut a road both ways. (*See note, infra,*)

Int. 2.—What was done, if anything, in regard to the title of this land, by either you or Dr. Tolmie, after he gave you notice that the Puget's Sound Agricultural Company claimed the land which you had taken ?

Ans.—I commenced a suit against Dr. Tolmie, before I surveyed the land, to quiet the title alleging that the Company had no title under the treaty, to this wild part ; showing that his employés on possession alone could claim it. I asked Dr. Tolmie, on behalf of the Company, if he would not agree on a case to try the title before the Supreme Court. He declined doing it. I then commenced the suit. I think he said he wanted to show his title by survey. There was a difficulty in his getting a surveyor. There was a great deal of animosity about it. I told him I would survey it myself for him. It was to see if there were any defined lines or boundaries to his claim. I surveyed it wherever they directed me, with particular observations as to whether there were any marks. I filed a case in Court, and asked an injunction. The court declined to grant one, because I was already in possession. The Puget Sound Agricultural Company did not come into Court, they would not do it, to try the title. I left them immediately afterwards, and have not been there since. (*See note, infra.*)

JOHN B. CHAPMAN,
With the corrections.

WASHINGTON, D. C., *April* 5, 1866.

When Mr. Chapman first read over the foregoing deposition, two days after it was taken, but as soon as my clerk could write out a fair copy, he (Mr. Chapman,) made the following corrections :

To the answer of the 1st Int., he says :· I was there in 1850,

1851, 1852. I know all the lands there, and I know of their claiming some on Puget Sound.

To the 6th Int. We commenced south of the Fort, between the mouth of the Nisqually and the Fort, at a station or stake made by myself. While plotting the survey Tolmie requested me to begin at the starting point, between the Fort and the Nisqually river, and run to the Sound below the mouth, and then meander the Sound north. I do not recollect how far we run towards the Steilacoom or Puyallup ; I do not think we crossed Steilacoom.

In answer to Int. 16. That answer ought to be corrected. They were the old employés of the Company, and remained on the lands they were put on by the Company, but did not any longer serve the Company, but claimed to be independent farm[er]s, British subjects, and when the word of the donation law of Congress came they filed intention of United States citizenship.

In answer to cross-Int. 1.—I answered thus : I am very deaf, but Mr. Stone wrote down the questions and read them very plain. I heard him distinctly, but before I answered any question you all appeared to be disputing among yourselves, and I had to wait, after I had commenced to answer the question, until you all subsided, and then answer word by word.

In answer to cross-Int. 7.—I never answered such a question in that way. I laid out a town-site and sold lots on land on the Sound, but did not believe it to belong to the Puget Sound Company. I said I used to be considered a good lawyer in Indiana, and thought I could construe a treaty, the supreme law of the land, too well to believe the Company had any title to that land. I never did, nor do not to this day, believe I was on the Company's land, as contemplated in the treaty.

In answer to cross-Int. 10.—I stated distinctly that the survey I made did not take in any of the Nisqually bottom, but run on high land, near the Fort, until we struck the bottom, and made a corner, and struck directly out from it through the timber country and swamps.

In answer to cross-Ints. 11, 14.—In a state of nature it is good pasturage, but if used much, it is destroyed.

In answer to cross-Int. 16.—I said I had travelled over great portion of the California and Oregon mountains, and my special notices were the soil, quality, and availability of every spot of ground; more exclusive travel and close observation of soil, climate, and topography, than any other man that visited the country.

Examination-in-Chief Resumed.

In answer to Int. 1.—Half a day the sun came out. It ought to have been inserted that after I had erected a house, he sent down a posse of British subjects with a written notice to leave, that he claimed it.

In answer to the 2d interrogatory.—I first proposed to the agent, Tolmie, to agree on a case in the Supreme Court of the United States to try the title of the land, under the treaty of 1846, but he refused to do so, and I then commenced a suit. I filed a declaration in the Supreme Court, at Oregon City. This was before I surveyed it. The Company would not appear, and the Court would not take further cognizance of the case. I stated that I came directly to Washington city, and took Joe Lane, a Hudson's Bay man, with me to President Fillmore, and stated the case and the claim of this British Company. He requested me to file the facts with the Secretary of State. (While I was engaged drawing up the case, I was taken sick here in Washington and filed what I drew up. I was sick a long time, and never recollected what I done.) I did so, and never went back.

J. B. CHAPMAN,
With the original.

Testimony of D. B. McKibbin.

D. B. McKibbin, being duly sworn according to law, says:

Int. 1.—What is your name, age, place of residence, and occupation?

Ans.—D. B. McKibbin; my occupation, that of an officer in the United States Army, brevet brigadier general of volunteers; thirty-six years of age; I have no particular place of residence.

Int. 2.—Have you not lived in Washington Territory? If yea, when and where did you reside in said Territory?

Ans.—I have. My permanent place of residence was Fort Steilacoom. I was there near about three years, in 1856, 1857, 1860, and 1861.

Int. 8.—Are you, or not, acquainted with the property claimed by the Puget's Sound Agricultural Company, between the Nisqually and the Puyallup rivers, called the Nisqually Plains?

Ans.—I am acquainted with the property, though not knowing the exact limits of their claim. I am acquainted with all that country between the Nisqually and the Puyallup.

Int. 4.—Please to describe, as minutely as you can, the character and the condition of the land at these plains; giving the quantity of arable land there, as compared with the prairie and woodland.

Ans.—On the plains, the soil is almost entirely gravel; there is a little black loam with it which is immediately washed out on cultivation, and there are spots of timber scattered over it, and lakes. Principally pine timber, some few oak trees—scrub-oak.

Int. 5.—Is any part of this land fit for tillage? If yea, what part, and what proportion does this tillage land bear to the whole tract?

Ans.—I suppose a great portion of it can be tilled, but not be productive. I think not one-twelfth part of it would be taken up by any man in a decent country, and that part only

moderately good, except some few spots; a very small proportion of that one-twelfth.

Int. 6.—What opportunities did you have, while at the fort,
to become acquainted with the character of the land at these
plains, and how often have you traveled over it?

Ans.—I have ridden over them hundreds of times—I could
not begin to count—in different directions, and in that way
had an opportunity of seeing and judging of the soil. I was
so well acquainted with them that I never took a road without
it went direct to a place, unless there was some obstacle in
the way. I mean by that that I was so well acquainted with
the country that I could go to any part of it without taking
the regular road, and could have ridden to almost any part of
it in the darkest night. I surveyed the roads and part of
the country for Mr. George Gibbs in 1856 or 1857.

Int. 7.—Were there any buildings or improvements when
you were there which were in the possession of the Puget's
Sound Agricultural Company? If yea, please to describe
them particularly.

Ans.—At Fort Nisqually there was a house in which the
chief trader, Dr. Tolmie, lived, which was the most valuable;
several small log houses used as stores, and others as out-
houses. Out at their farm, about Muck Creek, there were
one or two good log houses, and others that were not worth
much—very little indeed. Mr. Huggins put up a house there,
I think; I don't remember whether it was log or not; it was
one of the good houses there. I don't remember any other
houses. At the landing below Nisqually, and on the plains,
there were log huts; I did not consider them worth more than
the logs. There is a house there occupied by Dean, who was
formerly an employé of the Puget's Sound Company; but
whether it belonged to that Company or not, I can't say;
and also at Fort Steilacoom there were several log houses,
which were worth nothing but for fire-wood, save the improvements put on by officers at the fort.

Int. 8.—How much of the land at the plains which are
claimed by the Company was enclosed or fenced, if any?

Ans.—That would be a hard matter to say, as there was a

very little enclosed. I should not think the one-hundredth part was enclosed or fenced.

Int. 9.—Was there any tillable land at these plains, of any extent, except that which was on the edges of the streams and lakes?

(Objected to as leading.)

Ans.—There was not.

Int. 10.—What proportion of the land at these plains, if any, was, in your judgment, covered with pine timber and lakes and rocky tracts? I mean by rocky tracts, rocky and unproductive soil.

Ans.—The stony ground, pine timber, and lakes, and what I should say was unproductive ground, that is, ground used once or twice, is eleven-twelfths. I call the ground unproductive because the Puget's Sound Company, after farming it for a year or two, move their farms to another place.

Int. 11.—What use was made of the oak trees, if any, that grew on these plains?

Ans.—Fire-wood; I never heard it was used for anything else.

Int. 12.—What was the character of the pine or fir trees that grew on these plains, for purposes of timber, as compared with the fir trees that grew on the adjoining country, if you know?

Ans.—There was very little of it that was fit for spars; it was pretty much the same as timber in other parts of that country, only it could not be easily taken to the mills.

Int. 13.—How was the land on these plains affected, generally, by cultivation; was it improved or spoiled by tillage?

Ans.—It was utterly ruined. The gravel and sand all came up to the top, and the loam washed in. There was so little of the loam it could not be seen after one or two years' cultivation, except on the borders of the streams.

Int. 14.—Have you any knowledge of the value of this land at the plains? If yea, please to state what, in your opinion, is the average value of it per acre, limiting your answer to the land described on the map here produced, which was prepared at the request of Dr. Tolmie.

Ans.—In comparison with other public lands that I have seen for sale, as a general thing, I don't think it was worth one-fifth. I, certainly, if I was buying land, would not give twenty-five cents an acre for the whole plain. Its greatest value, as pasture land, has, in a manner, run out, because of a red sorrel which is spreading over it, and which can't be stopped.

Int. 15.—How many troops are generally stationed at the fort at Steilacoom, and when was this fort established?

Ans.—It varied from two to six companies, but I think the average would be about three, as far as I can recollect. I don't know when the fort was established.

Cross-Examination.

Int. 1.—At the time you resided at Fort Steilacoom, were you stationed there as an officer of the United States army? If so, what was your rank, and were you a graduate of West Point, or appointed from civil life?

Ans.—I was; I was a second lieutenant, and appointed from civil life.

Int. 2.—Are there not on the plains you have spoken of some one hundred and fifty settlers engaged in farming and agriculture?

Ans.—No, sir; I don't think there were; I don't think there were fifty.

Int. 3.—Do you not know that there were on this claim, as shown on the map, a grist-mill and several saw-mills for making timber?

Ans.—I don't at this time remember but one grist-mill and one saw-mill, both Judge Chambers', both on the same stream.

Int. 4.—Do you not recollect a saw-mill erected near the fort, above Judge Chambers', and another near the old Nisqually landing on Sequalitchew creek?

Ans.—I do. Bird had a saw and grist-mill in the same building, about a mile and a quarter from the fort; and Dr. Webber had a saw-mill at Sequalitchew, near the Nisqually landing.

Int. 5.—Do you not know that the land cultivated as a garden by the soldiers produced very largely, and that it was good land, though stony?

Ans.—I do. I don't that it was very stony. That was a little spot with a stream running through it. I don't suppose there was more than fifteen acres of it. I was asked generally.

Int. 6.—Did you ever cultivate any of this land, or any other land, as a farmer?

Ans.—Not on this land. I did out on Muckleshoot prairie, on White river, near the foot of the mountains. I also cultivated land at our camp up on the northwest boundary, the 49th parallel.

Int. 7.—Do you not know that the prairie called "Muck" is fertile land; and that all the swales, low grounds, and lands through which the small streams flow, are good tillable lands?

Ans.—I don't know that the whole of the Muck Prairie is good land; I know that part of it is moderately good. The largest stones that are to be found on the plain are found on Muck Prairie, and, as I said before, along the banks of the streams there is a little good land. As for low places, where the loam can wash down into them, it is pretty good land until it wears out, though it does not wear out so quick as the other.

Int. 8.—You state you were there three years; during that time did you see any of these low places worn out, or is this merely an opinion of yours?

Ans.—I have. There is the farm of George Gibbs, for instance, which has the wash from the hills, is in a low place on the bank of a stream, and in spite of manuring and everything else is completely worn out; and the land beside Dr. Tolmie's house, on the opposite side of the creek, is also pretty well worn out.

Int. 9.—When you speak of stony lands, do you mean lands covered with large stones, or not?

Ans.—I mean gravel, as a general thing. There are some of them as large as a hen's egg, most of them not half that size, and that intermixed with sand. There is a little loam with it, in its natural state.

12 P

Int. 10.—Do you not know that these plains are covered with grass and afford good pasturage for sheep and cattle?

Ans.—They have been, but were not so good when I left there as they had been. Red sorrel, in a measure, was spoiling them, and cultivation was wearing them out.

Int. 11.—With what lands do you compare them, when you say they are not worth one-fifth of them?

Ans.—I compare them with lands in the Mississippi Valley, lands at Whidbey's Island, the Muckleshoot Prairie, and Porter's Prairie. I was speaking more particularly of lands in the Mississippi Valley and the West, or lands that could be bought from the Government at the Government price.

Int. 12.—Are there any prairies on the Puget's Sound of equal extent, or as suitable for the pasturage of sheep and cattle as are these plains?

Ans.—No; I think not. None that I know of.

Int. 13.—Was not the garrison at Steilacoom generally supplied with beef by the Puget's Sound Agricultural Company?

Ans.—Yes, sir. It was up to the last few years, 1856–7, but not in 1860–1. I know it had been generally heretofore.

Int. 14.—Was not one of the buildings you have spoken of at Fort Nisqually a store house of some sixty by forty feet in dimensions, and one story and one half high?

Ans.—I really don't remember the measurement of it, nor of the one half story. There was a number of those log houses connected together.

Int. 15.—Might not these buildings have been larger than you have mentioned, and of better quality?

Ans.—There may have been one store-house of sixty by forty feet. I don't think there was more.

D. B. McKibbin,
Bvt. Brig. Gen. Vols.

Washington City, D. C., 28*th April*, 1866.

Testimony of Arthur A. Denny.

Arthur A. Denny, being duly sworn according to law, says:

Int. 1.—What is your name, age, place of residence, and occupation?

Ans.—Arthur A. Denny; aged forty-three years; residence, Seattle, Washington Territory; and occupation, at present, Delegate from Washington Territory to Congress.

Int. 2.—Are you acquainted with the property in Washington Territory, at and near Nisqually, claimed by the Puget's Sound Agricultural Company, which is indicated on the map here produced?

Ans.—I am somewhat acquainted with that piece of country.

Int. 3.—Have you any knowledge of the limits of the claim of this Company at Nisqually? If yea, please to describe them as nearly as you can.

Ans.—I can't say that I have any definite knowledge of the limits of the claim.

Int. 4.—Please to look at the map here produced, upon which is indicated the extent of the claim of this Company at Nisqually, and state whether you are acquainted with the country which is embraced in the lines indicated upon this map?

Ans.—I have been over or through that section of country represented on this map. I have traveled entirely across it in one direction and by one route, and traveled over it to some extent in addition.

Int. 5.—Please to describe this tract of land which is covered by this claim of the Company, giving the general character and the character of particular portions of it as fully as you can.

Ans.—That portion of it bordering on the Nisqually and smaller streams is generally a fine quality of soil. What we might call the uplands are rather poor and sterile. My impression of it is that the greater portion is prairie. The prairie portion is, generally speaking, of poor quality.

Int. 6.—Have you had any experience heretofore as a surveyor in Washington Territory, and has your attention or not been directed by your interests and pursuits to the value and character of land in Washington Territory?

Ans.—I have not followed surveying in Washington Territory as an occupation, but my attention has been directed to the character and value of lands in that Territory.

Int. 7.—What, in your opinion, is the value of the land per acre, which is embraced in the limits of this claim of the Puget's Sound Company at Nisqually, giving the value per acre as nearly as you can of the different portions, separating the good part from the bad, and giving also, if you can, what you should think would be a fair average price for the whole?

Ans.—There are portions of it which are comparatively valueless, and there are other portions which, being better, are valuable. My experience in those matters in that country is this: The poor lands would hardly sell at all, and the rich lands are in considerable demand.

Int. 8.—When did you first become acquainted, from your own observation, with the lands covered by this claim, and what caused you to observe them at that time?

Ans.—I first saw it in the spring of 1852. I was a new-comer in the country, and was looking with a view of locating and settling in the Territory.

Int. 9.—Did you, at the time, take special notice of these lands with a view to forming a judgment of their character and quality, and how much of this claim did you then observe?

Ans.—Yes, sir; so far as I traveled within the bounds of the lands designated. I did not travel extensively over the claim at that time, but principally in the vicinity of the old fort at Nisqually.

Int. 10.—Have you since then had occasion to examine and observe these lands; if yea, when, and to what extent, and for what purpose?

Ans.—Since then I have been over the land more extensively. So far as my observations have since extended, I have found the prairie to be of a very poor quality. The observations which I have made there, in the main, were casual, as I was passing through and over the country.

Int. 11.—Are you acquainted with the claim of this Company at the Cowlitz Farms, so-called, in Washington Territory?

Ans.—I have been at that point, but cannot say that I am particularly acquainted with it.

Cross-Examination.

Int. 1.—In passing over these plains, have not your travels been confined to the usually traveled road between Seattle and Olympia, running along the northern border of the claim, near the Sound?

Ans.—Yes, sir; that is so.

Int. 2.—With the exception of the observation you gave to the plains around the old fort, have you ever particularly observed any other portion of the plains off the traveled road?

Ans.—No, sir.

Int. 3.—Have you ever visited the Muck Prairies, or the farms located on the swales and lowlands?

Ans.—I have not visited the Muck Farms. I have seen farms on the swales or lowlands on the traveled road?

Int. 4.—Do you know anything of the productiveness of those farms you noticed on the traveled road?

Ans.—Yes, sir; they are considered very productive.

Int. 5.—Do you know that when these uplands are not too much depastured they afford good and valuable pasturage for sheep, cattle, and horses?

Ans.—Well, I should say this: they do for a short time, but are not durable.

Int. 6.—Are not those prairies the largest body of pasturage lands around the Sound in any direction?

Ans.—They are the largest body of prairie or plains, but not, in my judgment, affording the best pasture.

Int. 7.—What other body of lands afford better pasturage?

.166

Ans.—I regard the bottoms and the valley lands as affording the best pasturage.

Int. 8.—Do you know anything of these lands being hired in summer by drovers from Oregon, for pasturage for their stock?

Ans.—No, sir; I don't know that I do.

Int. 9.—Do you know that large numbers of stock are shipped from Steilacoom to Victoria?

Ans.—Yes, sir.

Int. 10.—How far is Seattle, your residence, from Steilacoom?

Ans.—I have usually estimated it at thirty-six miles.

Int. 11.—What is the extent of the largest of the prairies you know of outside of these plains, of the character you speak of, as being better for pasturage than those plains?

Ans.—I don't know of any other, unless it be Whidbey's Island. On the Sound I don't know of any.

A. A. DENNY.

WASHINGTON CITY, D. C., *May* 11, 1866.

TESTIMONY OF DR. GEORGE SUCKLEY.

Dr. George Suckley, being duly sworn according to law, says:

Int. 1.—What is your name, age, place of residence, and occupation?

Ans.—My name is George Suckley; aged thirty-five years; place of residence, New York city; I am a physician, but not in practice.

Int. 2.—Have you ever resided in Washington Territory? If yea, when and where, and for how long a period, and what was your occupation while there?

Ans.—I resided there twice. The first time from December, 1853, to about the 1st of August, 1854; the second time from January, 1856, to January, 1857. I lived eight months of the interim between these two periods at the Dalles, which was separated from Washington Territory by the Columbia river, and I frequently crossed. I was an assistant surgeon in the United States army.

Int. 3.—Please to look at the map, here produced, and state whether or not you recognize the same as a correct delineation of the country between the Nisqually and the Puyallup rivers, called the Nisqually Plains.

Ans.—In the main, it is correct.

Int. 4.—Are you acquainted with the country, indicated on said map by a black line, which is claimed by the Puget's Sound Agricultural Company? If yea, please to describe its character and condition as fully as you can.

Ans.—A great part of this tract I know very well. I hunted, and fished, and rode over it to see patients scattered for miles around Fort Steilacoom. The exact lines drawn on the map as a part of the claim I cannot swear to having been on, but the tract, as a whole, I know nearly as well as any man living. The country is very peculiar. There is a large amount of open ground that are called plain or prairie, also many patches of woods. The plains were crossed by streams and brooks; and there were many lakes, varying in size, most of which were margined by timber. In agricultural value, the soil of the untimbered parts was nearly identical with that of the Hempstead Plains, on Long Island, New York—a thin surface-soil on the higher ground, with many round pebbles intermixed. Around Fort Steilacoom the ground had been ploughed. The sod had apparently been destroyed, and the land looked nearly like desolation. There were swales, and in the vicinities of water-couses the land was much better; but compared to the whole tract, the amount of good ground was small. There were lines and depressions in these plains, frequently long, but very narrow, much richer than the ground on the general level of the plateau. The Hudson's Bay and Puget's Sound Companies had general control of that region before I went there. The pasturage had been over-used, and the grass nearly destroyed, partly by being eaten too closely, and partly by the introduction, as it was said, by the sheep, of sorrel, which had nearly exterminated the natural grasses. The increase of grasshoppers also greatly deteriorated the value of the pasturage. The plains were roamed over by large herds of cattle, in a very wild state ; they were neither guarded nor herded, but there were about twelve thousand sheep that were carefully tended by shepherds ; not in fenced enclosures, except about shearing time. The timber, where found, was very dense, as a rule, and many of the trees enormous. I have seen many on that tract fully five feet in diameter. In the vicinity of a farm there, called the Ross farm, on the map, there were many oaks like what we on the Atlantic call scrub-oaks ; but on the plains there were here and there scattered oaks of respectable size. Near Fort Steilacoom there were about a dozen, averaging about twenty inches in diameter, as near as I can recollect. This oak timber was not abundant, and was but seldom used. The timber which was most used for shipment or otherwise was a kind of fir, known to naturalists as the *Abies Douglassii*. There was another tree known to naturalists as the *Thuja gigantea* and to the settlers as the *cedar*, frequently of an enormous size.

Int. 5.—Have you paid, heretofore, considerable attention to botany and geology, and did you not while there observe carefully this tract of country with reference to its botanical and geological character ?

Ans.—I took great interest in the country in every way, and, perhaps, scientifically understood it better than any man there living at that time, except, perhaps, Mr. George Gibbs.

Int. 6.—Did you not, also, observe this country with reference to its agricultural and other uses ? If yea, please to state, in your judgment, for what uses it is mainly valuable, if at all.

Ans.—As a boy and a young man I lived a great deal on farms, and took much interest in crops and stock. As to the agricultural value of the so-called arable land near Nisqually, it was, compared to the quality of land in Ohio, Illinois, and Minnesota, very poor, except in the small swales and valleys. To make the plains proper, productive to an ordinarily desirable extent, it would require much labor, careful manuring, and great attention. There were small strips, however, which were very good.

Int. 7.—What buildings and improvements, if any, did you observe on this tract which was occupied by the Puget's Sound Agricultural Company, and what are their situation, character, and condition and value? Please to state as particularly as you can.

Ans.—I can't draw a line between the Hudson's Bay and Puget's Sound Companies' possessions. The main post was called Fort Nisqually. There were a number of rude buildings scattered about the country that were inhabited by men who were or had been servants or agents of the Puget's Sound Company. Fort Nisqually consisted of a number of buildings inside of a stockade built of posts, the area enclosed being, as near as I can remember, two hundred feet square. The buildings inside the stockade were of rough construction, and of a dilapidated appearance. I built a hospital in the army with soldiers' labor, which, intrinsically, seemed to me much more valuable, foot by foot and space by space. The stockade itself was of good solid posts. There was an excellent garden near the fort, and a fine stream of water close by, where the sheep of the Company were washed before shearing.

Int. 8.—Did you, while there, observe any cattle or sheep which you supposed to be the property of the Puget's Sound Agricultural Company? If yea, please to describe the cattle and sheep which you saw.

Ans.—The Nisqually Plains, when I first went there, were inhabited by deer, wild cats, Indian ponies, sheep, and cattle. The woods bordering the plains were infested with panthers—so much so that Dr. Tolmie spoke of the wild cats and panthers killing the calves; and in 1856 I got a lynx that was killed on the plains about midway between Fort Nisqually and Fort Steilacoom. I also got the skin of a panther, in 1854, that was killed within a mile and a half of Fort Steilacoom. I ate elk or moose meat killed within the same radius. The whole country is gloriously beautiful—almost a dead level for thirty miles, where Mount Rainier towers up, perpetually covered with snow, more beautiful and more superb than twenty Mont Blancs. At Fort Steilacoom we had the treasures of the deep salt water, in view of a snow-covered Alpine mountain ; the prairie, the forest, the lake, and the brook; oysters, star-fish, salmon, trout, venison, elk, wild cattle, bear, berries, flowers, and grouse, muscles, soft-shell crabs, wild pigeons, and a paradise of a climate, except when it rained. The garrison at Fort Steilacoom subsisted on the beef furnished by the Puget's Sound Company. The condition of the cattle, so far as flesh goes, was very poor. The cattle, as a rule, were killed like the buffalo—by shooting. I know that the cattle were in such a wild, unreclaimed condition that it was really dangerous to ride on the plains on a slow or obstinate horse.

Int. 9.—Have you any knowledge of Dr. Tolmie giving authority to any individual to kill any of the cattle of the Company? If yea, please to state what you know on this subject.

Ans.—I don't know.

Int. 10.—Have you ever visited or observed the Cowlitz Farms, so-called, which were occupied by the Puget's Sound Company? If yea, please to describe the character and condition and the value of these farms, when you visited there.

Ans.—The general section of country in which those farms lay was very rich, very good, and very productive. I have been to the Cowlitz Farm, I think it was in 1855. All that the Cowlitz Farms then needed was good transportation, and easy access to market, which it had not then and has not now. The buildings were of a general, cheap, home-made description, of the character of the Company's edifices found elsewhere in that section of country.

Cross-Examination.

Int. 1.—Was there not, during the time of your residence at Fort Steilacoom, a large number of settlers on these plains engaged in agricultural pursuits?

Ans.—Yes, sir.

Int. 2.—Did these settlers have stock of their own that pastured on the plains?

Ans.—Many of them had.

Int. 3.—Was there not, in the year 1859, at the time you

left there, a large amount of stock finding subsistence on these plains ?

Ans.—Yes ; stock belonging to the settlers, a large amount for that particular district, but not large as compared to a similar area of land in Ohio or Illinois.

Int. 4.—Were there not more cattle and stock in 1859 than in earlier years ?

Ans.—I can't answer that question, sir.

Int. 5.—Did these settlers you have spoken of depend on their cattle and stock alone, or were they also engaged in cultivating the land ?

Ans.—There were two classes of settlers ; one that depended more particularly upon their flocks and herds, and the other that relied principally on their grain and other crops. Nearly all had vegetable gardens.

Int. 6.—Did these men you speak of as raising grain and other crops, find land that did not need manure and careful attention to raise their crops in ?

Ans.—They found small patches and strips.

Int. 7.—Do you not know that there were large spaces of low prairies that were rich and fertile, lands, and swales, and low grounds on the rivers and streams that were also rich and fertile ?

Ans.—Compared to the whole size of the tract, there were not ; but often in a tract of six hundred and forty acres there would be a very handsome proportion of good land, but not in *every* six hundred and forty acres.

Int. 8.—Do you not recollect more than six hundred and forty acres of good land in one tract on this claim ?

Ans.—I never yet, to my knowledge, saw six hundred and forty acres of open ground lying together, as the United States surveyors lay off sections of six hundred and forty acres, within that tract, that was respectably rich.

Int. 9.—Did not these settlers you have spoken of dispose of and sell their claims occasionally ? If so, what was the common price for a three hundred and twenty acre tract ?

Ans.—Yes sir, they sold. The price received was according to the improvements, which consisted in the buildings and

fences. There was more land to be sold than there were
buyers; and the best farms were not offered for sale at all.
The Dougherty claim was a very valuable one. I never heard
that he wanted to sell it.

Int. 10.—Have you not, in describing these pasture lands,
compared them with the rich lands of the Ohio and Mississippi valleys?

Ans.—I compared these lands with the States of Ohio and
Illinois, and the Hempstead plains of Long Island.

Int. 11.—Do you know well the agricultural qualities of
any county or district in New York? If you do, state how
it compared with this tract, for say twelve miles square of
each.

Ans.—I am acquainted with Orange, Sullivan, Duchess,
and Ulster counties in the State of New York, very well, besides being acquainted somewhat with others. It is my belief
and conviction that twelve miles square of the Puget's Sound
land claimed by the Company is naturally of greater agricultural value than a tract of land of the same size in Duchess
county, New York.

Int. 12.—Do you know anything of the Victoria market,
since the mining discoveries, for produce and stock, and the
value of those lands as affording pasturage for stock for that
market?

Ans.—No, sir; not from my own knowledge.

Int. 13.—Are you well acquainted with the country around
the head and shores of what is known as Puget's Sound? If
so, state whether it is or is not generally a timbered country,
and whether the tract is not the only large and open prairie anywhere around the Sound.

Ans.—I was very well acquainted with the country, and my
remembrance of it is very clear. There was a very large
tract of prairie near the head of the Sound, not included in
the claim. There were a great many prairies of large and
small size scattered through the country; but as a rule, there
was not as large an amount of open land together in one body
as in the tract claimed by this Company. This strip of prairie commenced about five miles from Olympia, and ran down

to near Skookum Chuck. The mail road from Olympia to the Cowlitz passed through this open country. There were, however, patches of timber along the route, but the section was scarcely more heavily timbered than the Nisqually plains were in spots.

Int. 14.—Are not the shores of the Sound on the left, facing towards the ocean, from Olympia at the head, to Port Townshend at the foot of it, almost an unbroken forest, and on the right shore to the forty-ninth parallel of north latitude, with the exception of the prairies south of the Nisqually, and this great prairie called the Nisqually plains, is it not nearly all one forest?

Ans.—On the left bank, from Olympia to Port Townsend, there was scarcely any natural open ground at all; nearly all the land is very heavily timbered. The right shore (facing the ocean) is very densely timbered from the Puyallup to Bellingham Bay, except the salt marshes close to the water. From the Puyallup to the Nisqually, there is much open country.

Int. 15.—You have spoken of settlers selling their claims; do you not know of farms that could not have been bought of the claimants for less than a large sum above the value of the improvements on the Nisqually plains?

Ans.—There were good farms there that were held on to, the occupants holding on partly because the land was good in their estimation, and partly because they did not want to move, from a sort of *vis inertia.*

GEORGE SUCKLEY,
Late Surgeon and Brevet Col. U. S. Vols.
WASHINGTON CITY, D. C., *May* 19, 1866.

TESTIMONY OF HUGH A. GOLDSBOROUGH.

Hugh A. Goldsborough, being duly sworn according to law, says:

Int. 1.—What is your name, place of residence, and present occupation?

Ans.—Hugh Allan Goldsborough; I reside in Washington City, and am, at present, a chief clerk in a bureau of the Navy Department—the Bureau of Construction and Repair.

Int. 2.—Have you ever resided in Washington Territory? If yea, when and where, and for how long a period?

Ans.—Yes, sir; I resided principally at Olympia and Fort Steilacoom, (longer at Olympia than anywhere else in Washington Territory,) from 1850, to December, 1863, with occasional absences.

Int. 3.—Are you acquainted with a tract of land in Washington Territory called the Nisqually Plains?

Ans.—Yes, sir.

Int. 4.—Please to look at the map here produced, and state whether you are acquainted with the land there described as the land claimed by the Puget's Sound Agricultural Company.

Ans.—Yes, sir; I have been over a great portion of it very frequently.

Int. 5.—Please to describe, as fully as you can, the character and condition and value of the land embraced within the claim of the said Company, distinguishing between the portions that are capable of tillage, and the portions that are suitable only for pasturage, and the portions that are covered with wood, and the value of each.

Ans.—The portion of land claimed by the Puget's Sound Agricultural Company, that I understood, while residing there, from Dr. Tolmie, was almost entirely confined to the prairie land; it did not go down to the Nisqually river on the south, or the Puyallup on the north; when I say north and south, I mean northerly and southerly; but included generally the prairie land within the woods all around, extending eastwardly to the *foot-hills.* This I received from Dr. Tolmie, the agent of the Puget's Sound Agricultural Company. I was more impressed with the correctness of this understanding of the extent of the claim from a conversation I had with Dr. Tolmie with reference to the town of Steilacoom. He told me that the Puget's Sound Agricultural Company made no claim to the land on which the town of Steilacoom was situated, because it was in the woods and outside the prairies.

By far the larger portion of the claim is prairie, and, so far
as my judgment goes, with the exception of one-tenth, it is
very inferior land. For agricultural purposes, I would say
that nine-tenths of it is not worth fifty cents an acre. The
balance may be worth from three to five dollars per acre.
There is a small quantity of crooked and stumpy oak trees
scattered here and there; but the result of my personal observation with a friend, who was engaged in the saw-mill business, was that these oak trees were not worth the trouble and
expense of cutting down and transportation. I will also say
that in making this observation in regard to the oak trees, I
was myself engaged in the saw-mill business. I went there
for the purpose of seeing if I could get oak timber on the
plains. The testimony that I have given, in regard to the
value of this land and oak timber, has been, I believe, universally concurred in by a great number of persons with whom I
have conversed. (The statements made by Dr. Tolmie objected to, it not appearing to be within the limits of his
agency, and to be defining the limits of the principal's estate
by the mere careless statement of an agent, and as hearsay
also. The part in reference to the general statements of
others objected to as hearsay.)

Int. 6.—Were there any buildings or improvements of any
kind within the limits of this claim, which were owned and
occupied by the Company? If yea, please to describe their
character and value as fully as you can.

Ans.—There were some buildings owned by the Company
at Fort Nisqually. There was a stockade, probably three
hundred by four hundred feet, enclosing some log buildings.
About the year 1852 and 1853, when I first knew them, there
were some log buildings; they were comfortable; probably five
or six of them; worth together at that time three thousand
dollars. Outside the stockade they had a range of old stabling
and sheepcots; on Sequalitchew creek, I don't know what they
were worth; perhaps two or three hundred dollars. There
was also a rough log warehouse on the Sound, at the mouth
of the creek, that was worth probably two hundred and fifty
dollars. Subsequently to this period the agent of the Com-

pany, Dr. Tolmie, built for himself a more comfortable house, worth probably fifteen hundred dollars. The Company also had some very common log cabins and sheepcots out at a place called Muck. They may have had other log cabins and sheepcots on the plains that I am not cognizant of.

Int. 7.—Were there any saw-mills or water-power within the limits of the claim which were owned by the Company?

Ans.—They had remnants of a saw-mill, I believe, but I never saw them at work at the mill. Within my knowledge, a mill has been put up at the same site, by other parties, and was running when I left there. This mill was on the Sequalitchew creek. With my understanding of the extent of their claim, that was the only water-power embraced within it.

Int. 8.—Are you acquainted with the land of Cowlitz Farms, so-called, which were claimed and occupied by the Company? If yea, please to describe its extent and character and value as fully as you can.

Ans.—I know comparatively very little of that claim. I have been on it and through it fifty times probably, merely passing through on my way to Vancouver and elsewhere. The quality of the land is much superior to that of the Nisqually plains, and would probably be worth from eight to twelve dollars per acre.

Int. 9.—How is this land situated with respect to a market?

Ans.—There are two markets for the productions of the claim of the Cowlitz Farm; one down the Cowlitz river and up the Columbia and Willamette to Portland. This navigation down the Cowlitz river is particularly dangerous, from the many rapids in that river, and has been almost entirely abandoned within the last few years. The other market is Olympia, the road to which, for full one-half [the] year, is almost impassible for loaded wagons. The distance to these markets is about the same, fifty or sixty miles.

Int. 10.—Does this difficulty in respect to a convenient market affect the value of this land? If so, how.

Ans.—Certainly it does, from the cost of getting produce to market.

Int. 1.—During the time you resided in Washington Territory did you become a farmer on the Nisqually-plains, or become acquainted with the prices of agricultural produce?

Ans.—I did not become a farmer, but I had a general acquaintance with the price of produce. I kept a store at Olympia for a short time, which gave me a general acquaintance of the prices.

Int. 2.—Were you not, while at Steilacoom, chiefly employed in the Quartermaster's Department there, and connected with the military authorities?

Ans.—Yes, sir, for about half the time.

Int. 3.—You say you were acquainted with prices; did not the price of agricultural produce bear a high relative value to the cost of production?

Ans.—I should say, rather, yes. I could give the prices which I gave for articles, and which I sold them for. I don't know much of the cost of production, as I lived in town, and my attention was not called to it.

Int. 4.—Have you, in estimating the value of this land, given any attention to its rental or production, to the amount or number of stock a given number of acres would support, or to the price paid per head for pasturage of stock?

Ans.—Yes, I have, to a certain extent; I should judge it not worth much as grazing land, from the general appearance of the land itself, and from the circumstance of the Puget's Sound Agricultural Company moving their stock to Victoria, because whatever grazing qualities it may have originally possessed had been worn out, as I understood.

Int. 5.—Then you would say that the value you put on the grazing land, from its appearance, is derived from the fact that the moving of the Company's stock to Victoria was from the worn-out condition of the land, and that these worn-out pasture lands were only worth fifty cents per acre?

Ans.—I say that that land, that is, nine-tenths of it, is worth fifty cents per acre, as I saw it last, in 1863.

13 P

Int. 6.—Is your value put on this land placed upon it at the time you have last mentioned?

Ans.—It is the result of my experience, observation, and assertion for ten years prior to 1863.

Int. 7.—Is this opinion, your carefully conceived and studied opinion, often asserted by you, formed soon after you first saw the land, and continued to the present day?

Ans.—Generally, it is.

Int. 8.—Do I understand you to say that the land, in your opinion, was worth fifty cents an acre, in the year 1852, and the same price in 1863?

Ans.—What I meant to state is the result of my experience there for ten years; what my close observation, for a person who is not a practical farmer, could give it. It was something I took a great deal of interest in, and got my information from every practicable source.

Int. 9.—At what time, then, do you fix this price of fifty cents per acre; in 1852 or 1863, or at some intermediate time?

Ans.—The price that I thought the nine-tenths of that claim was worth, fifty cents per acre, may more probably be fixed from the years 1855 to 1857 generally, as I resided there in that period of years.

Int. 10.—Was there not much land there that, in your opinion, was worth more than fifty cents per acre?

Ans.—Yes, there was. As I previously stated, in my estimation, about one-tenth was worth more than fifty cents per acre.

Int. 11.—Is this statement you have made of one-tenth of good land, in your opinion, all the good land there was in this one hundred and sixty thousand acres; might there not have been more?

Ans.—I never understood the claim to equal anything like one hundred and sixty thousand acres. From Mr. Chapman's survey of it, some ten or fifteen years ago I think, I was given to understand that the claim was to embrace some seventy-five to eighty thousand acres, and my estimate of one-tenth was the aggregate of the best land that I could hear of on making inquiries from the settlers thereon.

Int. 12.—Suppose the survey shows one hundred and sixty thousand acres, would you change your estimate of the relative proportion of good lands?

Ans.—No, sir; I could not, from my acquaintance with what was generally called the Nisqually plains.

Int. 13.—You say you were connected with the Quartermaster's Department at Fort Steilacoom; were not the bands of mules, horses, and cattle of that post, during the years 1855, 1856, and 1857, pastured near the post, in the pasturage season, on these lands?

Ans.—Yes, sir; those that were not used for daily service. Some of them were pastured on the banks of the Puyallup river, which I did not understand was in the scope of this claim.

Int. 14.—Was not the stock of the post, during the Indian war of those years, pastured very near the post, and were there not at times more animals than usual at the post?

Ans.—Yes, sir.

Int. 15.—Was not the country in a disturbed state in the summer of 1856, so much so as to prevent the body of the settlers in Pierce county from returning to and cultivating their abandoned claims?

Ans.—Yes, sir, in their opinion.

Int. 16.—Where was the warehouse of the Company and the old saw-mill situated, and how far apart?

Ans.—On the landing on Puget's Sound; I don't remember, at this moment, precisely their relative positions, though I know they are far apart.

Int. 17.—Is there not a road leading through the woods from the Company's fort to the Sound, at or near the warehouse?

Ans.—Yes, sir.

Int. 18.—Do you mean to be understood as saying that the claim of the Company was bounded by the woods surrounding the prairie, and did not include any of the woodland, nor that it did not, in any portion of it, run out to the shores of the Sound?

Ans.—It certainly did run out to the shore of the Sound,

where the warehouse was. As I understood, the claim of the Company on the north and south, on the Puyallup and Nisqually—I mean the northerly and southerly boundaries of the claim running with the rivers Nisqually and Puyallup—did not include the Nisqually and Puyallup woods, but skirted them, including points of timber that made in. This is my impression, derived from conversations with Dr. Tolmie, Mr. Chapman, and others.

Int. 19.—Might not your impression, that the town site of Steilacoom was not included in the claim, have been as probably derived from what you were told by Chapman as from Dr. Tolmie?

Ans.—No, sir.

Int. 20.—At what time and place was this statement made to you by Dr. Tolmie, and what else did he say at the same time and in the same conversation?

Ans.—I cannot fix the time positively, as I had repeated conversations with Dr. Tolmie upon this and kindred subjects in connection with the claim; it was not long, however, after the establishment of the town of Steilacoom.

Int. 21.—If you cannot fix the time or tell what he said at any one time, can you tell whether it was in reply to a question by you, or whether it was an assertion on his own part?

Ans.—It was in reply to a question by me; such is my impression.

Int. 22.—Did the Doctor answer in words, or did he nod his head in acquiescence?

Ans.—He answered that question very plainly and emphatically.

Int. 23.—How near is the town of Steilacoom to the post and the buildings for which the military authorities were then paying rent to the Company?

Ans.—I think we used to call it one and a half miles.

Int. 24.—In what year, or about what year, was this statement made to you by Dr. Tolmie?

Ans.—I don't know the exact year, but think it was in 1851 or 1852.

Int. 25.—You were deeply interested in this question, as

you state, and have heard statements from so many people, and asked so many questions; do you feel certain, after the lapse of fourteen or fifteen years, that you can fix any particular statement, or the person by whom it was made?

Ans.—With regard to that particular answer of Dr. Tolmie I feel very certain.

Int. 26.—May not your memory now be dependent on the numerous times you have repeated this question to others?

Ans.—I am very confident I am correct in my recollection; I am as certain of it as I am of anything.

Int. 27.—Who was present at the time you put this question to Dr. Tolmie beside yourself and him?

Ans.—I think no one; I have no recollection of any one being present.

Int. 28.—Was it at his own house, or at the military post, or where was it?

Ans.—We were riding together on horseback on the plain; I think we were going to his house; I cannot positively state the precise place or the date of it.

Int. 29.—Who was with you at the time you looked at the oak trees?

Ans.—Michael T. Simmons; there was another party, I think, whom I do not now recollect.

Int. 30.—Is Michael T. Simmons a man of good repute, worthy of belief, of good judgment in matters of agriculture and milling, and one whose opinion on such matters would be of value?

Ans.—Simmons is a very clever man, natural judgment, strong sense, but violent prejudices. I would take his opinion on any ordinary subject in which his feelings did not come into operation.

Int. 31.—Whose opinion and knowledge was taken about the oak trees; yours, or that of Mr. M. T. Simmons?

Ans.—Mr. Simmons, at that time.

Int. 32.—Was not the saw-mill of M. T. Simmons some twenty-five miles from these oaks?

Ans.—Yes, sir, about that distance.

Int. 33.—Was not hauling by teams at that time very expensive in that section of the country?

Ans.—It was expensive.

Int. 34.—Did not the settlers on the Nisqually Plains, during the Indian war, leave their claims, and was not the country much injured in consequence?

Ans.—The settlers generally left their claims and came into the villages.

H. A. GOLDSBOROUGH.

WASHINGTON CITY, D. C. *June* 20, 1866.

DISTRICT OF COLUMBIA, ⎱ ss.
   County of Washington, ⎰

I, Nicholas Callan, a notary public in and for the county and district aforesaid, do hereby certify that the foregoing depositions hereunto annexed of John B. Chapman, D. B. McKibbin, Arthur A. Denny, George Suckley, and Hugh A. Goldsborough, witnesses produced by and on behalf of the United States, in the matter of the claims of the Puget's Sound Agricultural Company against the same, now pending before the British and American Joint Commission for the adjustment of the same, were taken before, me at the office of said Commission, No. 355 H street north, in the city of Washington, District of Columbia, and reduced to writing, under my direction, by Nicholas Callan, Jr., a person agreed upon by Eben F. Stone, Esq., attorney for the United States, and Edward Lander, Esq., attorney for said Company, beginning on the 5th day of April, A. D. 1866, and terminating on the 26th day of June, A. D. 1866, according to the several dates appended to the said depositions, when they were signed respectively.

I further certify that to each of said witnesses, before his examination, I administered the following oath:

"You swear that the evidence you shall give in the matter of the Puget's Sound Agricultural Company against the United States of America shall be the truth, the whole truth, and nothing but the truth, so help you God."

That after the same were reduced to writing, the deposition of each witness was carefully read to and then signed by him.

I further certify that Eben F. Stone, Esq., and Edward Lander, Esq., were personally present during the examination and cross-examination of all said witnesses and the reading and signing of their depositions.

In testimony whereof I have hereunto set my hand and [L. S.] official seal, this twenty-sixth day of June, A. D. 1866.

N. CALLAN,
Notary Public.

BRITISH AND AMERICAN JOINT COMMISSION

HUDSON'S BAY AND PUGET'S SOUND AGRICULTURAL COMPANIES' CLAIMS.

━━━━━ •••• ━━━━━

In the matter of the Claim of the Puget's Sound Agricultural Company against the United States.

The deposition of Horace R. Wirtz, brevet lieutenant colonel and surgeon in the United States Army, taken by agreement between Edward Lander, counsel for the Puget's Sound Agricultural Company, and E. F. Stone, of counsel for the United States. The oath was administered by United States Commissioner Osborn.

TESTIMONY OF HORACE R. WIRTZ.

Int. 1.—What is your name, place of residence, and occupation?

Ans.—Horace R. Wirtz; surgeon in the United States Army; place of residence, Fort Hamilton.

Int. 2.—Have you ever resided in Washington Territory? If yea, when, and where, and for how long a period?

Ans—I was stationed in Washington Territory for two or three years, during the years 1859, 1860, and 1861.

Int. 3.—Have you any knowledge of that tract of land bordering on Puget's Sound and lying between the Nisqually and Puyallup rivers, and extending easterly towards the foot-hills of the Cascade Range, called the Nisqually Plains, and claimed by the Puget's Sound Agricultural Company? If yea, please to describe the same, giving the character and extent of that part, if any, which is open and prairie land; the character and extent of that part, if any, which is woodland or swamp; the character and extent of that part, if any, which is suitable for grazing; the character and extent of that part, if any, which is suitable for tillage; and any other fact or circumstance which, in your judgment, may enter into a full description of the land in question.

Ans.—I was stationed for about two years at Fort Steilacoom, which I have always understood to be upon the land claimed by the Puget's Sound Agricultural Company. The character of the country in the neighborhood of the fort, and between there and Fort Nisqually, which is the Puget's Sound Agricultural Company's post, is an open prairie, interspersed here and there with low timber. The character of the soil is sandy, and generally barren; but sufficient for the purposes of pasturage and sheep-grazing, for which it has principally been used. There are certain points on the border of streams, in this tract of country, where the land is capable of cultivation and where gardens have been made. I know of one piece of land that had been cultivated by the Puget's Sound Agricultural Company, and of two or three others that had been cultivated by persons who had settled there; but, as a general thing, the whole tract of country is a prairie, covered with sparse grass and sandy soil. There are several ponds or lakes in the country, but I know of no marshes; and the quantity of land that is fit for agricultural purposes is very small indeed. There is no timber of any size; all the timber being generally stunted trees.

Int. 4.—Have you any knowledge of the extent of land at this place which was enclosed and cultivated by the Puget's Sound Agricultural Company? If yea, please to state what, in your judgment, was the quantity.

Ans.—I have very little knowledge of the quantity of land that was cultivated. I know that a gentleman named Huggins, who was connected with the Puget's Sound Agricultural Company, had a farm near Fort Nisqually; but I always regarded it more in the light of a kitchen-garden than anything else. I really do not know the extent of land that was under cultivation by him; I absolutely don't know how much there was; I never saw the place but once.

Int. 5.—State, if you know, what was the general condition of this tract of land claimed by the Company; whether it was for the most part in a wild and natural state, or enclosed and cultivated.

Ans.—I should describe it as a sandy prairie, covered with short grass. It was all in a wild natural state, except a small portion that was used for raising vegetables and such things, as far as I know.

Int. 6.—Do you know, from experience or observation, the effect of cultivation upon the condition of the soil of these plains? If yea, describe the same.

Ans.—I have a general theoretical idea of what land might be capable of cultivation, and what could not be cultivated. The only land that is capable of cultivation in that region of country is that bordering on the bottom of streams, and the proportion of that land to the whole amount is very small compared with the whole amount of country.

Int. 7.—Have you any knowledge of any cattle, or sheep, or horses, belonging to the Puget's Sound Agricultural Company, which were pastured upon these plains while you were there?

Ans.—I lived there about two years, and I never saw myself, and I used to ride about the country—I never saw any cattle, or sheep, or horses, whatever, on any of these plains; but I know there must have been sheep on the plains, because Dr. Tolmie, chief factor and agent of the Puget's Sound Agricultural Company, used to send me, when the sheep were cut, every spring, two or three gallons of what are called lambs-fries; and they must have had sheep, or they could not have had them; I imagined that there must have been a considerable number of sheep raised there, though I never saw any.

Int. 8.—Have you any knowledge of the fort and buildings and improvements belonging to the Puget's Sound Agricultural Company within the limits of the tract described? If yea, please to describe the same, giving their condition, and the character of their construction, as fully as you can, at the time you were there?

Ans.—I visited, a number of times, Dr. Tolmie, at what is

called Fort Nisqually. Fort Nisqually is a stockade, enclosing, I should think, about an acre of land; I cannot positively say how much, but I should think about an acre; perhaps more. Inside of this there was one very good frame house, in which Dr. Tolmie and his family resided, and two or three rows of dilapidated log huts. Inside of this enclosure there was a small store, about fifteen or twenty feet square, which was used for trading purposes with the Indians, and to some extent with the whites. This stockade was enclosed; but before I left the country most of the pickets were taken down and had not been replaced. The whole fort, as it is called, with the exception of the building in which Dr. Tolmie lived, was very old and dilapidated. What we used to call a fort, which I have just described, is the only place I know of personally that belonged to the Puget's Sound Agricultural Company—this enclosure. By that, I mean the only place where there were any buildings. I might state that there was a house where Mr. Huggins resided, which I never visited but once, and about which I don't recollect the extent, but it certainly was not large, not far from the fort. As far as I recollect, it was a log house, but I am not certain of that. I never was there but once, and that was at night.

Int. 9.—Have you ever observed upon these plains any oak trees? If yea, please to describe them, stating their numbers, and whether they were or were not suitable for timber.

Ans.—I never saw myself any oak trees, except stunted oak. They may have been there; I don't know; but I never saw myself any oak trees except stunted ones—none that I think would appear of any value for any purpose; I never saw any over twenty feet high at any rate.

Int. 10.—Was it your habit to ride about frequently over different portions of this tract, and did you take particular observation of its general condition and character?

Ans.—Yes; I have ridden over the whole of it, how often, I cannot say; but at different times I have certainly ridden over the greater portion of this tract. I never took particular observation of it, and I simply now state what my impressions are, though I have never looked at the country with any special view of finding out any particulars things, either in regard to the productions of the country or timber, but I simply record my impressions now to this date.

Cross-Examined.

Int. 1.—What time were you at Nisqually, at Fort Steilacoom ?

Ans.—I don't recollect any one time, but I can state that during the year 1859 I was there ; I don't recollect now without referring to my notes.

Int. 2.—Where were you stationed during the remainder of the time you spent about Puget's Sound ?

Ans.—I was stationed—I suppose it is called part of Puget's Sound—at Simiamhoo, on the 49th parallel ; but in 1859 I was at Steilacoom, and I stayed there about two years ; I cannot give you the exact date.

Int. 3.—Do you not know that a considerable amount of agricultural produce was raised upon these plains that you speak of, and that agricultural productions and cattle and horses were shipped from Steilacoom for sale at other points ?

Ans.—I never heard of anything of the kind being shipped from Steilacoom ; that is, in my experience, I never heard of anything of the kind ; indeed, I never heard of anything being shipped from there except lumber.

Int. 4.—Is there not a flouring-mill near Fort Steilacoom, on this claim of the Puget's Sound Company ?

Ans.—Yes, sir ; there is one close by the fort, owned by a Mr. Bird, I think. Mr. Bird had a flour-mill. He is the only one I know of.

Int. 5.—Do you not recollect the flouring-mill also of Mr. Chambers ?

Ans.—Yes, sir ; I think Mr. Chambers did have a small mill. Yes, sir ; Mr. Chambers and Mr. Bird both had mills.

Int. 6.—Are there not on these plains a number of settlers, from one hundred to one hundred and fifty, who have taken claims, opened farms, and are engaged in agricultural pursuits ?

Ans.—Well, I can state from my personal knowledge that I know of eight or ten; I don't know of any more; I could not positively call to mind any more who have opened farms, who have taken claims—or whatever you call them—farms on these plains; and with the exception of Judge Chambers, I don't know any one who is not living a miserable existence, that is, I don't know any one that is making more than what he can possibly live on. That is my own experience. I cannot call to mind any one else but Judge Chambers, and he is doing very well; but all the rest are just living from hand to mouth. What they raise I don't know, but it certainly cannot be much.

Int. 7.—Do you think you have ridden over these plains and visited the house of every settler on them, or nearly all the settlers on them?

Ans.—No, I don't think I have; but I have travelled about a good deal, and all I can call to mind—I cannot in fact call to mind more than eight or ten settlers, eight or ten farms.

Int. 8.—Have not your rides generally been confined to the road leading from the fort towards Fort Nisqually and Olympia, and the road leading up towards Puyallup?

Ans.—No, they have not; I have been forced to go, professionally, to a good many out of the way places, away from roads; but I must confess that there are other persons in the country, perhaps, who have ridden a great deal more than I have; but I have gone pretty much over the whole of this tract of country.

Int. 9.—Have your professional visits been confined to these eight or ten farmers' houses that you have mentioned, or have you visited any more of the settlers' houses than those you have spoken of?

Ans.—The farms I have spoken of were places that I passed in going to see other people, because the people I went to see generally, it could hardly be said that they had farms; they were very poor. The reason of that is, that I never practiced with a view of emolument. I never went to see anybody if he had any money, because I wished to go for charity when I did go.

Int. 10.—Was there a physician of the name of Ridgely at practice in Steilacoom when you were at the fort ?

Ans.—Yes, sir ; Dr. John Ridgely.

Int. 11.—Do you know where the grain that was supplied to the animals at the post at Steilacoom was raised ?

Ans.—My impression is, I have always thought they brought it from San Francisco ; that is my impression. The flour, or a portion of it, I know, was supplied by Mr. Bird and Judge Chambers ; but I don't think all of it was.

Int. 12.—Did you pay such attention to the agricultural products of those plains as to say with any exactness what amount of produce was raised upon them, and what quantity of cattle were pastured or fed on them ?

Ans.—No, I never did ; I never thought it amounted to anything ; that is my impression.

Int. 13.—Was not your attention, as a general thing, given to your profession, and to the study of it, and not diverted to determining points as to the fertility of lands, their productiveness, the population residing upon them, or anything of that nature ?

Ans.—Well, I only studied these things in so far as they related to my profession, and so far as any intelligent man would take an interest in such things who was not specially an agriculturist.

Int. 14.—Did you ever visit the Muck Prairie ?

Ans.—Yes, sir ; I have.

Int. 15.—Were there not some farmers upon that that were making money ?

Ans.—If I am right with regard to the Muck Prairie, I went there twice to see a man named Wren ; I think it was what they called the Muck Prairie ; and it was said he lived by stealing Hudson's Bay cattle, and Dr. Tolmie told me so. With regard to his farm, I don't recollect much about it. He lived in a little old log house. That is all I recollect about that part of the country.

Int. 16.—What is your opinion of the health of that climate, and its advantages for settlers in a sanitary point of view ?

Ans.—Well, I consider it a very fine climate on account of the temperature being so equable, there being no very great range of the thermometer between winter and summer, and I consider it, as far as climate is concerned, as an excellent country for people to settle in.

Int. 17.—Have you any experience as an agriculturist or farmer?

Ans.—Very little.

Int. 18.—Are you acquainted with the properties of soils?

Ans.—I am only acquainted with the properties of soils as a theoretical and practical chemist, and as far as chemistry bears on agriculture, I am acquainted with it.

Int. 19.—Did you ever make any examination of the soil of these plains, so as to decide upon the question whether they were fertile or not?

Ans.—I never did.

Int. 20.—Your impression then of the soil and of the land is derived by merely looking on it with your eyes when riding on horseback?

Ans.—Simply by riding over sandy prairies, I could see it was sand and gravel; that was all.

Int. 21.—Are not these prairies, especially in the spring of the year, covered with a fine growth of grass, affording pasturage to cattle and sheep?

Ans.—Well, there is a peculiar kind of weed that covers most of them, which, I understood from farmers, was injurious to agriculture, and which had probably been brought there and diffused by the sheep. What that weed is called I don't recollect now—it is called sorrel. There is almost as much sorrel in some places as there is grass, and it is stated to be diffused there by the sheep. I suppose they bring it there in their wool; but I know that it is said by farmers there to be a great draw-back to agriculture on these plains.

Int. 22.—Do you wish to be understood as saying that these plains produce sorrel alone, and that they are not covered in the spring of the year with grass?

Ans.—That is what I have understood. In some places there is as much sorrel as there is grass. I know I have heard that spoken of by the principal men there.

Int. 23.—Do you mean to say you know this to be the fact there, or that you heard it?

Ans.—I have had it pointed out to me, and I have also heard it spoken of frequently, and I have asked how it got there, and they said it was probably brought in the wool of the sheep, as I have said before.

Int. 24.—Have you noticed the soil yourself in more than a few instances, and is not what you have stated in reference to it derived chiefly from the information of others?

Ans.—As I have been riding out, I frequently had my attention called to it by persons who were with me; but I will say that I have heard it so much spoken of, that perhaps the universal opinion of the people that I have conversed with has had some influence on my opinion; universal statement among farmers.

Int. 25.—Are you prepared to say that these plains do not afford a good natural and nutritious grass for the pasturage of sheep and cattle?

Ans.—Oh, yes; I think the plains furnished a good pasturage for sheep and cattle.

Int. 26.—Are you prepared to say that there is not upon these plains a good deal of agricultural land susceptible of cultivation, as also many pieces of enclosed arable land, which have escaped your notice and observation?

Ans.—There may have been pieces of land that escaped my observation; but I state the general result of my observations, that on the borders of streams the land is, for a certain distance on each side, fertile; but that the country, if I were to give a general description of it, would be described by saying that it is a prairie, of a sandy quality, and covered with grass of different qualities, very good in some places, and not so good in others. If I were going through the country, I should describe it as a prairie, with here and there little spots that could be cultivated. That is my impression I brought away from that country. H. R. WIRTZ,
Surgeon and Brev't Lt. Col. U. S. A.

Sworn to before me this 13th day of July, A. D. 1866.

JOHN A. OSBORN,
U. S. Commissioner.

SOUTHERN DISTRICT OF NEW YORK, ⎫ ss.
    City of New York. ⎬

I, John A. Osborn, United States Commissioner, do hereby certify that the foregoing deposition of Horace R. Wirtz, a witness produced by and on behalf of the United States, in the matter of the claims of the Hudson's Bay Company against the same, now pending before the British and American Joint Commission, for the final settlement thereof, was taken before me, at my office in the city of New York, and reduced to writing, under my direction, on the 13th day of July, 1866.

I further certify that, before his examination, I administered to said witness the following oath:

"You swear that the evidence you shall give in the matter of the claims of the Hudson's Bay Company against the United States of America shall be the truth, the whole truth, and nothing but the truth, so help you God."

That after the same was reduced to writing, the deposition of said witness was carefully read to, and then signed by him.

I further certify that Eben F. Stone, Esq., attorney for the United States, and Edward Lander, Esq., attorney for the Hudson's Bay Company, were personally present during the examination and cross-examination of said witness.

And I do further certify that I am not of counsel nor attorney for either of the parties in the said deposition and caption named, nor in any way interested in the event of the cause named in said caption.

In testimony whereof I have hereunto set my hand and seal [L. S.] this 30th day of July, A. D. 1866.

        JOHN A. OSBORN,
    U. S. Comm'r South'n Dist. of N. Y.

14 P

BRITISH AND AMERICAN JOINT COMMISSION

HUDSON'S BAY AND PUGET'S SOUND AGRICULTURAL COMPANIES' CLAIMS.

In the matter of the Claim of the Puget's Sound Agricultural Company against the United States.

Deposition of Silas Casey, taken before Thomas S. Blackman, a United States Commissioner for the eastern district of Michigan, by consent of parties, in the matter of the claim of the Puget's Sound Agricultural Company against the United States, before the British and American Joint Commission on the Hudson's Bay and Puget's Sound Agricultural Companies' claims; said deposition being taken on the part of the United States to be used and read upon the hearing of said matter, subject only to all legal objections as to the relevancy and competency of the same. Wm. P. Wells, Esq., appears on behalf of the United States, for whom said deposition is taken, and Edward Lander, Esq., for said Puget's Sound Agricultural Company, and thereupon the said—

Silas Casey, being duly sworn, deposes, and says:

Int. 1.—Please give your name, residence, and present occupation.

Ans.—My name is Silas Casey; I reside at Fort Wayne, near Detroit, Michigan; I am a Brevet Major General in the United States Army.

Int. 2.—Have you ever resided in Washington Territory?

Ans.—Yes; I resided there for a period of about four years in all. I was there twice. I went there in 1855, and left finally in 1861; I had left once in the interval.

Int. 3.—About how long were you absent at the interval you mention?

Ans.—About one year, I think. I left there on January 12, 1858, and returned there in the following winter.

Int. 4.—At what place or places did you reside, and what places did you visit?

Ans.—I resided at Fort Steilacoom. I was stationed there in command of the United States troops, and a part of the time in command of the District of Puget's Sound. I was off on temporary duty to other places.

Int. 5.—Did you become acquainted with the tract of land at Nisqually Plains, so called, in Washington Territory, which is claimed by the Puget's Sound Agricultural Company?

Ans.—I have been at Fort Nisqually, and have crossed the plains several times, and am acquainted with the land which was known to be claimed by that Company. I have always understood that the Company claimed the country between Nisqually and Puyallup.

Int. 6.—Please describe the said tract.

Ans.—As I understand, the tract is bounded south by the Nisqually, north by the Puyallup, east by the foot of the Cascade Range of Mountains, and west by Puget's Sound. I state this merely from my belief and from general reputation as to the boundaries of the country.

Int. 7.—Are you able to estimate the number of square miles contained in the tract?

Ans.—I should think there were four or five hundred square miles; but I do not know. This is a rough estimate that I make from observation.

Int. 8.—About what portion of the tract is open or prairie land?

Ans.—So far as my observation extended, I should judge that three-quarters of it at least was prairie land, though I have never followed up the rivers to their source.

Int. 9.—About what portion is woodland and swamp?

Ans.—I should think one-fourth. It is a very high country, and very little of it is swamp. It is rather a peculiar country. There are places where you will find a little pond and some swamp about it. At these places there are always houses, because the land is very rich.

Int. 10.—What extent of the tract is suitable for tillage, and what for grazing or pasturing?

Ans.—A good deal of the open country, between Forts Steilacoom and Nisqually, the part which I am best acquainted with, is gravelly plains; grass very scarce, and a good deal of it has been so eaten by the sheep that it principally grows sorrel. There are parts of those plains where there is very good grazing and pasturing land. I should not think more than one-third of the open country is good grazing and pasturing land. There is a good deal of the land that will bear a pretty good crop of wheat in a wet season. It is what they call "leachy land," and soon wears out. It is not such land as our Western farmers would look at at all; farmers, I mean, who are used to good lands. To give you an idea of the country, I would state that the roads are always good and hard in the open country. When I was there, perhaps one nine-hundredth part of the open country was under cultivation. The population was very scarce. The river part of the country was more thickly settled than the balance. If the country were thickly settled, a great part of it would be cultivated; but our people would not consider more than one-third of the whole tract fit for cultivation.

Int. 11.—At the time of your residence, what crops were raised on the cultivated lands, and how much per acre?

Ans.—The principal crops raised while I was there, so far as I know, were oats and wheat—corn would not grow on account of the weather; it was too cold nights. I think, in the open country, the yield of wheat would be fifteen or twenty bushels to the acre, and in spots it would be more; I mean on the lands that were cultivated.

Int. 12.—What was the effect of cultivation on the condition of the soil?

Ans.—The effect was a deterioration of the soil; it was the general reputation there that it was leachy ground, and would not hold manure or water, and that it therefore required a good deal of water.

Int. 13.—Are you able to give an estimate of the money value of the different portions of the tract which you have described?

Ans.—If you estimate the value of land by what it will bring in market, I should say that the whole tract which they claim would not bring a dollar an acre, and I will give one reason: The Government had surveyed and sold land laying between these two rivers claimed by this Company, and the best lands so surveyed did not go off at the Government price, one dollar and a quarter an acre. This is what others have told me, and not what I know of my own knowledge.

(Counsel for the Company objects to the statement of the witness made upon information derived from others.)

Int. 14.—Will you please describe the farms, buildings, forts, and improvements of any kind which were claimed and occupied by the Puget's Sound Agricultural Company upon their land claim at Nisqually Plains, stating the construction of the buildings and the general condition of the improvements at the time of your residence.

Ans.—The principal buildings at Nisqually Plains were contained in Fort Nisqually and its neighborhood. So far as my knowledge extends, and I have been there a number of times, they were all log buildings. I was in but two of them. One was occupied by Dr. Tolmie, and was the best building there, I suppose; and the other was a store-house. The Doctor's building was a very fair building, and was ceiled inside, I think. The store-house was a very common building. The other buildings which I noticed were block-houses, four in number, and were very poorly constructed. There was a kind of picket around the fort. There were thirty to forty buildings there in all; some of them were stores and some dwelling-houses. Dr. Tolmie generally had thirty to forty Indians around him and some white people. I cannot give any estimate of the number of the people at the fort. I suppose there were forty or fifty acres of land there under fence, as near as I can estimate; there may have been a great deal more. This place that I have been speaking of was called the Main Post. There were other places about there, but I never visited any of them except this Main Post and Steilalacoom. Some of the improvements were in good order, and a part of them dilapidated.

Int. 15.—Have you any knowledge of the value of the improvements at Nisqually Plains, described in your answer to the previous question, including the cultivated lands, buildings, and other improvements?

Ans.—If they had been put up at auction with Fort Nisqually and the cultivated lands about it, I do not think they would have brought more than twelve thousand dollars. I include in this the fort and buildings, and the six hundred and forty acres immediately about the fort. They might have been worth more than this, but I do not think they would have brought more at auction.

Int. 16.—Were any cattle, horses, or sheep owned by this Agricultural Company pastured upon the plains at Nisqually? If so, state the number of each kind as far as you are able?

Ans.—I have seen sheep, cattle, and horses in the neighborhood of those plains, and which belonged, I suppose, to that Company, and I judge that the Company did own them, as I know that their agent, Dr. Tolmie, was a Government contractor, and contracted in behalf of the Company, as I understood, to supply the military post at Fort Steilacoom. I do not know how many cattle, sheep, and horses the Company had, and cannot give their value or any estimate of their value. My knowledge is too vague for that.

Int. 17.—Have you any knowledge of the land and farm, and improvements at Cowlitz river?

Ans.—I have not.

Int. 18.—Can you state any other matter or thing in your judgment affecting the claim of this Company against the United States?

Ans.—When I was stationed there the United States did not admit that the Company owned all the property there which it claimed to own. There was a claim owned by Judge Chambers with a mill on it near the fort. The town of Steilacoom was laid out within a mile of the fort, and within the territory claimed by the Company, and the citizens there bought and sold lots, and did not acknowledge the ownership of the Company. I suppose there were at most two hundred people in this town of Steilacoom while I was there. My impression is that the people there claimed title through the United States by what were called "Donation claims."

SILAS CASEY.

The foregoing direct examination having been taken on Saturday, September 29, 1866, the hearing for the further examination of said witness is adjourned by consent of parties until Monday, October 1, 1866, at 10 o'clock a. m.

THOMAS S. BLACKMAN,
U. S. Commissioner.

OCTOBER 1, 1866, 10 *o'clock a. m.*

The same counsel appear for the parties as before, and thereupon the said—

Silas Casey, being now further examined, deposes and says:

I wish to add a little to my testimony of Saturday last. I wish now further to state that there were a number of claimants in addition to Judge Chambers and those mentioned as occupying lots in Steilacoom. In fact, the whole of the claim of the Company which was within my knowledge was dotted over with claimants who did not acknowledge the rights of the Company. I recollect the names of a number of them. Two or three persons named Bird, who occupied a mill and the grounds connected with it; two persons named Keach; a man named Patterson, another named Follett, and others named Smith and Dowling, and there were several others. These persons whom I have named, held under the United States either by donation or otherwise. The claim of the Company was the subject of discussion very frequently.

With regard to the claim at Fort Nisqually, I wish to add that I considered it one of the best locations on the Company's whole claim. The fact that a fine spring of water flowed by the fort, well adapted to milling purposes, and on which, I think, there was a mill belonging, I suppose, to the Company, and the fact that this spot was connected with the waters of the Sound by a good landing and a good road, were sufficient causes, in my opinion, to enhance the value of this property of which I have spoken.

SILAS CASEY.

Being now cross-examined by Mr. Lander, the witness deposes and says:

Int. 1.—You state that you have travelled across these plains; please state in what directions you travelled, and by what roads.

Ans.—I have been over a portion of them. I have been to Puyallup river, which took me across Puyallup Plains. I have been to the Nisqually river *via* the Nisqually Fort, which took me across the Nisqually Plains. I do not suppose I have ever been more than ten miles directly east towards the Cascade Mountains.

Int. 2.—Is not the Company's fort at Nisqually about six miles from the military post at Steilacoom, and on the main road to Olympia; and does not that road run along the extreme western edge of the plains, and near to the woods, for the whole distance to the Nisqually river?

Ans.—The road from Steilacoom to Nisqually is nearer eight than six miles; something over seven miles, I think. It is on the main road to Olympia, and it does, for a large part of the distance, run along the western edge of the plains.

Int. 3.—Was not the road to Puyallup river a road also running along the western edge of the plains for a portion of the way, and the remainder through woods by a trail opened by your orders?

Ans.—I answer in the affirmative to the whole question.

Int. 4.—How often have you been to the east on these plains, and by what roads?

Ans.—I have been most frequently to the east on the road leading to the garden of the post, about six miles east of the fort.

Int. 5.—Did you usually keep to the main road in making

purpose of examining the country?

Ans.—I most frequently went on the main roads, but I have frequently left the main roads and ridden over the plains, and I generally notice a country pretty closely when I go over it.

Int. 6.—Is not your knowledge of these plains the best on that part of them which lie near the woods and on the main road between Forts Steilacoom and Nisqually, and immediately around those places?

Ans.—My knowledge of the portion which lay immediately on those roads is the best, but in my opinion I had a good knowledge of the country within ten miles of the fort, all around, though not so minute a knowledge as along the roads.

Int. 7.—Can you, of your own personal knowledge, give the results of any farming or gardening on any particular piece of ground?

Ans.—I can, with regard to the garden of about ten or fifteen acres belonging to the post. It was very well adapted to potatoes, turnips, beets, and peas, and onions. It would not raise corn or tomatoes. A portion of this garden, when I first went there, was a sort of a marsh, where the wild ducks used to roost. I caused that to be drained into a pond, and then ploughed it and planted potatoes, and on that particular spot where the ducks roosted I never saw such potatoes. The person who dug the potatoes said he had dug potatoes in England, Scotland, and Ireland, and that he never had seen such potatoes. I think they would have yielded seven to eight hundred bushels to the acre, and they were of an excellent qualtity and of very large size.

Int. 8.—In giving your account of these plains over their whole extent, is not a portion of the testimony that you have given derived from what you have heard from others?

Ans.—Yes, sir; the most of the testimony which I have given in regard to these plains, with the exception of those portions which I have myself been over, was derived from impressions produced upon my mind from the statements of others.

Int. 9.—At the time you visited Fort Nisqually, had a new-framed house for the chief factor been erected?

Ans.—When I visited Fort Nisqually the chief factor lived in a log house. I am strongly of the impression that it was a log house.

Int. 10.—Do you feel certain that the saw-mill or mill on the Company's land, that you speak of, on the stream running by the fort, was not built by and the property of American settlers?

Ans.—If the building which I suppose is meant is the one, I do not think it did belong to American settlers. There may have been no mill there. There was a dam there and a building which I took for a mill. I have seen them washing sheep there.

Int. 11.—In your examination in chief, you have stated that one-third of the open country is good grazing and pasturing land; do you mean to be understood that only one-third of it is suitable for pasturage?

Ans.—The difficulty in answering that question arises from the use of the word "suitable." I will explain what I mean by that; I think not more than one-third of it is good pasturing land.

Int. 12.—You have spoken of the ground being "leachy;" is that statement from your own knowledge or from information derived from others?

Ans.—With regard to its being "leachy," I have spoken from my own knowledge; in regard to water and in regard to manure, from information derived from others.

Int. 13.—Was this observation of yours about the ground being leachy made at Steilacoom or elsewhere?

Ans.—Mostly at and around Steilacoom, but somewhat in other localities.

Int. 14.—When you speak of the Government of the United States not acknowledging the claim of the Company, do you yourself know any facts which caused you to form that opinion?

Ans.—I know there were military reservations at Steilacoom and other places, plots of which were sent to Washington, and I supposed the reservations and plots were made by order of the Government.

SILAS CASEY.

EASTERN DISTRICT OF MICHIGAN, *ss.*

I, Thomas S. Blackman, one of the United States Commissioners for said district, do hereby certify that the foregoing deposition of Silas Casey was taken before me, at my office in the city of detroit, in said district, commencing on Saturday, September 29, 1866, and concluding on Monday, October 1, 1866, in the matter in which said deposition is entitled in its caption, and in behalf of the United States. That I was attended at said examination by William P. Wells, Esq. in behalf of the United States, and by Edward Lander, Esq., in behalf of the Puget's Sound Agricultural Company; that said witness, Silas Casey, was first duly sworn by me "to testify the truth, the whole truth, and nothing but the truth," in said matter, and was then orally examined in chief and cross-examined, and that the whole of his deposition was reduced to writing by me in his presence, and was then carefully read over by me to said witness, and was then subscribed by him in my presence; that said examination was commenced on Saturday, the 29th day of September, 1866, and not having been concluded on that day, the examination was adjourned by me, by consent of the counsel who appeared before me at said examination, until Monday, the first day of October, 1866, at 10 o'clock in the forenoon, at which last-mentioned time said examination was proceeded with and concluded.

That my fees for taking said deposition are twenty-five dollars.

[L. S.] In witness whereof I have hereto set my hand this second day of October, A. D. 1866, at Detroit.

THOMAS S. BLACKMAN,
U. S. Commissioner for the Eastern District of Michigan.

BRITISH AND AMERICAN JOINT COMMISSION

HUDSON'S BAY AND PUGET'S SOUND AGRICULTURAL COMPANIES' CLAIM.

In the matter of the Claim of the Puget's Sound Agricultural Company against the United States of America.

To any civil magistrate at the Fort Jefferson, Dry Tortugas, competent to administer oaths, or in his absence, to any officer thereof authorized by the revised regulations for the Army to take depositions:

Know ye, that in confidence of your prudence and fidelity, you have been appointed, and by these presents, you, or any one of you, is invested with full power and authority to examine Brevet Lieutenant Colonel Bennett H. Hill, on his corporal oath, as a witness in the above entitled cause, upon the interrogations annexed to this Commission on the part of the United States, and the cross-interrogatories thereto annexed by the Puget's Sound Agricultural Company.

Therefore, you are hereby required that you, or either of you, at certain days and places to be appointed by you for that purpose, do cause the said Brevet Lieutenant Colonel Bennett H. Hill to come before you, and then and there examine him on oath on said interrogatories and cross-interrogatories, and reduce the same to writing in conformity with instructions hereto annexed; and when the said deposition shall have been completed, you will return the same annexed to this writ, closed up under your seal, and addressed by mail to George Gibbs, Esq., Clerk of said Commission, at the office thereof, in the city of Washington.

Witness,

ALEXANDER S. JOHNSON,
Commissioner.

JOHN ROSE,
Commissioner for Great Britain.

INSTRUCTIONS.

BRITISH AND AMERICAN JOINT COMMISSION ON HUDSON'S BAY AND PUGET'S SOUND AGRICULTURAL COMPANIES' CLAIMS.

In the matter of the Claim of the Puget's Sound Agricultural Company against the United States of America.

INSTRUCTIONS FOR THE EXECUTION OF THE COMMISSION.

The deposition may be preceded by the following heading:

"Deposition of ———, a witness sworn and examined in the Island of Dry Tortugas, State of Florida, by virtue of this Commission, issued by the Hon. John Rose and the Hon. Alexander S. Johnson, Commissioners, to me directed for the examination of a witness in the matter of the claim of the Puget's Sound Agricultural Company against the United States of America."

The Commissioner then calls the witness before him, and administers to him the following oath, namely:

"You swear that the evidence you shall give in the matter of the claim of the Puget's Sound Agricultural Company against the United States of America shall be the truth, the whole truth, and nothing but the truth, so help you God."

The witness having been thus sworn, the evidence given by him will be reduced to writing, thus:

"Bennett H. Hill, brevet lieutenant colonel in the Army of the United States, now on duty at the Island of Dry Tortugas, a witness produced on the part and behalf of the United States, in answer to the following interrogatories and cross-interrogatories, deposeth and says as follows."

When the deposition of the witness is concluded, he must subscribe his name thereto.

The deposition, with all documents and papers, if any, accompanying the same, will be returned before the Commissioners with all convenient diligence.

In returning this Commission, your attention is called to the certificate required by the revised Regulations for the Army, Article 1031.

Attest: GEORGE GIBBS,
               Clerk.

In the matter of the Claim of the Hudson's Bay Company, now pending before the British and American Joint Commission, on the Claims of the Hudson's Bay and- Puget's Sound Agricultural Companies against the United States.

Interrogatories to be addressed on behalf of the United States to Brevet Lieutenant Colonel Bennett H. Hill, now stationed at Fort Jefferson, Dry Tortugas.

Ques. 1.—What is your name, place of residence, and present occupation?

Ques. 2.—Have you ever resided in Washington Territory? If yea, where, and when, and for how long a period?

Ques. 3.—Have you any knowledge of the tract of land at Nisqually Plains, so-called, in Washington Territory, which is claimed by the Puget's Sound Agricultural Company? If yea, please to describe the same, giving, as fully as you can, the character and extent of that part, if any, which is woodland or swamp, the character and extent of that part, if any, which is suitable for tillage. the character and extent of that part, if any, which is suitable for grazing, and any other facts or circumstances, which, in your opinion, may enter into a full description of the land in question.

Ques. 4.—Have you any knowledge of the value of the different portions of this tract at the time that you resided in Washington Territory? If yea, please to state what, in your opinion, was their value at that time.

Ques. 5.—Have you any knowledge of the fort and buildings and improvements connected therewith, which were within the limits of this claim at Nisqually, and were occupied by the servants of this Company? If yea, please to describe the same, giving their condition, and the character of their con- struction as fully as you can.

Ques. 6.—Have you any knowledge of the value of the fort and buildings and improvements referred to in the previous question? If yea, please to state what, in your judgment, was their value at the time you were acquainted with them.

Ques. 7.—Have you any knowledge of any cattle, or sheep, or horses, which were owned by the Puget's Sound Agricultural Company, and pastured upon the plains at Nisqually? If yea, please to state, if you know, the number of such which were pastured by the Company upon said plains at the time that you were there.

Ques. 8.—Have you any knowledge of the character of the different breeds of cattle and horses and sheep, which are referred to in the previous question? If yea, please to describe the same, and state, if you know, whether they were of a superior or inferior quality.

Ques. 9.—Have you any knowledge, from experience or observation, or otherwise, of the effect of cultivation or condition of the soil, for the most part, on the plains at Nisqually? If yea, unless this point be substantially covered by a previous answer, please to describe the same as particularly as you can.

Ques 10.—Have you knowledge of any other matter which may affect the claims of the Puget's Sound Agricultural Company against the United States? If yea, please to state the same as fully as if you were specially interrogated in relation thereto.   C. CUSHING,
Counsel for the United States.

In the matter of the Claims of the Puget's Sound Agricultural Company, now pending before the British and American Joint Commission on the Claims of the Hudson's Bay and Puget's Sound Agricultural Companies against the United States.

Cross-Interrogatories to be addressed, on behalf of the Puget's Sound Agricultural Company, to Brevet Lieutenant Colonel Bennett H. Hill, now stationed at Fort Jefferson, Dry Tortugas.

Int. 1.—While you were stationed at Fort Steilacoom, did you pay any attention to agricultural pursuits, or were you attending to your professional duties?

Int. 2.—Is not your knowledge of the quality of the soil, its division into arable and pasture lands, and the proportion of each kind of land, if you have any knowledge on these subjects, derived from your rides along the roads leading over the plains, and chiefly to the road leading to the Company's Fort at Nisqually and the town of Olympia?

Int. 3.—At the time you were stationed at Steilacoom, was not the number of settlers quite small on the plains, and the

15 P

amount of arable land on the river and creek bottoms and in the swales unknown?

Int. 4.—If your rides extended in any direction off the main roads mentioned in the second interrogatory, did you pay particular attention to the soil for any purpose other than to find the best road to ride upon?

Int. 5.—Did you, at any time, give especial attention to these plains with a view to ascertain their productive quality or to discover how much arable land there might be upon them, or what farms might be made when a demand for produce should stimulate settlement and agricultural activity?

Int. 6.—In estimating the value of those lands, did you take into consideration the facts mentioned in interrogatory 5?

Int. 7.—In estimating the value of those lands, when you were there, did you take into consideration the scarcity of prairie land compared to the vast extent of forests in the Puget's Sound country, the cost of clearing land of the large trees for either cultivation or pasturage, and the probabilities of future settlement or not?

Int. 8.—Did you while at Fort Steilacoom buy or sell any lands, or know the saleable value of these lands?

Int. 9.—If you answer that you do know of sales or the saleable value of these lands, please state whether anything was conveyed to the purchaser except the mere possession?

Int. 10.—Did not the forces of the United States occupy and pay rent for certain buildings of the Puget's Sound Agricultural Company while you were at Fort Steilacoom?

Int. 11.—Had you, while at Fort Steilacoom, any practical knowledge of the price of labor or cost of lumber?

Int. 12.—Have you ever paid enough attention to the erection of buildings, the amount of lumber required in one of a certain size, as to be able to tell the amount of lumber in any particular building, or the cost of erecting it?

Int. 13.—Did you buy or sell any buildings at this time or have any means of ascertaining the value of buildings in that section of the country?

Int. 14.—Did you make any particular inquiry into the number of cattle, horses, or sheep on the plains belonging to the Puget's Sound Agricultural Company, while you were there, or is your estimate of their number merely the result of observation made while riding?

Int. 15.—Were not the plains, to the best of your knowledge, at the time you first came to Fort Steilacoom, covered and depastured by the horses, cattle, and sheep of the Puget's Sound Agricultural Company?

Int. 16.—Are you prepared to state the different breeds of sheep, cattle, and horses owned by the Company? If so, state what portion of the sheep were imported South-Down and Leicester, and if you can, what number of their cattle were of American breeds. How many of their horses were American, how many Indian, how many Spanish?

Int. 17.—Do you know of your own personal knowledge, of any piece or pieces of ground on the Nisqually Plains that had been ploughed and cultivated, and have you noticed personally the effect produced by it? If so, state where this piece or pieces of land were situated, how much land there was in that piece; and who cultivated it.

Int. 18.—Did not these plains afford good pasturage to the stock you saw ranging there?

Int. 19.—What was your rank in the Army of the United States when you were at Fort Steilacoom?

CHAS. D. DAY,
Counsel for the Puget's Sound Agricultural Company.

Deposition of Lieutenant Colonel Bennett H. Hill, Brevet Brigadier General U. S. Army, a witness sworn and examined in the Island of the Dry Tortugas, State of Florida, by virtue of this Commission, issued by the Honorable John Rose and the Honorable Alexander S. Johnson, Commissioners, to me directed for the examination of a witness in the matter of the claim of the Puget's Sound Agricultural Company against the United States of America.

TESTIMONY OF BVT. BRIG. GEN. BENNETT H. HILL.

Brevet Brigadier General *Bennett H. Hill*, Lieutenant Colonel U. S. Army, now on duty at Fort Jefferson, Dry Tortugas, Florida, a witness produced on the part and behalf of the United States of America, in answer to the following interrogatories and cross-interrogatories, deposeth and says as follows:

Answers to Questions.

Ques. 1.—My name is Bennett H. Hill, my present residence Fort Jefferson, Florida, and I am by occupation an officer of the United States Army.

Ques. 2.—I was stationed, as an officer of the army, at Fort Steilacoom, Washington Territory, and commanded that post from September, 1849, until some time in the early part of 1853, with the exception of an interval of some months that I was on leave of absence.

Ques. 3.—The knowledge that I have of the Nisqually Plains is that derived from having been stationed at Fort Steilacoom, which is on the tract claimed by the Puget's Sound Company, from having ridden over many parts of the tract in question, and from the information obtained from officers, soldiers, and citizens, who hunted over or explored the country. These plains lie very high above the level of the waters of the Sound, from one hundred and fifty (150) to two hundred (200) feet, I should think. The soil is most generally sandy and gravelly. I considered very little of it fit for cultivation; the grass on those plains was also very short and sparse. There was generally a belt of pine timber extending back from the shores of the Sound about a mile. There were several small lakes and streams in the plains, whose banks were fringed with timber; also some scattered oak trees here and there on the plains. I do not remember to have seen or heard of any swamp lands on those plains. I cannot give the extent of the woodland, and my opinion was that the plains in question were unsuitable for cultivation, by reason of the sandy and gravelly soil and dry summers, except in a few patches of limited extent, and that the plains afforded very indifferent grazing.

Ques. 4.—I had no knowledge of the value of the different portions of the tract in question. At the time I was there the Government donated land to actual settlers, and they sought the most favorable locations; but few settled in the Nisqually Plains except for other reasons than cultivation of the soil.

Ques. 5.—I visited the Puget's Sound Company's fort at Nisqually frequently when I was stationed at Fort Steilacoom. As I remember it, it was a square stockade work, formed of light logs, set upright; how large I cannot state, but my recollection is that each face was about one hundred (100) yards; I think, also, there was arrangement for flank defence. There were quarters inside the work for Dr. Tolmie, who was in charge, also quarters for a few employés, and store-house or store-houses. These buildings were, as I remember them, plainly and rudely built, either of logs or boards. There were a few out-houses and barns outside of the fort, and cabins for Indian em-ployés, and about one hundred acres of ground under fence; there was also a store-house on the beach at the foot of the hill. I understood, also, that there were some shepherd's cabins on the plains, but I do not remember now to have seen any of them.

Ques. 6.—I first visited Fort Nisqually about 1st September, 1849, and presumed it had been built before the price of labor and material was increased by the discovery of gold in California, and I supposed that Indian labor entered largely into its construction and into the improvements made; but I do not know how long it had been built, or with what kind of labor. The fort itself was of value only for the purposes for which it had been built. It is impossible for me now to estimate, with any degree of accuracy, the value of the fort and improve-ments at the time I was in Washington Territory.

Ques. 7.—The Puget's Sound Agricultural Company owned and raised cattle and sheep. They were far from numerous, compared to the ground over which they grazed, and I think they were being sent to Vancouver's Island as often as oppor-tunity offered. I cannot state the numbers of cattle or sheep owned by that Company. No horses were owned, except those for ordinary use, and I never understood that the Company pretended to raise horses on the Nisqually Plains.

Ques. 8.—The cattle were of inferior quality; they were generally small and thin, and very wild. I supposed they were of Spanish or mixed breeds. The sheep were, so far as I knew and understood, of very good quality. As I pre-viously stated, the Company had only a few horses at Fort Nisqually. These were the common Indian horse.

Ques. 9.—None other, except the observation of the effect of cultivation by the Puget's Sound Company, and experience in gardening. The Puget's Sound Company cultivated some fields near Fort Steilacoom one or two seasons. The crop was wheat, and the yield was reaped and sold for forage to the quartermaster of the post, if I remember rightly. The season after my arrival at Fort Steilacoom, a post-garden was attempted, with the view of supplying the officers and soldiers with vegetables, and a piece of ground selected near the post that seemed to offer the best prospect of success, but it failed entirely;-the ground was too sandy and gravelly and poor. I then had an examination of the country about the post made, and about three or four miles from the post a small piece of very good land was found. There were only twelve or fourteen acres of it, which I caused to be fenced in, and here we were very successful in gardening.

Ques. 10.—The claim of the Puget's Sound Agricultural Company was, as I understood it to be, about ten miles (10) square. The metes and bounds of that claim were not, however, marked off, to my knowledge, when I arrived at Puget's Sound; but a man, as I remember, was engaged in the winter of 1852 and 1853 to run and mark the extent of the claim. Steilacoom had been a farm, and was in the possession of the Puget's Sound Company when I arrived on Puget's Sound. The farm buildings were rented by the acting assistant quartermaster on the part of the United States. The barn was converted into quarters for my company. It was built of small logs, and roofed with bark. So also the farm-house, which I occupied myself as quarters, but subsequently improved. There was also a granary, kitchen, and other outbuildings, all roofed with bark, and, like all the buildings of the Puget's Sound Company on the Sound, very rudely built.

Answers to Cross-Interrogatories.

Int. 1.—I paid no attention to agricultural pursuits, except so far as is mentioned in answer to Question 9; and I was engaged in attending to my professional duties.

Int. 2.—The opinion formed and expressed in answer to Question No. 3 was derived from riding along the road leading to Fort Nisqually, along the road leading to the upper crossing of the Nisqually—I mean the road to the Cowlitz farms—along the road leading from Fort Steilacoom to the Puyallup river, to rides over the country in the neighborhood of the post of Steilacoom, and to the information I would obtain from officers, soldiers, and citizens who either hunted over or explored the country.

Int. 3.—There were but few settlers on the plains; but the amount of arable land on the river and creek bottoms, &c., was well known, I believe, to all interested on the subject.

Int. 4.—My rides off the main roads were for pleasure, and I had no object in paying particular attention to the soil.

Int. 5.—I did not give especial attention to these plains to ascertain their productive quality, except so far as is mentioned in answer to Question No. 9.

Int. 6.—I have not expressed an opinion of the value of the lands in question, except that they were, in my opinion, unsuitable for cultivation, and very inferior for grazing purposes; and I do not think I ever heard any other opinion expressed of them by persons who examined the lands.

Int. 7.—I have not estimated the value of the lands in question.

Int. 8.—I did not buy or sell any lands whilst I was at Steilacoom; nor do I think any lands were sold whilst I was there. It may be that premiums were paid for squatters' rights to claims.

Int. 9.—I have replied that I do not know of sales of land whilst at Fort Steilacoom.

Int. 10.—The United States paid rent for certain buildings that were in the possession of the Puget's Sound Agricultural Company when I arrived on Puget's Sound, and continued to pay rent for them while I was at Steilacoom.

Int. 11.—I had practical knowledge of the price of labor and cost of lumber only so far as it was employed or purchased by the United States at Fort Steilacoom.

Int. 12.—I have paid no attention to the erection of buildings or their cost, except such buildings as would be erected on the frontier by the labor principally of the troops.

Int. 13.—I did not buy or sell any buildings in Washington Territory. I have not estimated the value of the buildings in that section of the country. The buildings in that section of the country at the time I was there were of a very rough, plain character.

Int. 14.—I have not given an estimate of the number of cattle or sheep owned by the Puget's Sound Company. I have no doubt but that I inquired the number, but I do not remember at this time. I have stated that the Puget's Sound Company did not own at Nisqually any horses beyond the number required for their ordinary use. This information I must have

Int. 15.—The plains were not covered with cattle, sheep, and horses at the time of my arrival at Steilacoom. The grazing, I remember, was very indifferent; in fact, it was so poor that it would not support the ox teams we had to employ at that time, and the difficulty of purchasing forage occasioned great inconvenience.

Int. 16.—I cannot state the breeds of sheep owned by the Puget's Sound Company. They were generally esteemed, if I remember rightly, of excellent quality. The cattle were very inferior, small, lean, and wild. I considered that they were of Spanish or mixed breeds. The horses in use by the Company at Fort Nisqually were the common Indian horse.

Int. 17.—I can give no other answer to this interrogatory than that contained in answer to Question No. 9. I may have also seen the effect of cultivation on the fields of the Puget's Sound Company near Fort Nisqually, but I do not remember to have done so. The fields I refer to in my answer to Question No. 9 were situated near to Fort Steilacoom. They were cultivated for the Puget's Sound Company by its servants, and I do not remember to have seen the ploughing of them. I think the fields contained some fifteen or twenty acres.

Int. 18.—I considered that they afforded very inferior pasturage.

Int. 19.—I was a captain in the army of the United States at the time I was at Fort Steilacoom.

B. H. HILL,
Lt. Col. 5th U. S. Art'y, and Bvt. Brig. Gen'l U. S. A.

The above depositions, in answer to questions on behalf of the United States, and in answer to cross-interrogations on behalf of the Puget's Sound Agricultural Company, were duly sworn and subscribed to before me this twentieth day of October, 1866.

B. W. RITTENHOUSE,
1st Lieut. 5th U. S. Art'y, Bvt. Major U. S. A.

FORT JEFFERSON, FLORIDA,
October 22, 1866.

I certify on honor that there is not a civil magistrate at this post competent to administer oath, that there is not a judge advocate at the post, nor is there a garrison or regimental court in session, nor an adjutant of a regiment.

B. H. HILL,
Lieut. Col. 5th Art'y, and Bvt. Brig. Gen'l U. S. A.

BRITISH AND AMERICAN JOINT COMMISSION

ON THE

HUDSON'S BAY AND PUGET'S SOUND AGRICULTURAL COMPANIES.

———•◦•———

In the matter of the Claim of the Puget's Sound Agricultural Company against the United States of America.

To Robert McPhail Smith, Esq., Clerk of the United States Circuit Court, Nashville, Tennessee, Notary Public, Nashville, or any other person duly authorized to take depositions in the State of Tennessee:

Know ye, that in confidence of your prudence and fidelity, you have been appointed, and by these presents, you, or any one of you, is invested with full power and authority to examine Brevet Brigadier General August V. Kautz, on his corporal oath, as a witness in the above-entitled cause, upon the interrogations annexed to this commission on the part of the United States, and the cross-interrogatories thereto annexed by the Puget's Sound Agricultural Company.

Therefore, you are hereby required, that you, or either of you, at certain days and places, to be appointed by you for that purpose, do cause the said Brevet Brigadier General August V. Kautz to come before you, and then and there examine him on oath on said interrogations and cross-interrogatories, and reduce the same to writing, in conformity with instructions hereto annexed. And when the said deposition shall have been completed, you will return the same, annexed to this writ, closed up under your seal, and addressed by you, by mail, to George Gibbs, Esq., Clerk of said Commission, at the office thereof in the city of Washington.

    Witness:

ALEXANDER S. JOHNSON,
Commissioner.

JOHN ROSE,
Com. for Great Britain.

INSTRUCTIONS.

BRITISH AND AMERICAN JOINT COMMISSION ON HUDSON'S BAY AND PUGET'S SOUND AGRICULTURAL COMPANIES' CLAIMS.

In the matter of the Claim of the Puget's Sound Agricultural Company against the United States of America.

INSTRUCTIONS FOR THE EXECUTION OF THE COMMISSION:

The deposition may be preceded by the following heading:

"Deposition of ———— ————, a witness sworn and examined in the city of New Orleans, in the State of Louisiana, by virtue of this Commission, issued by the Honorable John Rose and the Honorable Alexander S. Johnson, Commissioners, to me directed, for the examination of a witness in the matter of the claim of the Puget's Sound Agricultural Company against the United States of America."

The Commissioner then calls the witness before him, and administers to him the following oath, namely:

"You swear that the evidence you shall give in the matter of the claim of the Hudson's Bay Company against the United States of America shall be the truth, the whole truth, and nothing but the truth, so help you God."

The witness having been thus sworn, the evidence given by him will be reduced to writing, thus:

"*August V. Kautz*, Brevet Brigadier General in the army of the United States, now on duty at the city of New Orleans, a witness produced on the part and behalf of the United States, in answer to the following interrogatories and cross-interrogatories, deposeth and says as follows:"

When the deposition of the witness is concluded, he must subscribe his name thereto.

The deposition, with all documents and papers, if any, accompanying the same, will be returned before the Commissioners with all convenient diligence.

Attest: GEORGE GIBBS,
                                 Clerk.

In the matter of the Claims of the Puget's Sound Agricultural Company, now pending before the British and American Joint Commission on the Claims of the Hudson's Bay and Puget's Sound Agricultural Companies against the United States.

Interrogatories to be addressed on behalf of the United States to Brevet Brigadier General August V. Kautz, of New Orleans, in the State of Louisiana.

Ques. 1.—What is your name, place of residence, and present occupation?

Ques. 2.—Have you ever resided in Washington Territory; if yea, when and where, and for how long a period?

Ques. 3.—Have you any knowledge of the tract of land at Nisqually Plains, so called, in Washington Territory, which is claimed by the Puget's Sound Agricultural Company? If yea, please to describe the same, giving, as fully as you can, the character and extent of that part, if any, which is open prairie land, the character and extent of that part, if any, [which is] woodland or swamp; the character and extent of that part, if any, which is suitable for tillage; and the character and extent of that part, if any, which is suitable for grazing; and any other fact or circumstance which, in your opinion, may enter into a full description of the land in question.

Ques. 3*a.*—Have you any knowledge, from experience or observation, of the effect of cultivation on the condition of the soil at the Nisqually Plains, so called? If yea, please to describe the same as particularly as you can.

Ques. 4.—Have you any knowledge of the value of the different portions of the tract at the time that you resided in Washington Territory? If yea, please to state what, in your opinion, was their value at that time.

Ques. 5.—Have you any knowledge of any fort, or buildings, or improvements of any kind, which were claimed and occupied by the Puget's Sound Agricultural Company, and were within the limits of their land claim at Nisqually Plains? If yea, please to describe the same, giving their condition and the character of their construction as fully as you can.

Ques. 6.—Have you any knowledge of the value of the fort, and the buildings and improvements connected therewith, referred to in the previous question? If yea, please to state what, in your judgment, was their value at the time that you had an opportunity to observe them.

Ques. 7.—Have you any knowledge of any cattle or horses or sheep which were owned by the Puget's Sound Agricultural Company, and pastured upon the plains at Nisqually? If yea, please to state, if you know, the number of such kind which were pastured upon said plains at the time you were there.

Ques. 8.—Have you any knowledge of the character of the different breeds of cattle and horses and sheep which were owned by the Puget's Sound Agricultural Company? If yea, please to describe the same, and state, if you know, whether they were of a superior or inferior quality.

Ques. 9.—Have you any knowledge of any other matter which may affect the claims of the Puget's Sound Agricultural Company against the United States? If yea, please to state the same, as fully as if you were specially interrogated in relation thereto.

C. CUSHING,
Counsel for the United States.

In the matter of the Claims of the Puget's Sound Agricultural Company, now pending before the British and American Joint Commission on the Hudson's Bay and Puget's Sound Agricultural Companies' Claims against the United States.

Cross-interrogatories to be addressed, on behalf of the Puget's Sound Agricultural Company, to Brevet Brigadier General August V. Kautz, now stationed at New Orleans, in the State of Louisiana.

Int. 1.—For what length of time were you stationed at Fort Steilacoom, and in what years?

Int. 2.—Were you ever engaged in agricultural pursuits while at Fort Steilacoom, or were you occupied in the duties of your profession?

Int. 3.—Is not your knowledge of the quality of the soil of the Nisqually Plains, their division into arable and pasture lands, and the proportion of each kind of land, derived, if at all, from what knowledge you acquired from your rides in certain directions, for fishing and perhaps hunting, and on the roads leading to the Puyallup river and the town of Olympia?

Int. 4.—During the Indian war, when you were traveling off these roads in search of hostile parties of Indians, were you not giving more attention to the finding of the enemy than to the examination of the soil?

Int. 5.—Is there not in bottoms of the creeks and rivers, in the swales and lower grounds of these plains, a considerable amount of land suitable for cultivation, and much of it that would be called rich farming land?

Int. 6.—Did you remain at Fort Steilacoom until the settlers had located some one hundred and fifty farms on these plains? If not, how many settlers were there when you left?

Int. 7.—Do not the whole of those open lands, that are not cultivated, afford good pasturage for sheep and cattle?

Int. 8.—Can you, from your own personal knowledge, say that you ever saw any portion of those plains under the plough, and afterwards noticed the effect which that cultivation or ploughing had on that particular portion thus ploughed and cultivated?

Int. 9.—When you first came to Fort Steilacoom, were not the forces there quartered in buildings owned by the Puget's Sound Company, for which rent was paid at the rate of $50 per month? If you do not know the fact as to the payment of rent, please answer the first part of the question.

Int. 10.—Were there not scattered around those plains log buildings, used by shepherds of the Company?

Int. 11.—In answering the six interrogatories-in-chief, as to the buildings of the Company and their value, does your estimate include the new house, built by the agent in charge, or is it made before that building was erected?

Int. 12.—Was there not at the main post of the Company, at the time you left there, a large and good barn and sheds, one new, and for that country, valuable dwelling-house, one older dwelling-house, two store-houses, besides the smaller dwellings of the employés of the Company?

Int. 13.—Are you a builder or mechanic, accustomed by the eye to estimate the size of buildings and the quantity of lumber required to build them, or have you such an acquaintance with the price of lumber, the cost of labor, and the cost of transportation, for a series of years, as to enable you to say what these buildings cost the Company, or what they were worth in 1846, or at any time since then to the present date?

Int. 14.—Is your idea of the value of these lands derived from any estimate based upon their productiveness and the value of produce, and have you taken into consideration the value of pasturage, the price of beef, the market value of sheep and wool, and the adaptation and fitness of those lands for sheep and cattle-raising?

Int. 15.—In estimating their value, have you taken into consideration the fact that this is the largest and most important body of open lands on the shores of Puget's Sound suitable for pasturage?

Int. 16.—At the time you were at Fort Steilacoom, had the great demand for cattle for the Victoria market began? If so, have you thought of that in valuing these lands?

Int. 17.—At what date is your estimate of value made?

Int. 18.—What do you know of any sales of land on these plains, of your personal knowledge?

Int. 19.—Was there not an Indian war going on during a considerable portion of the time you were stationed at Fort Steilacoom, and were you not personally very active in it?

Int. 20.—At the time you were stationed at Fort Steilacoom, had not the original cattle of the Company nearly disappeared, and were not those then owned by the Company chiefly what were called American cattle?

Int. 21.—Had not the Company large flocks of sheep pasturing on those plains?

Int. 22.—Were there not, at the time you left Fort Steilacoom, besides sheep and cattle of the Company, all the cattle and sheep of the settlers, pasturing on these plains?

Int. 23.—If you know the number of cattle and sheep belonging to the settlers at the time you left, please state the number.

Int. 24.—If you have been unable to answer the 23d interrogatory particularly, state if they had not a large number of cattle and sheep pastured on those plains at the time you left Steilacoom.

Int. 25.—What was your rank in the army of the United States when you were stationed at Fort Steilacoom?

CHAS. D. DAY,
Counsel for the Puget's Sound Agricultural Company.

UNITED STATES OF AMERICA, }
State of Tennessee, City of Nashville. }

BRITISH AND AMERICAN JOINT COMMISSION ON HUDSON'S BAY AND PUGET'S SOUND AGRICULTURAL COMPANIES' CLAIMS.

In the matter of the Claim of the latter Company against the United States of America.

Deposition of August V. Kautz, Lieut. Colonel 34th Infantry, and Brevet Major General United States Army, now awaiting orders at Nashville, Tennessee, a witness sworn and examined in the city of Nashville and State of Tennessee, by virtue of the annexed commission issued by the Hon. John Rose and the Hon. Alex. S. Johnson, Commissioners, to me directed, for the examination of said witness in the matter of the claims of the Puget's Sound Agricultural Company *vs.* The United States of America.

TESTIMONY OF BVT. MAJ. GEN. AUGUST V. KAUTZ.

Said witness, produced on behalf of said United States, being duly sworn to speak the truth, the whole truth, and nothing but the truth, in the matter of the claim last aforesaid, in answer to the annexed interrogatories and cross-interrogatories, deposeth and says as follows, his answers being numbered to correspond with said interrogatories and cross-interrogatories.

Answers to Direct Interrogatories.

1. My name is August V. Kautz; I am an officer of the United States Army, and at present awaiting orders at Nashville, Tennessee.

2. I was stationed in Washington Territory first from January to March, in the year 1853, at Fort Vancouver, and then from March to July of the same year, at Fort Steilacoom. In February, 1856, I returned to Fort Steilacoom from Oregon, and remained there until October, 1858, when I was stationed at Simiahmoo Bay until April, 1859. I then left the Territory, and returned to it again in the fall of 1860, and was stationed at Gray's Harbor until May, 1861.

3. I became well acquainted with the tract known as the Nisqually Plains during the three years I was stationed at Fort Steilacoom. They comprise an area of about ten or twelve miles square, and constitute a table-land comparatively level, about 200 feet above the Sound waters, and they are interspersed with patches of woods, swamps, thickets, and lakes. The lakes, swamps, and wooded portions I estimate as together constituting from one-fifth to one-fourth of the whole tract. The land is very poor and unproductive. When I was last there, all the land regarded as worth tilling was already claimed by settlers, and under cultivation. This however, in my opinion, did not exceed one-twentieth of the entire tract. Very little of the ground under cultivation would be considered as worth tilling in Illinois. The soil is very gravelly, and yields a very sparse, thin grass. This is good, but of such slow growth and so thinly scattered, that I should call the lands poor grazing-lands. The wooded parts were generally either wooded knolls or swamps. The former were more unproductive than the open plains; the latter, in some cases, were capable of being drained and tilled to some extent.

3 *a.* I know the soil to be very poor, and the extent of cultivation very limited. We had the garden for the post, a small tract of about eight acres, between four and five miles distant, and the settlers could not supply enough grain to feed the public animals at the post, numbering about ninety.

4. I cannot give the money value of the land, as it was not in the market while I was there. When claims were sold the improvements constituted the greater part of their value. Good agricultural land was chiefly valuable there on account of its scarcity, which was very great.

5. I know respecting the post at Fort Nisqually, which, when I first saw it in 1853, consisted of a stockade twenty feet high, with two block houses on opposite corners, one or two dwelling-houses, and two storehouses, and a number of smaller houses for the servants and employés of the Company. These were all log buildings—some of them of hewn logs; but the whole establishment was in a dilapidated condition, and between the time I first and that I last saw it much of the stockade had fallen down and been replaced, and the dwelling-houses and one of the storehouses had been replaced by two board buildings. There were a number of outbuildings, including a barn, also quite old and rotten. They had other buildings, on other portions of the tract, one of which was known as the Muck Farm and another as the Dean Farm. I believe there were also a few others, but I did not know much about them. The Muck and Dean Farms each consisted of a farm-house and a number of outbuildings, built of logs, and not of very great value. Each one of these places had some land enclosed and under cultivation; but these tracts were not large—somewhere between twenty and forty acres each.

6. Fort Nisqually, with all its improvements, fencing, outhouses, &c., may have cost the Company from $10,000 to $15,000, and the two farms from $1,000 to $2,000 each; but they were not worth that when I saw them, as they were in a decaying condition. The two new board buildings, I should say, cost together about $6,000.

7. I do not know the number of horses, cattle, and sheep. I remember that I saw several large droves of wild cattle on the plains, in 1853, belonging to the Company, none after that. I saw a great many sheep belonging to the Company, after I went back in 1856; of the number of horses I have no particular knowledge. I do not remember to have seen more than three or four hundred head of cattle in one drove, more

16 P

than a thousand head of sheep, nor [more] than from fifteen to twenty head of horses; but I have reason to believe that they had two or three droves of this description, perhaps one of each to each post or farm.

8. I know something of the quality of the cattle and horses; the cattle were of what is called in that country the Spanish breed, very wild and only good for beef; the horses were such as are bred by Indians generally, and of inferior quality. I know nothing about the quality of the sheep.

9. I may state that many of the settlers were followers and discharged employés of the Company, who gave the Company much trouble. Some of them pre-empted the land they were engaged to hold and work for the Company. Large claims were taken, which secured, however, only a comparatively small part for tillage to each farm. A small fertile spot of a few acres was sufficient to locate a farm; that included all the good land, and the full extent of the claim was made up of the best that could be found around the more fertile spot. The Company obtained a contract to supply the military post with fresh beef for several years; I remember the lowest price was thirteen cents, and the highest eighteen cents and a fraction. The Company had sheep-folds located on various parts of the plains, convenient for changing the grazing, which, on account of the poor character of this, had to be done very often. The settlers coming in with more or less stock, together with the stock of the military post, made the grazing very poor for all parties, although, when I left that country, there was not more than one animal to ten acres of open land. I understood the Puget's Sound Agricultural Company to claim from the Nisqually river to the Puyallup river, and from the waters of the Sound to the mountains east. The plains do not cover more than one-fourth of this area, and all the improvements of the Company were confined to the plains; the rest is woodland.

Answers to Cross-Interrogatories.

1. I was stationed, about three months in 1853, and about three years, from February, 1856, to October, 1858, at Fort Steilacoom.

2. I never was engaged in agricultural pursuits on my own account, but some of the duties I had to discharge necessarily rendered me acquainted to some extent with the resources of the country. I sometimes had charge of the post garden, and as quartermaster and commissary, purchased many of the supplies; and, indeed, the post was the principal market for the settlers of the Nisqually Plains.

3. My knowledge of the tract of land is derived, in part, from hunting and fishing excursions, and I am more familiar with the roads mentioned than with any other; but I also rode about a great deal on duty, making purchases, and for other purposes, and the public animals, for which I was responsible, were grazed in part on the plains.

4. During the Indian war, my excursions extended beyond the Nisqually Plains, but my attention was directed to every quality of the country passed through, as we are generally required to make reports of the character of the country passed over, and to furnish maps of the route.

5. All the grounds that were considered good for farming were in the swales and creek-bottoms and the edges of swamps; but very little of it could be called good farming land. I remember only one creek of any extent, Muck Creek and its tributaries; Steilacoom Creek and the creek near Fort Nisqually are short outlets to lakes, and the good land forms a very small portion of the whole tract.

6. I don't think there were as many as 150 settlers on the plains when I last had an opportunity of learning; my opinion is there were fewer than 100.

7. The pasturage could not be considered rich, though the cattle did very well on it till they became too numerous. There was no good pasturage there when I last saw it; it had been eaten off and injured very much.

8. I know quite a number of tracts. The post garden was a tract of seven or eight acres; that made a very good garden for a year or two, but after that required manure. I saw the cultivation and produce of a number of other farms.

9. I know that $50 per month was paid for part of the buildings occupied by the troops. In 1857 the buildings were

so unserviceable that new buildings were erected and the old ones torn down, and the $50 a month was continued for the land on which the post stood, to compensate for the buildings torn down.

10. There were quite a number of buildings at different points on the plains used by the employés of the Company.

11. My estimate of the value of the two new houses exceeds my estimate of the original cost of the fort.

12. I do not remember a good barn. The new dwelling-house I remember, and also the dwellings alluded to.

13. I have had considerable experience in building, and believe I can estimate the cost of building in that country. I had charge of the building of Fort Steilacoom in 1857 and 1858, where the buildings were better and more numerous than at Fort Nisqually, and which cost the United States. Government about $35,000, and I therefore know the cost of all the means and materials used in building at the time I was there. I don't know what it was in 1846, but am of the opinion that the expenses increased very much after the discovery of the gold mines in 1849. The work on the buildings at Fort Nisqually, except the two new houses, was very rough work, and was not done by skilled workmen.

14. I believe I have taken into consideration every element mentioned in the interrogatory, though I have not estimated the money value of the land.

15. I am aware of the fact stated in the interrogatory.

16. Victoria had become quite a market when I was last on Puget's Sound, but I don't think that market materially affected the price of lands on Puget's Sound.

17. I have not fixed the value of the land at any time. I never knew it to have any established value while I was at Fort Steilacoom.

18. I know of no sales of land. I only know of offers to sell claims, and always understood them to be estimated mainly from the amount of improvement on the claim.

19. The Indian hostilities, while I was at Fort Steilacoom, existed only from the time I joined, in February, to July of 1856, and during the time I was active in it.

20. When I was first at Fort Steilacoom, in 1853, I think there were very few American cattle on the plains. Before I left, most of the wild cattle had disappeared, and I know that Dr. Tolmie, the agent of the Company, became quite a dealer in Oregon cattle.

21. The Company had a large number of sheep; I should say three or four thousand, although there may have been more.

22. The settlers used the pasturage all they could.

23. I don't know the number, but the proportion of cattle and sheep to the amount of land was necessarily very small.

24. This is answered in my 23d answer.

25. In 1853, I was Brevet Second Lieutenant. In 1856, and up to the time I left, I was First Lieutenant.

AUGUST V. KAUTZ,
Lt. Col. 34th Infantry, Brev't Maj. Gen'l.

UNITED STATES OF AMERICA, }
   Middle District of Tennessee. }

I, R. McP. Smith, clerk of the United States district court for said district, and commissioned as per the annexed commission by the Hon. Jno. Rose and the Hon. Alex. Johnson, to take the deposition of the witness aforesaid, hereby certify that said deposition, hereto annexed, was taken by me on the annexed interrogatories and cross-interrogatories, pursuant to the within instructions, at my office in Nashville, Tennessee, on November 8, 1866; that the caption prefixed to said deposition is true; that said witness subscribed his name to said deposition in my presence, and that said deposition was reduced to writing by me, and retained unaltered in my possession until mailed in the post office at Nashville by me, as directed per the annexed instructions.

In testimony whereof I subscribe my name hereto and affix the seal of said court this 8th day of November, 1866, and in the ninety-first year of our Independence.

[L. S.]

R. McP. SMITH,
Clerk Dist. Court of the United States
for the Middle District of Tennessee.

BRITISH AND AMERICAN JOINT COMMISSION

HUDSON'S BAY AND PUGET'S SOUND AGRICUL-TURAL COMPANIES' CLAIMS.

————•—•——————

In the matter of the Claim of the Puget's Sound Agricultural Company against the United States.

Deposition of Rear Admiral Charles Wilkes, United States Navy, sworn and examined in the city of Charlotte, county of Mecklenburg, State of North Carolina, in behalf of the United States of America, by virtue of an agreement between Chas. C. Beaman, Jr., Esq., agent and attorney for the United States of America, and Edward Lander, Esq., agent and attorney for the Puget's Sound Company, before me, Chas. Overman, a justice of the peace in and for the city of Charlotte, county of Mecklenburg, State of North Carolina.

TESTIMONY OF REAR ADMIRAL CHARLES WILKES.

Int. 1.—What is your name, residence, and occupation?

Ans.—Charles Wilkes; Washington, D. C.; rear admiral, Navy.

Int. 2.—Were you connected with the Navy in the years 1838, 1839, 1840, 1841, and 1842; and if so, in what particular service were you engaged?

Ans.—Command of the United States Exploring Expedition on a voyage of discovery and survey around the world.

Int. 3.—What report of this expedition has ever been made, and by what authority has it been published?

Ans.—It was made by the direction of the Congress of the United States, and published by their authority, and at the expense of the Government.

Int. 4.—Was the report so published written by you; and, if so, from what was it prepared?

Ans.—It was written by me entire—prepared from my own notes and from official reports made by the officers under me, in the carrying out of orders issued by me.

Int. 5.—During this expedition did you visit Nisqually, a station or fort on Puget's Sound; and, if so, how long did you remain?

Ans.—I did; and remained there upwards of three months, with an interval of a few days' absence, in the year 1841, from April to latter part of July.

Int. 6.—What is its situation?

Ans.—It is situated on a bank two hundred (200) feet high, running back on a level plain to some several miles. Situation of the fort measures about ($\frac{1}{2}$) a half mile.

Int. 7.—What was its value for commercial purposes?

Ans.—Very little; the anchorage is dangerous, from the immediate shelving of the bank to a great depth of water, and an entire exposure to the westerly winds. The bank is very difficult of ascent, and no space at its base to afford any building site.

Int. 8.—Of what did the fort consist?

Ans.—Of a small stockade, two bastions at the corners, two hundred (200) feet square, with a central gate. In the interior there were several wooden buildings, some of logs and others of plank. Attached to the fort was a garden of a few acres.

Int. 9.—What other buildings around the fort, for the purpose of storing grain or folding sheep?

Ans.—At the time of my visit there a few small shanties, probably three or four, a short distance from the fort; but none suitable for granaries. Sheep and cattle were folded at night in movable pens, containing about one acre.

Int. 10.—What was the value of all these buildings—of all the buildings at Nisqually?

Ans.—I should think five thousand dollars ($5,000) would have built them all, including the fort.

Int. 11.—On what knowledge do you found your estimate?

Ans.—Upon the fact of my having built buildings for the

accommodation of my ship's crew, some two hundred men in number, houses for myself and officers, and for making pendulum experiments and observations for drafting, bakeries, and brewing. The space comprised of some six hundred (600) feet square, outside of which was a line of picket houses, some two hundred (200) yards distant, I suppose for the sentries—the whole assuming quite the appearance of a village.

Int. 12.—What number of persons were employed by the Company at Nisqually?

Ans.—I think Mr. Anderson, the officer in charge of the fort, informed me that there were about twenty, (20,) exclusive of the women and children; and, to my own knowledge, there were no more.

(Any statement made by Mr. Anderson to the witness objected to as incompetent.

Int. 13.—How much land had been enclosed by the Company?

Ans.—Besides the garden, there was a field of fifteen or twenty acres of wheat, or some other grain, and, in addition, some two or three hundred (200 or 300) acres being prepared for cultivation by movable pens, but only enclosed. While the fence was there, this last land had not yet been planted.

Int. 14.—What was the character of the soil under cultivation?

Ans.—I should call it a gravelly loam.

Int. 15.—Whether or no it was well adapted to produce grain?

Ans.—I should say *not*, from its deficiency in moisture; this was evident from their being compelled to bring water from the creek for their kitchen and garden, as the season advanced.

Int. 16.—Whether or no the Company used other portions of land about the fort for grazing purposes?

Ans.—The whole country, from the Nisqually river back to East, was entirely open and free—extensive prairies, divided by narrow strips of wood.

Int. 17.—What was the value of this prairie land?

Ans.—I should have been sorry to have given 6¼ cents per

acre; beautiful to look at; clay, gravelly soil; the upper prairie.

Int. 18.—Whether or no the Company claimed any distinct portion of this prairie land besides that you have already described as enclosed?

(Question objected to.)

Ans.—I think they did not; I never heard of any. Two (2) missionaries and their families established themselves within three quarters (¾) of a mile of the fort, on the borders of one of the prairies, with a view of settling there.

Int. 19.—Did the Company object to your using land in that neighborhood for erecting buildings upon, or for cutting timber from; and did they charge you anything for such use?

Ans.—I never heard of any objections; if there were any, they were never intimated to me by any one whatever. I cleared about ten or twelve acres, I suppose, sawed the logs for plank for my houses, and used the wood for firewood for the squadron.

Int. 20.—Whether you know of any map of the Company's claim, as Nisqually, having been made before or being made in the year 1841.

Ans.—I know of none.

Int. 21.—About what number of cattle were there at Nisqually in 1841?

Ans.—I should say there were less than fifty (50.)

Int. 22.—What was the value of these cattle per head, and what particular opportunities did you have during this expedition for judging of the value of cattle in this section?

Ans.—The cattle were few in number, as is shown in the fact of their declining to sell all that belonged to the Company. Dr. McLaughlin presented the crew with two (2) on the 4th of July. I sold cattle belonging to Mr. Slocomb [? Slacum] for ten (10) dollars per head to Dr. McLaughlin, in the Willamette valley, the price fixed upon them by Dr. McLaughlin. This was to close Mr. Slocomb's estate.

Int. 23.—Whether you remember the creeks, Steilacoom and Sequalitchew, and whether there were any mills upon them when you saw them?

Ans.—Steilacoom creek is about seven miles to the north; I doubt whether any person but an Indian had ever been there before our visit.

Int. 24.—What value would you put upon these creeks as water power?

Ans.—Don't consider the water power at all; if turned into them, shows that the country is deficient in streams.

Int. 25.—Whether the country is deficient in streams.

Ans.—Entirely so.

Int. 26.—About how many oak trees were there per acre in the tract of land from the Nisqually river on the one side to the Puyallup river on the other, and back to the coast range of mountains from the Sound?

Ans.—I should think there were about one to three acres.

Int. 27.—What was the average value of an oak tree situated in this tract, and suitable for building purposes?

Ans.—Value was in cutting it down; it then might be found valueless.

Int. 28.—Whether or no you have any particular knowledge for estimating the value of timber in this section?

Ans.—From experience in procuring timber and spars for the squadron, I found a vast many of the trees defective; when cut down, [they] were found useless for our purposes.

Int. 29.—Whether or no the most of the timber at Nisqually was far back from the Sound?

Ans.—There were groves or strips of oaks which divided the open prairie on the Nisqually Plain, but the great body of dense forest rose from the foot of the mountains up their sides.

Int. 30.—Whether you made a map of the country about Nisqually? If so, state whether you marked out or knew of any claim made by the Puget's Sound Company at this post.

Ans.—I made a map of the country, but I never knew or heard of any claim whatever, except, perhaps, to the land occupied by the buildings and under cultivation.

Int. 31.—Are you acquainted with the post or station occupied by the Puget's Sound Agricultural Company, and known as the Cowlitz Farms?

Ans.—I am, as far as two visits to the place would enable me to be so; perhaps one day at each time.

Int. 32.—What is its situation?

Ans.—It is situated on the right bank of the Cowlitz river, on the bank (200) two hundred feet high, and comprises an area of about a square mile.

Int. 33.—What buildings had been erected there by the Company?

Ans.—There were various buildings, consisting of dwelling-houses and barns.

Int. 34.—What would you estimate the cost of all these buildings to have been?

Ans.—I suppose something about three thousand ($3,000) dollars.

Int. 35.—About how much land was under cultivation?

Ans.—About six hundred (600) acres.

Int. 36.—What was the character of this land, and how valuable was it per acre?

Ans.—Its yield was about ten bushels of wheat to the acre. The crop that I saw on the ground, I was told, yielded about twelve. Value about three (3) dollars per acre, judging from this yield.

Int. 37.—What number of cattle and sheep should you estimate the Company to have had at Cowlitz?

Ans.—None but those for agricultural purposes that I saw then; no herds of cattle. When I was there in the dry season, I saw them cutting nutritious flags from across the river; low grounds.

Int. 38.—What kind of boundaries were there to this land which you have described as containing a square mile?

Ans.—Rail and hurdle-fences; outside of the fence were small patches of ground cultivated by the settlers, some distance from the fence.

Int. 39.—How was Cowlitz situated as regards access from Puget's Sound or from the Columbia river?

Ans.—From Puget's Sound, almost impracticable. By the Cowlitz, some three months during a freshet it was navigable for batteaux.

Int. 40.—Do you know anything of the formation and purposes of the Puget's Sound Agricultural Company? If so, state what you know.

Ans.—I do. My knowledge is derived from Dr. McLoughlin, Mr. Ogden, Mr. Douglas, Mr. Anderson, Captain McNeil, and, I think, Mr. Burney, and Mr. Forrest, superintendent of the Cowlitz Farms.

(The statement of any knowledge derived from the persons mentioned, or any statements made to the witness by these persons, objected to as incompetent and irrelevant.)

The charter of the Hudson's Bay Company did not permit them to engage in anything but in the trade of furs and peltries; it was therefore found necessary to organize a new company under the title of the Puget's Sound Agricultural Company, and various localities then in possession of the Hudson's Bay Company were assigned to the Puget's Sound Company, under articles of agreement to supply the Hudson's Bay Company's post with the requisite provisions. The nominal capital of the Company was, I think, five hundred thousand pounds, (£500,000,) to be exclusively taken by the officers and employés of the Hudson's Bay Company. The capital actually paid in was somewhere about twenty thousand (20,000) pounds. The officers of the Puget's Sound Company were those belonging to the Hudson's Bay Company; Dr. McLoughlin was their superintendent. The profits that were expected to accrue were held out as a reward for those who had rendered services in the Hudson's Bay Company.

Int. 41.—Had the Puget's Sound Company, at that time, declared any dividend?

Ans.—I was informed they had not.

Cross-Examination.

Int. 1.—Is all your knowledge of the Company posts derived from your visits to them at the times you have mentioned in the year 1841?

Ans.—It is from myself and officers.

Int. 2.—In the answers which you have made, has your

memory been assisted by any reference whatever to the report, which you state was written by you, of an exploring expedition?

Ans.—No.

Int. 3.—Have you seen the report made by you within the last few days, and.have you examined it at all, in the parts which have reference to the lands and farms and buildings of the Puget's Sound Agricultural Company?

Ans.—I have seen it, in volumes, in the last few days; naturally spoken of them in my family. I had not examined it with reference to that part; I made a cursory view of it.

Int. 4.—How long after the time you saw these posts of the Company was this report written?

Ans.—I kept a diary during the expedition, of every day's proceedings and occurrences throughout the whole time embraced in the publication, written daily, before I retired to rest. It had been my practice long before the expedition, and has been ever since.

Int. 5.—Does this report embody a correct and accurate transcript of the substance of your diary, made by you in reference to the lands, farms, buildings, and stock of the Puget's Sound Agricultural Company?

Ans.—Of my own diary, as well as the official reports of the officers and scientific corps under my orders and attached to the expedition.

Int. 6.—Was this statement made by you in your report, about the station at Nisqually, as follows: "Near by were to be seen fine fields of grain, large barns and sheep-folds, agricultural implements, and workmen with cattle engaged in the various employments of husbandry?" If so, what portion of this statement is of your own personal knowledge, and what portion is derived from official reports?

Ans.—It is in my report. It is all my own knowledge, but it must be taken comparatively of my own situation and that of country. Large barns would be comparative, as to the size, in a new country, and the number of cattle would be so considered, although they did not embrace more than fifty (50) head.

Int. 7.—Did you make use of this language in your report, in speaking of the garden at Fort Nisqually: "Here I saw peas a foot high, strawberries and gooseberries in full bloom, and some of the former nearly ripe, with salad that had gone to seed three feet high, and very large and thrifty?"

Ans.—Yes, sir.

Int. 8.—Did you make use of this language in your report, speaking of the fort, and how much of it was derived from your own personal knowledge: "It is constructed of pickets, enclosing the space, about two hundred (200) feet square, with four (4) corner bastions; within this enclosure are the agent's stores and about half a dozen houses, built of logs and roofed with bark?

Ans.—I made use of this language in my report; it is my personal knowledge.

Int. 9.—In speaking of the Company's establishment at Nisqually, did you make use in your report of this language, and how much of it is of your personal knowledge: "In connection with the Company's establishment at Nisqually they have a large dairy, several hundred head of cattle, and among them seventy (70) milch cows. They have also large crops of wheat, peas, and oats?"

Ans.—I made use of this language; that is derived from Mr. Anderson, the superintendent.

Int. 10.—Did you not see a dairy at or near the Company's establishment?

Ans.—No, sir.

Int. 11.—You have stated in your examination-in-chief that the cattle were few in number, and less than fifty, (50.) In making this answer, do you wish to be understood as saying that there were not more than fifty (50) cattle belonging to the Company at Nisqually, or that you yourself only saw fifty, (50)?

Ans.—I wish to be understood as saying that I only saw fifty (50), and of my own knowledge. In the part of the report referred to, in interrogatory 9, I gave the number derived from others, good authority, as I believe, but I deemed it somewhat exaggerated, for I saw no force large enough to take care of and milk so many cows.

Int. 12.—You have stated in answer to interrogatory 13 that there was a field of fifteen (15) or twenty (20) acres of wheat or some other grain. Do you wish to be understood as saying that there were not other fields in which were large crops of wheat, peas, and oats, or only that this field was the only one you saw near the fort and garden?

Ans.—It was the only one I saw, nor did I hear of any other.

Int. 13.—Have you made use in your report of this language: "It is also their intention, when they shall have succeeded in breeding a sufficient stock of cattle and sheep, to export hides, horns, tallow, and wool to England in the return ships. In this way it may readily be perceived that they will be enabled to drive a profitable trade, particularly when it is considered how little care the cattle require in this Territory, in consequence of the grass and natural hay which the soil affords at seasons?" If so, are you now of the same opinion as to the profitable trade which you have expressed?

Ans.—I am not of the same opinion now, as cultivation destroys the natural grasses.

Int. 14.—In the same report, did you make use of this language: "These operations are conducted by [a] farmer and dairyman brought from England?" If so, did you see this farmer and dairyman, or either of them?

Ans.—I made use of this language. That these persons were there, I learned from Mr. Anderson.

Int. 15.—In the report, have you made use of this language: "A few Indians are engaged in attending the flocks?" If so, did you see these Indians thus engaged?

Ans.—That information is likewise obtained from Mr. Anderson.

Int. 16.—In the report, did you make use of this language: "A large supply of milk was also sent to us daily from the dairy, and many other little kindnesses and attentions were received?" If so, do you wish now to make the same statement?

Ans.—I made use of this language. The supply of milk was two (2) pails full, I think, which was a large supply for myself and officers. I presume it came from the dairy. The other little kindnesses were cranberries, gooseberries, and lettuce.

Int. 17.—Were you at Nisqually during the time of harvest?

Ans.—I think I must have been.

Int. 18.—Did you not receive from the officers of the Puget's Sound Agricultural Company all the attention in their power; and did they not afford you every facility that they could in carrying out the objects of your expedition?

Ans.—For the first week, I did not. I understood from the gentlemen that they were precluded from giving me aid until they received instructions from Vancouver. Afterwards, in arranging my traveling parties, procuring horses from the Indians, and giving us models and instructions for making saddles for the horses, they were very kind. As regards the surveying duties, they afforded me no assistance.

Int. 19.—Was there any government in the country when you were there?

Ans.—There was none, nor did I look for any.

Int. 20.—How many vessels, and how large a force of men, had you while at Nisqually?

Ans.—A sloop-of-war and a brig-of-war, with two (2) launches and some ten (10) boats. The crews comprised upwards of three hundred (300) men.

Int. 21.—Did you ever ask the officers of the Company at Nisqually to point out the boundaries of their claim, or did you ever have any conversation with them in reference to it?

Ans.—I never asked the officers of the Company relative to any claim they had. I know and believe they had none. I had frequent conversation with the officers of the Company upon the subject of my explorations and the tenure of the country. In all of them they never gave me any intimation relative to any rights they possessed in the country.

Int. 22.—Did you ask their leave to occupy and use the landing and road, or to cut timber?

Ans.—Never.

Int. 23.—How far from Nisqually Plains was it to the places where you sold the cattle of the deceased Mr. Slocomb [Slacum] for ten ($10) dollars per head, and was the communication between the two places easy and secure?

Ans.—The cattle were at Willamette Valley, where the most active operations, at that time, were going on; and I presume the cattle were more valuable there than at any distant post. The distance from Willamette Valley to Nisqually may be one hundred and fifty (150) miles.

Int. 24.—In answer to interrogatory 30, you stated you made a map of the country about Nisqually; was that map the result of your own observations, or was it made from the examination of your officers?

Ans.—Of course it was made by the examinations of myself and of my officers, under my directions.

Int. 25.—Was not the map you speak of a general map of the whole country, within one hundred (100) or more miles of the coast?

Ans.—It extended back to the Blue Mountains, nearly three hundred (300) miles from the coast. The map was a general map, made up of particular maps.

Int. 26.—Did you ever cross Steilacoom Creek on the plains going to the eastward?

Ans.—I may have frequently done so without knowing its name.

Int. 27.—Do you recollect crossing over any creeks on the Nisqually Plains, except the creek near your encampment?

Ans.—I do.

Int. 28.—Did you see a lake or lakes on these plains?

Ans.—I saw some small ponds.

Int. 29.—How long did you stop at the Cowlitz Farm the first time you visited it; at what time of the day did you arrive, and at what time did you leave?

Ans.—I was there nine or ten hours during daylight; I arrived about 9 a. m., and left about 7 p. m., the same day.

Int. 30.—Is this statement as to your being there in the day, and the time you were there at your first visit, from your distinct recollection, or is it derived from an examination just made by you of your report?

Ans.—It is derived from my distinct recollection, corrobo-
17 P

rated by the astronomical observations I took while I was there, for both longitude and latitude.

Int. 31.—Your statement then is, that the examination of the report has not refreshed your memory?

Ans.—It will be very difficult to decide; but reading the paragraph confirms me in my recollection, having recalled the observations made, and the result of them, in latitude and longitude.

Int. 32.—Did you, in your report, make use, in reference to the Cowlitz Farm, of this language: "At this farm the Company have a large dairy; large numbers of cattle were being brought in for the night." If so, what portion of the statement is of your own personal knowledge?

Ans.—There are two distinct paragraphs of my report. The first, about the dairy, is derived from Mr. Forrest, the superintendent; the second is from a view of some fifty or sixty cattle coming in, as we passed towards the landing, about one mile distant below the farm. The reason for driving them in, which, derived from Plumondon, follows in the report; these may have been those I saw before in the early part of the day.

Int. 33.—Were these the only cattle you saw at Cowlitz at either visit?

Ans.—I recollect seeing no other cattle in a body.

Int. 34.—Were you at the Cowlitz at the time the wheat was cut, or when it was threshed?

Ans.—I don't think I was.

Int. 35.—Do you consider yourself competent, from seeing wheat growing in the field, to estimate the number of bushels produced to the acre?

Ans.—I think I do.

Int. 36.—Did you, at the time, estimate the amount of bushels to the acre of the wheat you saw growing at Cowlitz Farm?

Ans.—Mr. Forrest told me that the field would yield ten bushels of wheat to the acre; my estimate, from the appearance of the crop, was much less.

Int. 37.—Did any one else tell you that the crop yielded more than ten bushels to the acre?

Ans.—Both Mr. Drayton and Mr. Walden, [? Waldron] of my party, who were associated with me, thought less favorably of the crop than I did. I see in a note to my report now before me, that the crop of 1841, at the end of the season, produced seventhousand (7,000) bushels. I presume I got this from Mr. Douglas or Mr. McLoughlin, or some one in high authority.

Int. 38.—In your report, have you used this language in reference to the Cowlitz Farm: "The grounds appear well prepared, and were covered with a luxuriant crop of wheat?"

Ans.—Yes, sir; I did use it in writing of the landscape view.

Int. 39.—In this report, did you make use of this language in speaking of the Cowlitz Farm; "With several large granaries, a large farm-house, and numerous out-buildings to accommodate the daily workmen, cattle, *et cetera?*" If so, how much of the statement is derived from your personal observation?

Ans.—I used the language in the report. I say now, that in the word "large," which was used relative to the new country, elsewhere, in a settled community, they might be deemed small and insignificant.

Int. 40.—In your report, did you make use of this language: "The superintendent's dwelling is large, and built of well-hewn logs, with workmen's houses, *et cetera;* it forms quite a village?" If so, is that statement all derived from your personal knowledge?

Ans.—It is my own personal knowledge. I made use of the language, "The degree of progress resembled that of a settlement of several years' standing in our Western States, with the exception, however, of the remains of the conquered forest. Here the ground was ready for the plough, and nature seems as it were to invite the husbandman to his labors."

Int. 41.—At your second visit to the Cowlitz Farm, how long did you remain there, what time did you arrive, and at what time did you leave?

Ans.—I must have remained there about twenty-four hours. I arrived on one morning, and departed the next.

Re-Examination.

Int. 1.—Whether or no you visited any Mission station near the fort at Nisqually? If so, state what you saw.

Ans.—I visited the station of Mr. Richmond and Mr. Wilson. On the borders of the prairie, three-quarters of a mile east of Fort Nisqually, there were two comfortable log cabins, in which they had located.

Int. 2.—Whether or no you used this language in your report in regard to the soil: "This is composed of a light brown earth, intermixed with a large portion of gravel and stones. It requires an abundance of rain to bring a crop to perfection;" and whether or no you made this of your own knowledge, and now remember the same to be as accurate and true?

Ans.—I made use of this language. I made my own observations, and know it to be accurate and true.

(The above question and answer thereto are objected to, as incompetent and irrelevant.)

Int. 3.—Do you think that cattle could swim across the Columbia river when it is low?

Ans.—Yes.

(Question and answer objected to, as incompetent and irrelevant.)

Cross-Examination Resumed.

Int. 1.—How much rain, if any, fell during your stay at Nisqually?

Ans.—I think there was very little rain during our visit there.

Int. 2.—Were not the trees which you cut down to make spars for the Vincennes, and which proved to be more or less defective, cut at Fort Discovery, a harbor on the Straits of Fuca?

Ans.—Many of them were.

Int. 3.—Did you not, by letter from Fort Discovery, request the officers of the Company to send you a pilot? And were you joined at Pilot's Cove by the first mate of the Hudson's Bay Company's steamer, sent down to pilot up your ship?

Ans.—I wrote a note, and sent it up by an Indian, asking for a pilot. I therefore proceeded in the Vincennes up the Admiralty Inlet some sixty or seventy miles, where I anchored for the night at Pilot's Cove for the tide. Early the next morning the man joined me, who reported that he had come down to act as pilot. From this circumstance I called the place Pilot's Cove. In conversation with him I soon found that he was ignorant of a pilot's duties.

Int. 4.—Have you not stated, in speaking of your arrival at Nisqually and anchoring there, "That twelve miles more brought us to the anchorage off Nisqually, where both vessels dropped their anchors about 8 o'clock. Here we found an English steamer undergoing repairs. Soon after we anchored I had the pleasure of a visit from Mr. Anderson, who is in charge of the fort, and Capt. McNeil. They gave me a warm welcome, and offered me every assistance in their power to aid me in my operations?"

Ans.—That is a correct extract from my report; but as I imagine it may have been misunderstood, I will add a few words in explanation. From Mr. Anderson I learned that the receipt of my note by the Indian created a great surprise; and from the Indian's description they thought a large military expedition had arrived in their waters. They had great hesitancy about sending me a pilot, and forthwith dispatched messengers to Vancouver to know what their course of action should be. We were nearly a week from Fort Discovery in reaching Puget's Sound. Mr. Anderson and Capt. McNeil determined to send the mate of the steamer to Fort Discovery on their own responsibility. Told me that they thought that my ship would not move from there. I was half way up the Sound when he met me. Capt. McNeil admitted to me that he was little of a pilot; and I am well satisfied now if he had had the ship in charge she would have been wrecked in passing through the narrows. Personally, these gentlemen extended to me all the civilities I could wish for or expected. But they distinctly told me they had to await their orders from Vancouver. The messenger arrived the day after their interview.

Int. 5.—Was there not, at the time of your arrival at Nisqually,- a well-constructed road, of easy ascent, going up the hill-side at the landing?

Ans.—There was. I never used it; but I made a better one to my own encampment.

Int. 6.—Have you not, in reference to the establishment of an observatory, made this statement: "A suitable site was found on the top of the hill within hail of the ship. Here the instruments and tocks [? books] were landed, and put up in a small clearing, whence the trees had been cut in order to supply the steamer with fuel?"

Ans.—I have, sir, in my official report. The place is not near the road nor the landing.

Int. 7.—Did not Mr. Anderson, on the 13th of May, and within two or three days of your arrival at Nisqually, present you with two bullocks for the crews, and a quantity of vegetables?

Ans.—He did; it is so stated in my report.

Int. 8.—Was not the ox which was barbecued on the 5th of July sold to you by the Company's agent?

Ans.—Yes. The present of two oxen I looked upon as something like a peace offering, when they had become satisfied that our object was not warlike, and the gift had no doubt emanated from Vancouver.

Int. 9.—Did Dr. McLoughlin arrive at Nisqually before the morning of the day after the celebration, the morning of the 6th?

Ans.—He did not arrive before the morning of the 6th, as he was detained on the way.

Int. 10.—Have you not stated, in reference to the farm at Nisqually, that "on this farm there were about two hundred acres of land under cultivation, which I was informed would yield (15) fifteen bushels of wheat to the acre?"

Ans.—I have made this statement in my report. The (15) fifteen bushels to the acre refers to fifteen or twenty acres or the acres that were sown in wheat. The rest was being prepared for cultivation.

Int. 11.—Have you not, in speaking of the future prospects of the Puget's Sound Company, made use of this language: "[In] the event, however, of the country becoming the abode of a civilized community, the farms and other land possessed by this Company must become very valuable, as the posts occupy all the points most favorably situated for trade, and the agricultural establishments have been placed in the best position for farming operations?"

Ans.—I have made this statement. It is an extract from my published report.

CHARLES WILKES.

CITY OF CHARLOTTE, }
County of Mecklenburg, State of North Carolina. }

I, Charles Overman, a justice of the peace in and for the county and State aforesaid, do hereby certify that the foregoing deposition, hereto annexed, of Rear Admiral Charles Wilkes, United States Navy, a witness produced by and on behalf of the United States of America, in defence to the claims made against the United States by the Puget's Sound Agricultural Company before the British and American Joint Commission for the adjustment of the same, was taken before me, at the office of the First National Bank of Charlotte, in the city of Charlotte, North Carolina, and reduced to writing, under my direction, and in my personal presence, by P. P. Zimmerman, a person agreed upon by Chas. C. Beaman, Jr., Esq., attorney for the United States, and Edward Lander, Esq., attorney for said Company, beginning on the 31st day of December, A. D. 1866, continuing from day to day, until 4th day of January, 1867, when it was signed according to the date appended to said deposition.

I further certify that said deposition was taken before me, in pursuance of the written agreement, hereto annexed, between said Chas. C. Beaman, Jr., Esq., and Edward Lander, Esq.

I further certify that to said witness, before his examination, I administered the following oath:

"You swear that the evidence which you shall give in the matter of the claim of the ‚Puget's Sound Agricultural Company against the United States of America shall be the truth, the whole truth, and nothing but the truth, so help you God."

That after the same was reduced to writing, the deposition was carefully read to, and then signed by said witness.

I further certify that Edward Lander, Esq., attorney for said Company, was personally present during the examination and cross-examination of said witness, and the reading and signing of his deposition.

In testimony whereof I have hereunto set my hand at said office, the 4th day of January, A. D. 1867.

CHARLES OVERMAN, J. P.

CITY OF CHARLOTTE, }
County of Mecklenburg, State of North Carolina. }

Puget's Sound Company in the Matter against the United States in the above cause.

It is agreed by the undersigned that the testimony of Rear Admiral Wilkes, United States Navy, a witness produced by and on behalf of the United States of America, in defence to the claims made against the United States by the Puget's Sound Agricultural Company before the British and American Joint Commission for the adjustment of the same, shall be taken before Charles Overman, a justice of the peace for and in the county and State aforesaid, this 31st day of December, A. D. 1866.

EDWARD LANDER,
Of Counsel for Hudson's Bay Company.
CHARLES C. BEAMAN, Jr.,
Attorney for the United States.

BRITISH AND AMERICAN JOINT COMMISSION

ON THE

HUDSON'S BAY AND PUGET'S SOUND AGRICULTURAL COMPANIES' CLAIMS.

---•••---

In the matter of the Claim of the Puget's Sound Agricultural Company against the United States.

Deposition of Simpson P. Moses, taken at the request and in behalf of the United States, by agreement between C. C. Beaman, on behalf of the United States, and Edward Lander, on behalf of the Puget's Sound Agricultural Company.

TESTIMONY OF SIMPSON P. MOSES.

Int. 1.—What is your name, place of residence, and present occupation?

Ans.—Simpson P. Moses; Washington city, D. C.; am a lawyer by profession.

Int. 2.—Have you resided in Washington Territory; if yea, when, where, and how long?

Ans.—I have, at Olympia, the now capital of Washington Territory, from the 10th November, 1851, to middle of August, 1856.

Int. 3.—How were you employed, or what office did you hold while at Olympia?

Ans.—I was the United States collector of customs for the district of Puget's Sound, of which district Olympia was then the port of entry. This office I held from November, 1851, to 27th September, 1853.

Int. 4.—Are you acquainted with the tract of land in Washington Territory called the Nisqually Plains?

Ans.—I have been to Fort Nisqually several times, and have rode over the plains several times.

Int. 5.—What was the character of the post at Fort Nisqually?

Ans.—Within the picket enclosure, about one hundred feet square or more, there was a very comfortable residence, occupied by the gentleman in charge, Dr. Tolmie. I remember a ware-house; it was a log building; it is adapted to contain one year's supply for their trade. There were some smaller buildings, occupied by the employés; also an old building used for storing hides and wool for shipment.

Int. 6.—To what time does your description of the buildings at Nisqually refer, and what would you estimate the cost and value of all these buildings to have been?

Ans.—The summer of 1853. There was great difference in the age of the buildings; while some were crumbling with decay, others were in pretty good order. I think the original cost of all the buildings, including the picket, did not exceed $10,000. The buildings, at the time I saw them, would, I think, have been worth to any one who needed them $3,000.

Int. 7.—What was the character of the soil about Nisqually?

Ans.—It was very inferior, gravelly, and well exhausted. The growth of sorrel seemed to have destroyed the fertility of the land.

Int. 8.—What would you estimate to have been the value per acre of the land at Nisqually?

Ans.—I should consider the value of the Company's claim, regarding part of it as fertile and the other part as sterile, at $1 per acre. The value of these lands fluctuated with the hopes or disappointments of increased population. The value I have given to the lands around Nisqually is the average of different years.

Int. 9.—What would you estimate to have been the number of oak trees per acre on the Company's claim around Nisqually?

Ans.—Liberal to say two trees to an acre.

Int. 10.—What was the character of these trees, and what were they worth, considering their position?

Ans.—The quality of the oak through that region is very inferior, scrubby; many of what I called oak trees would not be considered trees of any value in an oak country. These trees were of no value, except where knees might be obtained for ship-timber. Most of the value of these trees was in the labor of cutting them and expense of hauling them.

Int. 11.—In estimating the value of the land and the number of trees on the land claimed by the Company at Nisqually, are your answers applicable to the whole claim of the Company at Nisqually, as is marked out on the map now shown you?

Ans.—They are.

Int. 12.—Are you acquainted with the station of the Puget's Sound Agricultural Company known as the Cowlitz Farms?

Ans.—To a limited degree only; the lands are of good quality, excellent. Though I have heard of estimation of lands in that locality at from $10 to $20 per acre, yet I have never known or heard of any sales over $10 per acre.

Int. 13.—State whether you know anything about the cattle claimed by the Company at Nisqually.

Ans.—Yes; the Company made shipments of cattle to Vancouver Island. They furnished beef two years or more to the town of Olympia. They also had contract for, and furnished beef to the forces at Fort Steilacoom. The cattle furnished at Olympia had to be shot like deer. The cattle had become wild, and were of inferior breed. During the very severe winter of 1852–3, the quality of the beef furnished was very poor. During this severe winter of 1852–3 the American settlers lost a large portion of their cattle. Hon. Gilmore Hays and his associates, American settlers, had a large number of cattle, and they lost nearly all of them. They lost $40,000 worth of cattle. As they took more care of their cattle than the Company did of theirs, the Company must have sustained a severe loss in cattle that winter. The snow was two feet two inches deep for several weeks.

Int. 14.—State whether or no the cattle sent by the Company to Vancouver's Island were raised by the Company.

Ans.—They were, to a great extent; but Dr. Tolmie, the officer in charge for the Company at Nisqually, purchased of the American settlers' their improved stock of cattle, and shipped them also to Vancouver's Island. The cattle of their own raising, shipped by the Company, were for consumption, and not for breeding.

Int. 15.—State whether or no the Puget's Sound Agricultural Company used Steilacoom or Nisqually as a harbor.

Ans.—They used Nisqually.

Int. 16.—What do you know of the various prices which have been asked and obtained for lands in Washington Territory?

Ans.—There were no perfected titles in the American settlers until about 1855. The claimants of land held under the donation act, which required a five years' residence, many of them after residing on their lands some time, and spending all their earnings on the improvements, sold for a very much less sum than they had expended in the improvements.

Int. 17.—State whether or no lands were held at high prices at the time you were on the Pacific coast; and whether or no they have since been sold for a much less price.

Ans.—The depreciation of the price of lands has been very great. The population of the country has not increased.

Int. 18.—State whether or no you were ever acquainted with any lands owned by R. M. Walker, in Thurston county, Washington Territory. If so, state whether or not parts of that were more valuable than average lands in the Territory, and why.

Ans.—The lands owned by R. M. Walker were on the main route of travel, were near the saw-mills, and were also about one mile from Olympia, the capital of the Territory, and they were well timbered with fir and cedar.

Simpson P. Moses.

Examination Resumed.

Int. 19.—Whether or not you know one William B. Bolton, a witness examined in behalf of the Puget's Sound Agricultural Company against the United States, a resident of Pierce county, Washington Territory, who describes himself in his direct-examination on behalf of the Company as a "shipwright," and having resided in Pierce county from 1850 to 1859.

Ans.—I do know said William B. Bolton.

Int. 20.—Whether or not you are acquainted with said Bolton's claim below Steilacoom.

Ans.—Yes, I am acquainted with the fact that he was the occupant of a land-claim below Steilacoom.

Int. 21.—Whether or no there were any three acres of ground, or any thirty acres, in any one section of the land occupied by Bolton, or any other land upon the plain between the Nisqually and Puyallup rivers, from which four hundred oak trees suitable for shipping could have been cut.

(Mr. Lander objects to this question as incompetent.)

Ans.—I Have visited Bolton's claim several times. From my observation and information I have no reason to believe that such a number of oak trees suitable for shipping purposes could have been cut from thirty acres of land in the locality referred to, or any where in that part of the country.

Int. 22.—What do you know of the shipment of oak trees by said Bolton during the years 1852, 1853, and 1854?

Ans.—My answer cannot come down later than September, 1853, up to which time, commencing at November, 1851, when vessels were being loaded at, opposite, and in the vicinity of Steilacoom by contractors, to furnish cargoes of piles, and so forth, for shipment, Bolton had sub-contracts to furnish small numbers of ship-knees.

(Mr. Lander objects to the above answer as incompetent.)

Int. 23.—Can you estimate the number of knees shipped by said Bolton during the time above referred to by you, and do you know from what tract of country they were obtained?

Ans.—I estimate about 200. They were obtained from land claimed by himself, and also from land of the United States.

Int. 24.—What would be the average height of the branches of the oak trees on the claim set up by the Puget's Sound

Agricultural Company, and what was the character of these trees; what were they used for, and what were they fit for?

Ans.—Regarding every oak scrub as a tree, a liberal estimate would be six feet to the branches. These trees were stubbled, scrubby, and of the most inferior quality; and whilst it is possible to procure a few joints for ship-knees, I consider the oak trees to have had no other use except for fuel. In that part of the country oak had, as fuel, only a nominal value.

Int. 25.—What do you know of Bolton's ship-yard, the vessels built by him, and what he proposed to use as knees?

Ans.—He had a ship-yard of limited capacity, adapted to such repairs as vessels might require, and to the building of small craft suitable for trade about the Sound. I remember his building two or three small vessels of the kind already alluded to in this answer. Bolton told me, in reply to my remark about the scarcity of oak, that from the roots of the fir trees he could get good enough ship-knees.

(Mr. Lander objects to the statements made by Bolton as incompetent.)

Int. 26.—Are you acquainted with what is known as Steilacoom creek? If so, say of what size it is.

Ans.—Yes; I have been up Steilacoom creek different times. I think a dock might be made up there; but large vessels entering that dock at spring tide would have to wait for another spring tide to make their exit. But I consider there are better locations for docks in those waters.

Int. 27.—How wide and how deep is Steilacoom creek at its mouth at an average tide?

Ans.—I should say about 100 feet wide. Ordinarily the creek is shallow.

Int. 28.—What is the average rise of tide at Steilacoom?

Ans.—My recollection is about 12 or 13 feet.

Int. 29.—Are you acquainted with the land claim of M. Walker, situated in Thurston county, Washington Territory?

Ans.—I am. His land was along the main road about one mile from Olympia, the capital of the Territory, about half a mile from the sawmills at Newmarket, and was a timbered claim.

Int. 30.—What, considering the location of Walker's claim in regard to Olympia and the sawmills, would be the value of the timber on an average acre of this claim?

(Mr. Lander objects to this question as argumentative and leading.)

Ans.—Though the country generally is so abundantly supplied with timber, I regard this claim as valuable, worth say $15 an acre, from its proximity to the two towns and sawmills, which had exhausted to a great degree the other timber in reach at moderate expense of hauling.

Int. 31.—What harbor or anchorage did the Hudson's Bay Company use for their vessels in Puget's Sound?

Ans.—The harbor of Nisqually, in front of their own road and warehouse.

Int. 32.—Whether or no the Puget's Sound Agricultural Company had to your knowledge ever cut any road from Steilacoom down to the water?

Ans.—I do not know of their ever having made such road.

Int. 33.—What was the breed and character of the Company's cattle on the plains?

Ans.—The officers of the Company told me the cattle were of the Spanish breed.

(Mr. Lander objects to the statements of the officers of the Company on this subject.)

Int. 34.—What do you know of flocks of sheep sent by the Company or its officers from Nisqually?

Ans.—The Company sent two or three large droves of sheep from Nisqually to Oregon for sale, and parties from California came to Nisqually and purchased sheep for the California market. The Company also sent a flock of sheep to San Juan island, and the impression at the time was that it was done to take possession of the island.

Cross-Examination.

Int. 1.—At the time you went to Fort Nisqually, did you go by boat or on horseback?

Ans.—Sometimes by boat and sometimes on horseback.

Int. 2.—How many times were you there on horseback?

Ans.—Half a dozen times.

Int. 3.—At any one of those times that you were at the fort on horseback did you go beyond the fort, and if so, in what direction and where to?

Ans.—North and west. I went to Fort Steilacoom, Judge Chambers' farm, and a place occupied by a man named Myers.

Int. 4.—Are not Fort Steilacoom and Chambers' farm near together and both in a northern direction from Fort Nisqually?

Ans.—They are near together, and are both in a northern direction from Nisqually.

Int. 5.—In what direction is the house of Myers from Fort Nisqually, and how far distant is it?

Ans.—It is about east of north, and about the same distance from Fort Nisqually as Fort Steilacoom is, according to my recollection.

Int. 6.—How far to the northward of Fort Steilacoom or Chambers' farm have you been on horseback?

Ans.—I presume I have not been beyond Chambers' farm to the northward. This was about the extent of my rambles on horseback. I have been by boat on the Sound to the mouth of the Puyallup, where I walked about in the timber. This point, by water, was about 12 or 14 miles from Bolton's place.

Int. 7.—Where and on what part of the Company's claim, and in riding over what road, did you see the growth of sorrel you have spoken of?

Ans.—Upon that portion of the Company's claim, stretching out eastwardly and northeastwardly from Fort Nisqually, the land is red with it as far as the eye can reach. I saw this in riding along the main road from Olympia, via Fort Nisqually, to Fort Steilacoom.

Int. 8.—Did you observe the oak trees around Nisqually as you rode along the main road you have mentioned?

Ans.—I think I observed all the oak trees from the crossing of the Nisqually river to as far north as I stated I have traveled on horseback.

Int. 9.—In averaging the size of oak trees seen by you, have you taken to account the oak brush or small trees along the side of the road between the Nisqually river and Fort Nisqually?

Ans.—I have.

Int. 10.—Have you ever walked upon the Nisqually Plains; if so, to what distance, and on what occasion?

Ans.—I have walked upon the plains between Fort Nisqually and the Nisqually landing, when I visited there by boat, on a number of occasions.

Int. 11.—How far is the house of Mr. Bolton from Olympia?

Ans.—About twenty-five or twenty-eight miles.

Int. 12.—How far below the present town of Steilacoom?

Ans.—About three or four miles.

Int. 13.—Did you not always go to the ship-yard of Bolton by boat?

Ans.—I did.

Int. 14.—State how many times you visited that ship-yard by boat.

Ans.—Three or four times.

Int. 15.—The first time you visited there, where were you going, and on what business?

Ans.—In December, 1851; I was there on a visit to Steilacoom, to charter a vessel for the relief of shipwrecked persons on Queen Charlotte Islands.

Int. 16.—What time of the day were you at Bolton's ship-yard and house?

Ans.—It was late in the afternoon.

Int. 17.—How long did you remain there?

Ans.—Not over one-half to three-quarters of an hour.

Int. 18.—What were you doing while you were there?

Ans.—Conversing with Bolton.

Int. 19.—When did you make your second visit to Bolton?

Ans.—I cannot so definitely fix the time of this visit; but, to the best of my recollection, it was in April, 1852.

Int. 20.—Where were you going at that time, and on what business?

Ans.—On that trip I traveled about 500 miles in my open boat, on a general trip of reconnoisance through my district.

18 P

Int. 21.—How long did you stop at Mr. Bolton's on this occasion ?

Ans.—About half an hour.

Int. 22.—When was the next occasion you visited Bolton's, and on what business ?

Ans.—I can only answer this by saying that I was there on subsequent occasions, but cannot fix the times.

Int. 23.—Can you state the time of day, or the length of time of your visits to Bolton's on the occasions subsequent to your two first visits ?

Ans.—My visits to Mr. Bolton's place were generally early in the morning or late in the afternoon, on account of my making Steilacoom my stopping place for the night.

Int. 24.—Did you find any horses at Bolton's to ride out into the country upon ?

Ans.—I did not.

Int. 25.—Is not the residence of Mr. Bolton immediately at the ship-yard, and in a small clearing made in large and thick fir woods ?

Ans.—It is, according to my recollection.

Int. 26.—Did you go on foot through that timber until you came to the prairie on any occasion; if so, on which of your visits was it ?

Ans.—I never penetrated to the prairie from Bolton's landing, though I went some distance into the timber.

Int. 27.—Are not the woods near Mr. Bolton's house, and along the shores of the Sound near it, of very heavy and thick fir trees ?

Ans.—The growth along there is very dense, and of large firs, though there had been some thinning out of piles or ship's spars for shipment.

Int. 28.—Were not the vessels employed in the lumber trade sailing generally under a coasting license ?

Ans.—The majority of them were. There were some trading with foreign ports that were registered.

Int. 29.—Do you not know that vessels sailing under a coasting license do not send manifests of their cargo to the collector of the district from which they sail ?

Ans.—I know that they are required to exhibit their manifests, when called upon, to the officers of the customs, and that it was the usage to call for them in my district.

Int. 30.—Is your knowledge of the shipments of Mr. Bolton derived from the manifests called for by you or your officers?

Ans.—I speak of the shipments of oak made by various persons, but furnished by Bolton, my information being derived from the manifests.

(Mr. Lander objects to this as not responsive to the question.)

Int. 31.—Had piles, ship-knees, or oak timbers been purchased of Mr. Bolton for shipment from the district, and delivered by him, would not the manifests show these articles in the name of the purchaser and shipper?

Ans.—They would appear in the name of the shipper. Most, if not all the oak furnished to shippers in that locality was by Bolton.

Int. 32.—Is not the difference between extreme high and extreme low water at Olympia about 18 feet?

Ans.—I should think so.

Int. 33.—Is not the claim of R. M. Walker separated from the main road by the claim of Mr. Crosby?

Ans.—I always thought Walker's claim extended out to the road.

Int. 34.—Was not the dwelling-house of Mr. Walker about one-fourth of a mile from the road?

Ans.—It is some distance from the road, but not, I think, so far.

Int. 35.—Are there not between Mr. Walker's claim and Sylvester's claim, on the north half of which the town of Olympia is situated, the land claims of Offutt and of Wilson?

Ans.—Yes.

Cross-Examination Resumed, February 15, 1867.

Int. 36.—What was the population of the place called Tum-water or Newmarket in 1854–'5?

Ans.—I should suppose from 100 to 150.

Int. 37.—Are not the trees growing on the land around the town of Olympia and on Walker's claim generally of too large a size for the purpose of making what are called saw-logs?

Ans.—I think not generally, though some of them are.

Int. 38.—Do you know yourself what distance logs can be hauled on land to be paid for at the usual price at Puget's Sound?

Ans.—From a half to one mile, anywhere in the vicinity of Tum-water mills. When I was there choice timber was then worth about $23 a thousand. This is stated according to the best of my recollection.

Int. 39.—Is not the whole of the east half of Walker's claim more than a mile from any saw-mill?

Ans.—I think his front line is about half a mile from the mill, or perhaps not so far.

Int. 40.—What would it cost, from your experience, to clear an acre of timbered land on Walker's claim so as to render it free from stumps?

Ans.—Upon a claim so conveniently located the saw-logs and cord-wood have a marketable value. The destruction of the refuse and eradication of the stumps would then cost many times more than the land would sell for after being cleared. Much land is cultivated in that country without being entirely cleared.

Int. 41.—Do you know of any, or did you yourself ever make, or cause to be made, any soundings at the mouth of Steilacoom creek?

Ans.—I never did.

Int. 42.—Have your statements with reference to the shipments of oak timber been confined to times anterior to September, 1853?

Ans.—They were.

Cross-Examination Resumed, May 27th, 1867.

Int. 1.—In your examination-in-chief you have spoken of the cattle of the Hon. Gilmore Hays that were killed by the severe weather during the winter season. Do you not know that these cattle, at the time you speak of, were near the Dalles, in a section of the country separated from the Puget's Sound section by the Cascade Range of Mountains?

Ans.—I referred to the Hon. Gilmore Hays' loss of cattle, which occurred at the Dalles in the winter of 1852 and 1853, as illustrative only. The deep snow, severe cold, and the privation were experienced as well all over the western portion of northern Oregon (now Washington Territory) as at the Dalles.

Int. 2.—Were you at the Dalles yourself during that winter, or at the place where these cattle were kept?

Ans.—I was not at the Dalles, nor where the cattle were kept; but my information concerning the weather and suffering there was obtained from Judge Hays himself, and others. I was at Fort Vancouver, and all along the route, from the mouth of the Cowlitz river to Olympia, which was not more than ten miles from the Nisqually river, which is the southern boundary of the land claimed by the Puget's Sound Agricultural Company, and along this route the snow was of the depth and remained on the ground as stated in my examination-in-chief. The snow was two feet two inches deep, and laid several weeks.

Int. 3.—Do you know, of your own knowledge, of any cattle dying on the Nisqually Plains that winter?

Ans.—I do not; but the poor quality of the beef delivered at Olympia by the Puget's Sound Company bore every evidence of having perished.

SIMPSON P. MOSES.

In the matter of the Claims of the Puget's Sound Agricultural Company against the United States.

Deposition of Charles T. Gardner, taken at the request and in behalf of the United States, by agreement between Caleb Cushing, on behalf of the United States, and Edward Lander, on behalf of the Puget's Sound Agricultural Company.

TESTIMONY OF CHARLES T. GARDNER.

The said *Charles T. Gardner* being duly sworn, deposeth as follows:

Int. 1.—Please to state your name, the profession to which you are educated, the employments you have filled, the places of those employments, and your present residence.

Ans.—My name is Charles T. Gardner; I was educated at Columbia college, D. C.; I went into the coast survey in 1853, with Captain M. Woodhull, and we surveyed Sandy Hook; Romer Shoals, from there to Monomoy Point, end of Cape Cod; the Elizabeth Island, York river, Maine. I left this service September 1, 1853; started from New York September 20th, 1853, for Oregon, with my father; went immediately to Oregon City; I started in April, 1854, from Oregon City as a partner of Mr. Joseph Hunt, and as deputy surveyor; in 1858 engaged in the boundary survey, and continued in that to 1861; since then I have been in the army until November, 1865, and am now at Washington City, a clerk in the Third Auditor's office, the Treasury Department.

Int. 2.—Are you acquainted with the Cowlitz Farm, so-called, claimed and occupied by the Puget's Sound Agricultural Company? If yea, please to describe its extent and character, so far as you remember.

Ans.—Yes, sir. I can't describe its extent. The land which had been cultivated was good. I know nothing about the difference between private land-claims at that point and that of the Puget's Sound Agricultural Company. The lands which I refer to as being cultivated, were cultivated in wheat and corn, without being able to discriminate which part belonged to the Company.

Int. 3.—How many times have you visited that region of country, and at what periods?

Ans.—I went there first in 1854, and remained there until Christmas day, 1854, when I went down the river Cowlitz.

Int. 4.—What market or markets has the tract of country called the Cowlitz Farms?

Ans.—Olympia, Washington Territory, and Portland, Oregon.

Int. 5.—What is the condition of the roads for loaded wagons, between Cowlitz and Olympia, at different seasons of the year?

Ans.—In the winter they are impassable for, I should think, at least seven or eight months.

Int. 6.—In what conveyance did you descend the river Cowlitz?

Ans.—In an Indian canoe. I started from a point called Cowlitz Landing, and landed at Monticello; stopped there all night; went the next day to St. Helen's, on the Columbia river, and took the steamboat from St. Helen's to Portland, Oregon, up the Columbia and Willamette rivers.

Int. 7.—Did you observe any falls or rapids in the Cowlitz river, between Cowlitz Landing and Monticello?

Ans.—Yes; there is a landing on the river at a rapid nearly half way down.

Int. 8.—Whether or not those rapids constitute an obstacle to the convenient commercial navigation of the Cowlitz up or down the river?

Ans.—They constitute a serious obstacle to commercial navigation.

Cross-Examination.

Int. 1.—Did you travel over the road between the Cowlitz Farm and Olympia during the winter season? If so, how often.

Ans.—I have traveled over portions of the road frequently, but never went directly through but twice.

Int. 2.—Is there not at all seasons of the year a good wagon road from the crossing of the Schookum Chuck to Olympia?

Ans.—There was, except a few crossings at Scatter Creek, and that in very high water.

Int. 3.—How far is it from the crossing of Schookum Chuck to the Cowlitz Farm; and from the same crossing to Olympia?

Ans.—I think the whole distance is about fifty miles; from the crossing to Cowlitz Farms was about twenty; from the same crossing to Olympia about thirty miles.

Int. 4.—Is not the portion of the road between the Cowlitz Farms and the Schookum Chuck, a road, for three fall months in the year, which is used by farmers to wagon wheat to mill?

Ans.—Parts of it; but most of it is impassable during the fall for wagons.

Int. 5.—At what dates did you cross over that portion of the road which you pronounce impassable for wagons in the months of September and October?

Ans.—I was passing over the road I have described as impassable continually.

Int. 6.—Is that portion of the road which you pronounce impassable the old road running through Saunders's Bottom, so-called, on the east bank of the river?

Ans.—Yes.

Int. 7.—Are your statements in reference to this road made from your experience of it while you were engaged in surveys in 1854?

Ans.—Yes; they were.

Int. 8.—Do you know of a road on the opposite bank of the river, leading from north of the Schookum Chuck, near the crossing, to Cowlitz Farm, built by the Government of the United States? If so, state as nearly as you can, when it was constructed.

Ans.—I think they commenced in 1854; I know they were working on it then.

Int. 9.—Have you any knowledge of the navigation of the Cowlitz river, nearly as far up as the Cowlitz landing, by a steamer constructed for the purpose of navigating it?

Ans.—I have none; I have heard such project was entertained.

Int. 10.—Did not the farmers on the Cowlitz Farm find a

market for their produce at a place called Rainier, opposite the mouth of the Cowlitz, on the south bank of the Columbia river ?

Ans.—Yes; I made a mistake in naming St. Helen's; Rainier was the place I stopped at after leaving Monticello.

Int. 11.—Is not the produce of the Cowlitz Farm easily taken down the Cowlitz river in canoes, either to Monticello or Rainier, when the river is at a proper stage ?

Ans.—Yes; it can.

Int. 12.—Do you know what amount of freight the large baggage canoes of the Indians will carry ?

Ans.—I do not.

CHAS. T. GARDNER.

January 30, 1867.

In the matter of the Claim of the Puget's Sound Agricultural Company against the United States.

Deposition of General Benjamin Alvord, witness examined on behalf of the United States, by agreement between C. C. Beaman, counsel for the United States, and Edward Lander, counsel for the Puget's Sound Agricultural Company.

TESTIMONY OF GENERAL BENJAMIN ALVORD.

Int. 1.—State your name, residence, and occupation.

Ans.—Benjamin Alvord; residence, New York city; paymaster in the United States Army.

Int. 2.—Have you ever visited Nisqually, a post of the Puget's Sound Agricultural Company ?

Ans.—I have, often; first in 1855, and frequently since as paymaster, *en route* to Fort Steilacoom.

Int. 3.—What was the character of the buildings of this post ?

Ans.—A stockade, surrounded with pickets. On the left, as you entered the gate, a house occupied by the officer of the

Company in charge; opposite, a store-house; beyond that, another store-house, the lower story of which was used as a store; opposite to this latter, a building occupied by the servants of the Company.

Int. 4.—Are you acquainted with the character of the lands around Nisqually?

Ans.—I have traveled them a good deal on horseback.

Int. 5.—What is their character?

Ans.—The soil is gravelly; in arable tracts it was very thin and poor, covered with sorrel some seasons of the year; four or five pretty lakes, surrounded with a few oaks; the ground very level; natural macadamized road-ways in every direction; some patches on the stream with a little more fertility.

Int. 6.—What would be the average value per acre of a tract of land at Nisqually, extending along the shores of Puget's Sound from the Nisqually river on the one side, to the Puyallup river on the other, and back to the Coast Range of Mountains?

Ans.—I don't think it is worth more than seventy-five cents an acre.

Int. 7.—About what number of oak trees would there be per acre on the tract of land described in the previous question?

Ans.—Not more than one to an acre; large tracts without any at all; they were in clumps—small.

Int. 8.—What was the character of these oak trees?

Ans.—They were good for fuel; could be put to little use in wagon-building or ship-building.

Cross-Examination.

Int. 1.—Is not your acquaintance of that tract of country known as the Nisqually Plains derived from your official visits to the fort at Steilacoom, as paymaster?

Ans.—Yes; every four months.

Int. 2.—Did you not, in going to that post, go through Olympia; and from there, by the road leading from Olympia by Fort Nisqually, to Fort Steilacoom?

Ans.—Generally that route; sometimes over the military road east of Olympia.

Int. 3.—How far from the military post at Steilacoom are the lakes you have spoken of, and how often have you visited them?

Ans.—A few miles. I visited them very often ; but made repeated tours of payments to troops at Muckleshoot Prairie, on the White River, beyond the Puyallup, twenty miles east of Fort Steilacoom.

Int. 4.—Is there not a direct traveled road from the fort at Steilacoom to the crossing of the Puyallup, upon the route to the Muckleshoot Prairie?

Ans.—I went on horseback. There was a path, not deserving the name of a road.

Int. 5.—Is there not a well-defined trail, which you may call a path, which you followed on your way to the Muckleshoot Prairie ?

Ans.—I went by a horse-path, north of the military road; returned by the military road, paying troops at two other block-houses, and thus had to traverse a large share of that country.

Int. 6.—Have you, in your answer to the questions put to you in the examination-in-chief, described any portion of the Nisqually Plains, other than that seen by you when traveling on the routes you have described, and to and from the lakes you have mentioned ?

Ans.—I made frequent pleasure trips, as well as business trips, on horseback and in carriages.

February 27, 1867.

Cross-Examination Resumed this 28 *February,* 1867.

Int. 7.—State how many pleasure trips you have made.

Ans.—Several, every summer.

Int. 8.—Did you, in any instance, go off the traveled road or path? If so, state how often, in what directions, and to what distances.

Ans.—In the excursions on horseback with ladies and gentlemen, we often left the roads and paths. It was an open prairie.

Int. 9.—Can you give the names of any persons whose claims you visited or passed by in the pleasure rides you speak of?

Ans.—There were two or three settlers north of Steilacoom; one by the name of Chambers, one at the post garden seven miles from Fort Steilacoom, and George Gibbs' place, east of the fort. I was not very familiar with their names, as I was not stationed at the post.

Int. 10.—Is not the house of Mr. Chambers about a mile from Fort Steilacoom?

Ans.—I think it was.

Int. 11.—Did you ever visit a prairie called "Muck?"

Ans.—I don't know.

Int. 12.—Do you ever recollect visiting or being upon the claim of one Bolton?

Ans.—No.

Int. 13.—Were not the post garden, the lakes, and Mr. Gibbs' claim the usual places to which these pleasure rides you speak of were directed?

Ans.—Yes. Sometimes we went further.

Int. 14.—Has your observation of these plains been other than a general one, gained when riding or driving in the different directions you have mentioned?

Ans.—The quality of the land there came under my observation because the commanding officer at Fort Steilacoom had to go seven miles to establish a post garden. I used to ride with him, General Casey, exploring for some other place.

Int. 15.—Is not this land you have spoken of as covered with sorrel, land lying near Fort Nisqually?

Ans.—Near Fort Steilacoom and Nisqually both.

Int. 16.—Do you know of any sale of lands on the Nisqually Plains, or have you ever purchased any land there?

Ans.—No.

BENJ. ALVORD,
Paymaster and Brev. Brig. General U. S. Army.
February 28th, 1867.

DISTRICT OF COLUMBIA, }
   County of Washington. }

I, Samuel J. Huntington, Clerk of the United States Court of Claims, do hereby certify that the foregoing depositions hereto annexed of Simpson P. Moses, Charles T. Gardner, Benjamin Alvord, and the direct examination of Edward J. Allen; witnesses produced by and on behalf of the United States in the matter of the claims of the Puget Sound Agricultural Company against the same, now pending before the British and American Joint Commission, for the adjustment of the same, were taken at the city of Washington, in the District aforesaid, and reduced to writing under my direction, by a person agreed upon by Charles C. Beaman, Jr., Esq., attorney for the United States, and Edward Lander, Esq., attorney for said Company, beginning on the said 20th day of January and ending on said 28th day of February, 1867, according to the several dates appended to said depositions when they were signed respectively.

I further certify that to each of said witnesses before his examination, I administered the following oath:

"You swear that the evidence you shall give in the matter of the claim of the Pugets' Sound Agricultural Company against the United States of America, shall be the truth, the whole truth, and nothing but the truth. So help you God."

I further certify that Charles C. Beaman, Jr., and Edward Lander, Esq., were personally present during the examination and cross-examination of all of said witnesses, and the reading and signing of their depositions.

In testimony whereof, I have hereunto set my hand and official seal this 26th day of June, A. D. 1867.

[L. S.]   SAM'L J. HUNTINGTON,
                      Clerk Court of Claims.

BRITISH AND AMERICAN JOINT COMMISSION

ON THE

HUDSON'S BAY AND PUGET'S SOUND AGRICULTURAL COMPANIES' CLAIMS.

In the matter of the Claims of the Puget's Sound Agricultural Company against the United States.

Deposition of a witness (on behalf of the United States) sworn and examined in the City of Philadelphia, Eastern District of Pennsylvania, before me, Charles Sergeant, United States Commissioner in and for said Eastern District of Pennsylvania, by virtue of a verbal agreement made and entered into between C. C. Beaman, Esq., as Counsel for the United States, and Edward Lander, Esq., as Counsel for the Puget's Sound Agricultural Company.

TESTIMONY OF GEORGE DAVIDSON.

George Davidson being duly sworn, deposes and testifies as follows:

Ques. 1.—What is your name, residence, and present occupation?

Ans.—George Davidson; Germantown, Philadelphia. I am Assistant United States Coast Survey.

Ques. 2.—Are you the same person that has already testified in the Hudson's Bay Company *vs.* The United States?

Ans.—Yes, I am.

Ques. 3.—Have you ever visited Puget's Sound? If so, state whether you are acquainted with Steilacoom creek.

Ans.—I had charge of the astronomical, triangular, and

topographical work of all the waters of Washington Territory, from the entrance to the Straits of Fuca, and am familiar with most of them as high as Steilacoom. I have worked and visited in the vicinity of Steilacoom in 1853, 1855, and 1857, and am acquainted with and have landed at the mouth of Steilacoom creek.

Ques. 4.—Whether or no you have had any experience that would enable you to judge of the true value and proper location of a dry-dock?

Ans.—Having made naval architecture one of my studies, to a certain extent, in concert with my brother, Thomas Davidson, Jr., naval constructor in the United States Navy, and also investigated the properties of dry-docks and similar constructions, I think I am enabled to make a fair estimate of the importance of any specified location for the construction of a dry-dock.

Ques. 5.—Describe Steilacoom Creek, and state what you consider to be its suitability for a dry-dock.

Ans.—My recollection of Steilacoom Creek is, that for about a third of a mile from the entrance it has a width between the banks at high-water of about one hundred and fifty yards. That there is not a large supply of water in this creek, as I judged by the amount flowing out at low-water, where it was very narrow and shallow. That I commanded the United States brig Fauntleroy, drawing about ten feet of water, and should never have hazarded an attempt to get her in this creek at the highest tide by any appliances whatever. In fact, I would consider it totally impracticable to get a vessel drawing ten feet of water in there. As an engineer, I do not consider it practicable, without accurate surveys and a large amount of capital, to construct a dry-dock in the basin of this creek. I believe there are other localities on these waters much better suited for the purpose.

Cross-examination waived.

GEORGE DAVIDSON.

UNITED STATES OF AMERICA, }
Eastern District of Pennsylvania. }

I, Charles Sergeant, United States Commissioner, duly appointed and commissioned by the Circuit Court of the United States in and for the Eastern District of Pennsylvania, do hereby certify that the foregoing deposition of George Davidson was taken and reduced to writing by me in the presence of said witness; and from his statements on the sixth day of May, 1867, at my office, No. 123 South Fifth street, Philadelphia, in pursuance of a verbal agreement made in my presence by C. C. Beaman, Esq., as counsel for the United States, and Edward Lander, Esq., as counsel for the Puget's Sound Agricultural Company.

I further certify that to said witness, before his examination, I administered the following oath:

"You do swear that the evidence you are about to give in the matter of the claim of the Puget's Sound Agricultural Company against the United States shall be the truth, the whole truth, and nothing but the truth, so help you God."

I further certify that said deposition was by me carefully read to said witness, and then signed by him in my presence.

In testimony whereof I have hereunto set my hand and official seal at Philadelphia, this seventh day of May, 1867.

[L. S.]

CHARLES SERGEANT,
U. S. Commissioner.

BRITISH AND AMERICAN JOINT COMMISSION

ON THE

HUDSON'S BAY AND PUGET'S SOUND AGRICULTURAL COMPANIES' CLAIMS.

In the matter of the Puget's Sound Agricultural Company against the United States.

Deposition of a witness, (on behalf of the United States,) sworn and examined in the city of Philadelphia, eastern district of Pennsylvania, before me, Charles Sergeant, United States Commissioner in and for said Eastern District of Pennsylvania, by virtue of a verbal agreement made and entered into between C. C. Beaman, Esq., as counsel for the United States, and Edward Lander, Esq., counsel for the Puget's Sound Agricultural Company.

TESTIMONY OF MAXIMILIAN MOGK.

Maximilian Mogk, being duly sworn, deposes and testifies as follows:

Int. 1.—What is your name and residence?

Ans.—My name is Maximilian Mogk; I reside 1,082, Germantown Road, Philadelphia.

Int. 2.—Were you ever at Fort Steilacoom, Washington Territory?

Ans.—Yes, sir.

Int. 3.—In what years, and in what capacity?

Ans.—From 1855 to 1857. I was a soldier in the United States Army, company C, 4th infantry. I was at first private, afterwards corporal and sergeant; I was discharged as orderly sergeant in 1857.

19 P

Int. 4.—Are you acquainted with the tract of land, as set forth on the map, entitled "Plan of the Puget's Sound Agricultural Company's Land Claim at Nisqually, Washington Territory," marked B, and hereafter to be annexed to your deposition?

Ans.—I am; I have been over the whole ground gunning, and know every inch of it as well as anybody can. I was engaged to keep the officers' mess in game, so I had a good chance to see the whole country. I have been out gunning nearly every day for a year at a time. I went both on foot and on horseback, and frequently a distance of from ten to fifteen miles from the fort. I have also been engaged to take charge of parties cutting wood for the fort.

Int. 5.—Will you describe the general character of the land embraced in the map marked B?

Ans.—The general character of the land is gravelly, without any soil on it. Useful for cultivation except on the low bottoms. These bottom lands were small in extent and far apart. The land was so gravelly it never made any mud. You could ride anywhere. It would rain for four weeks without making any mud. The grass was very clumpy, short and sour grass, with a great many bare spots where there was no grass at all.

Int. 6.—What particular knowledge have you of the fitness of this soil for agriculture?

Ans.—I know that several of our men tried to cultivate the ground within a mile around the barracks, but it would not repay their labor to cultivate it, for nothing whatever could be grown. They never tried it after the first year, because they could not raise anything. There were also several farmers of my acquaintance who tried to raise on the high ground, but it would not pay their labor. I know a man, but do not remember his name, who built a block-house on a claim two or three miles north of the post or fort, and abandoned it altogether after two years.

Int. 7.—What do you know of the post garden?

Ans.—The post garden is a very good piece of ground of about five acres, made so by great labor. We took about thirty loads of manure there every year from the fort. It is about five miles north of the fort. It is the best piece of ground I saw from the fort to Olympia. The garden had been selected several years before I went there. They always kept a garden there. He had a block-house there.

Int. 8.—What would you estimate to be the value per acre of the land embraced on the map marked B?

Ans.—It is not worth much. I would not take it for a gift if I had to pay taxes for it; that is, I mean, for cultivation. It is a pretty good pasture country. It is not fenced in. For pasturage, and including the timber on it, I would value it about fifty cents an acre. I now speak of the whole tract.

Int. 9.—What is the character of the oak trees on this tract?

Ans.—They are very short, crippled trees, worth nothing else but to be used for fire-wood. The general height of them is such that a good-sized man could catch the branches. Their average thickness is about ten inches through. I never saw one more than about eighteen inches through; never saw one two feet through. Their quality is very poor, not fit for building or other timber use; white prickly oak, scrub oaks.

Int. 10.—What do you know of the number of the oaks on this tract of land, known as Nisqually Plain?

Ans.—The number of them is very spare, except on one or two places where they stand a little thicker. I don't think they would average one to an acre. You will find one here, and then you might go over a hundred acres before coming to another one. They stand so far apart and are so low they throw little or no shade. I know only one place, of about sixty acres back of the fort, that would average from ten to twelve to an acre. I know of no other tract where they would average more than one to an acre.

Int. 11.—Whether or no there were any cattle upon these plains? If so, describe them.

Ans.—There were a great many cattle on the plains and in the woods. They were wild and dangerous on the plains, for men either on foot or horseback, for I saw, myself, a bull upset a hay-wagon with a pair of oxen to it. I killed several myself in self-defence.

Int. 12.—How were these cattle killed?

Ans.—They were killed by shooting them in riding after them on horseback. I often have seen, in my travels over the plains, the Hudson's Bay Company men shoot the cattle in this way. I have often helped them myself. The cattle were very wild to be got at; they had always to be surrounded by the horsemen, and then it took very good horses to overtake them on the plains before they reached the woods. When in the woods they were wilder than the deer. I would undertake to shoot two or three deer before I would be able to get in gun-reach of any of those cattle.

Int. 13.—Whether or no these cattle were branded or marked?

Ans.—I never saw any either branded or marked any way at all.

Int. 14.—Whether or no you knew of any of these cattle being killed by the Indians?

Ans.—Yes, I have seen the Indians killing them myself. They used to cut up the best parts of the meat in long strips to dry it, to stow away for winter use. We often found, when fighting with the Indians, in 1855 and 1856, whole huts full of this dried beef.

Int. 15.—What do you know of the supply of beef to the garrison at Fort Steilacoom?

Ans.—We were supplied by the Hudson's Bay Company. We used to get beef six days in the week. Dr. Tolmie's carts fetched the beef in twice a week to the fort from Fort Nisqually.

Int. 16.—What was the average number of men at the garrison?

Ans.—From two to four companies at a time; each company averaged about sixty men.

Int. 17.—Are you acquainted with Fort Nisqually?

Ans.—I often passed, and have been in Fort Nisqually. I was engaged at one time as mail-carrier from Fort Steilacoom to Olympia, and had to pass Fort Nisqually twice every time I went to Olympia; I brought Dr. Tolmie's mail with the rest.

Int. 18.—Will you describe the fort?

Ans.—It is a square place, fenced in with stockade-fence. There were about six buildings inside of the stockades. There was only one house, the dwelling-house of Dr. Tolmie,. of any value; the rest of them were one-story block-houses.

Int. 19.—What would you estimate to be the value of this fort ?

Ans.—It would be of no use to any farmer, except as a fort; it is a safe place in case the Indians should break out; for the land around the fort is very poor; has been cultivated once, but is now abandoned; that is, it was abandoned and lying waste when I knew it.

Int. 20.—Whether or no you have any particular knowledge which would enable you to estimate the length of time it would take a given number of men to erect such a fort?

Ans.—I have seen several such buildings built in our fort, and I think I can estimate how much time it would take a given number of men to erect such a fort as that.

Int. 21.—How long do you think it would have taken ten men to have built Fort Nisqually ? And regard in your answer the character of the post, and the location of the proper timber.

Ans.—I think it would have taken ten men between eight and ten months to build a place like Fort Nisqually. I think in this time they could have got out all the timber and put up the place.

Int. 22.—What was the condition of Fort Nisqually when you knew it?

Ans.—I think it was rather in a careless state; I think the stockades round the fort were in rather a dilapidated state; I think the doors were off; I never saw any there shut.

Adjourned till May 9th, at 10 o'clock.

May 9th, 1067. Present, Mr. Beaman and Judge Lander.

Cross-examination by Judge Lander.

Int. 1.—Of what nation are you ?

Ans.—I am a German born.

Int. 2.—At what age did you come to the United States?

Ans.—At nineteen years of age.

Int. 3.—What was your occupation before you enlisted in armies of the United States?

Ans.—I was employed in a grocery store.

Int. 4.—What do you mean by a grocery store?

Ans.—A store where they sell groceries, liquor, and such things; where they sell liquor by the glass. The store was in Williamsburg, New York.

Int. 5.—What is your present occupation?

Ans.—I am bar-tender.

Int. 6.—What time in the year 1853 did you arrive at Steilacoom?

Ans.—I can't state exactly the month; we left Vancouver in the spring of 1853, and went to Steilacoom.

Int. 7.—Who was in command of your Company at the time?

Ans.—First Lieutenant De Lancey Floyd-Jones.

Int. 8.—What year did you hunt for the officers' mess, and what was your rank in the company at that time?

Ans.—I hunted in 1853 for the mess, and was private at that time.

Int. 9.—What time did you carry the mail, and what was your rank in the company at that time?

Ans.—I think it was in 1855; I was then private.

Int. 10.—When did you leave Fort Steilacoom?

Ans.—I left Fort Steilacoom in 1857.

Int. 11.—Did you carry the mail through the whole year 1855?

Ans.—I carried it about six months; in the fall of the year, I believe.

Int. 12.—How often did you go to Olympia?

Ans.—Twice a week.

Int. 13.—Do you feel certain you carried the mail in the fall of 1855?

Ans.—I think it was in the fall of 1855.

Int. 14.—When was the Indian war in that country?

Ans.—In 1856 and 1857.

Int. 15.—Were you away from the fort with your company any portion of that war?

Ans.—Yes, sir.

Int. 16.—Under whose command were you then, and where did you go?

Ans.—Captain Maloney was in command of the expedition after the Indians; we went up into the Cascade Mountains, on White and Green river.

Int. 17.—Do you know what year this was in?

Ans.—I can't say exactly; it is ten years since I have been back; I did not take particular notice.

Int. 18.—Did you go on any other expedition? If so, state where, and under whose command.

Ans.—I went on several expeditions after Indians who had been murdering white settlers. I have been under Major Larned one time, and Lieutenant Von Kautz another time.

Int. 19.—At what time did you go with Major Larned; what year, and what season of the year?

Ans.—I can't state the year or the season, but the time that Major Larned got drowned; it was before the war broke out.

Int. 20.—Where did you go with Lieutenant Kautz, and when?

Ans.—We went down the Sound, stopped at Bellingham Bay, and at other different islands in the Sound; I can't say when; but it was before the Indian war.

Int. 21.—During the Indian war, did you go on any other expedition besides that of Captain Maloney's?

Ans.—That is the only one I went on.

Int. 22.—Did you not remain in the garrison from the time of the expedition under Captain Maloney until the end of the Indian war?

Ans.—I remained in the fort, while I was wounded; in the hospital; I went out again after my wounds were healed up; I returned to my command, which was lying at Porter's Prairie.

Int. 23.—Were they not in garrison there in a block-house?

Ans.—Not at the time I was there; that fort was built

after we went back to our fort, as I understood; I never saw it.

Int. 24.—Did not the wood parties you speak of get their wood within a mile or two of the fort?

Ans.—Yes; they got the wood inside of a mile, for the fort joined right on to the wood.

Int. 25.—Were, not the cattle, horses, and mules of the garrison pastured, during the war, immediately round the fort?

Ans.—The horses and mules were pastured round the fort, but we had no cattle.

Int. 26.—Was not the land immediately round the fort injured, and the grass destroyed, by this close pasturage?

Ans.—There was nothing to destroy, for there was not much pasturage there; the horses and mules were driven in in the evening, and fed on barley or oats or whatever we had; they were let out more for recreation than pasturage.

Int. 27.—Do you know anything of a claim taken up by Mr. George Gibbs?

Ans.—I don't recollect that man's name.

Int. 28.—Do you know the claim of Mr. Chambers?

Ans.—I do.

Int. 29.—How near to the fort is it, and was he not a resident upon it during all the time you resided at Fort Steilacoom?

Ans.—His claim was about a mile from the fort; he resided on it; but I think it was not for the cultivation of his claim, as he had a saw-mill there; he staid there for the saw-mill, not for the land.

Int. 30.—Did not this man Chambers have a large band of cattle and horses?

Ans.—All I seen was a few horses and a few milch-cows.

Int. 31.—Did you ever see any of the land on the Nisqually Plains enclosed and kept for pasturage?

Ans.—I seen small pieces of it fenced in on certain farms for the safe keeping of young stock.

Int. 32.—How is the beef of that country, as served out to you—pretty good or bad?

Ans.—The beef is pretty good.

Int. 33.—Who was the man that built a house within two or three miles of the fort, and abandoned it?

Ans.—I do not remember the name.

Int. 34.—Did he not abandon during or about the time of the Indian war?

Ans.—No; he abandoned it before the war?

Int. 35.—Was he not a discharged soldier?

Ans.—I think he was a discharged soldier from the second artillery, that was stationed there before we came there.

Int. 36.—Of what nation was he, Irish or German?

Ans.—I don't know; he spoke English; I don't know whether he was Irish or American.

Int. 37.—Give the name of any farmer of your acquaintance "who tried to raise on the high land," and state where he lived, and how far from the fort, and at what place.

Ans.—I know one man by name, of the name of Murray, a Scotchman, about four miles from the fort, to the left going from Fort Steilacoom to Fort Nisqually. I know of another man, but I forget his name; he lived about seven miles from the fort, back of the soldiers' garden.

Int. 38.—Is not that the man who tried to jump the garden?

Ans.—It was not.

Int. 39.—Do you know where the Elk Plain is?

Ans.—I have been on it.

Int. 40.—Have you ever been on the Muck Plain?

Ans.—I never heard of it.

Int. 41.—Have you ever been on the prairies which lie to the north or left of the roads leading from Fort Steilacoom to the crossing of the Puyallup river?

Ans.—I have.

Int. 42.—How far to the north or left of the road have you been?

Ans.—I have been way back into the woods all around, all over the prairies. I don't believe there is an inch where I have not been.

Int. 43.—On what part of the plains and how far from the fort did you shoot any cattle?

Ans.—I helped to shoot cattle close to the fort, and so up the plains to back of Fort Nisqually; in fact I helped to shoot them wherever I met them, that is, the Company's people.

Int. 44.—Where did you kill one of these in self-defence, and what had the animal done to you before you shot him?

Ans.—I killed one about a mile, say two miles, from Fort Steilacoom, on the road to Fort Nisqually. He was tearing up the ground, bellowing, and made for me. I took up my gun and killed him.

Int. 45.—Have you not often seen in Germany bulls pawing the ground and bellowing?

Ans.—I did, and I have seen bulls kill people in Germany.

Int. 46.—Do you know of any cattle being killed by the settlers on the plains?

Ans.—I never saw any so killed.

Int. 47.—State where you saw an Indian killing any one of these cattle; how far it was from the fort, and at what time it was.

Ans.—I saw Indians killing cattle in the woods running to the right of the road going to Fort Nisqually, about three miles from Fort Steilacoom.

Int. 48.—How many times did you see this done?

Ans.—I saw it two or three times.

Int. 49.—Was this before or after the war?

Ans.—This was before the war.

Int. 50.—Do you know these were not Indians employed by Dr. Tolmie to kill beef for him?

Ans.—I know they were not, for when they see me come they run away, thinking I was one of the Hudson's Bay men; but after they saw who I was they came back and cut up the beef.

Int. 51.—Was it at this time or at some other time that you saw the Indians cutting the best parts of the meat into long strips?

Ans.—I saw it at this time.

Int. 52.—How long did you stop to see it?

Ans.—Three or four minutes, and then I went on my way gunning.

Int. 53.—Were you on foot or on horseback?

Ans.—I was on foot.

Int. 54.—Were you walking along the road?

Ans.—This was in the woods; there were no roads.

Int. 55.—Have you not, when riding on horseback, passed under the branches of oak trees on the plains?

Ans.—Well, I did, stooping down on the horse's neck.

Int. 56.—Do you think your recollection of this circumstance is as correct as the rest of your testimony?

Ans.—Yes, for I remember more than once to have stooped while riding on horseback.

Int. 57.—Are there not many oak trees on the road from Olympia to Fort Nisqually, under the lowest branches of which a man on horseback can easily ride?

Ans.—There are but very few oak trees on the road from Olympia to Fort Nisqually; there may be a few where a man could ride under, but they were very scarce.

Int. 58.—Did you ever go upon the enclosed fields back of Fort Nisqually and to the right of the road leading past the fort to Fort Steilacoom?

Ans.—I never saw any enclosed fields round the fort.

Int. 59.—Do you not know that during the rainy season it is not usual for men to work in the open air in that section of the country?

Ans.—Well, I do not suppose they would work anywhere in the rain if they could help it. I have seen our own men working in the rain, cutting wood and repairing the road.

Int. 60.—How long does the rainy season continue in that country?

Ans.—I think about three months.

Int. 61.—Do you know where the farm of a man by the name of Lane was?

Ans.—I don't recollect that name.

Int. 62.—Do you recollect a settler by the name of Rigdon?

Ans.—I do not.

Int. 63.—Do you recollect a settler by the name of Downie?

Ans.—No. I was not acquainted with all the farmers' names, for I had not much to do with them.

Int. 64.—How many settlers should you say were on the plains at the time you say you hunted over them?

Ans.—I could not recollect the number of the settlers that were living on the plains.

Int. 65.—How often have you been ten miles away from the fort on hunting expeditions?

Ans.—A good many times.

Int. 66.—State, if you can, any particular occasion on which you were away that distance from the fort, the time of the year, the game you brought home, and the length of time you were gone from the fort.

Ans.—I can't state any particular occasion, but have been away often; have brought home ducks, geese, and deer; have left before daylight, and have not returned till ten and eleven o'clock at night.

Int. 67.—Did you hunt upon the plains during the Indian war?

Ans.—I did not.

Int. 68.—You speak of manure being used on the post garden; could not manure have been used equally well on other portions of the plain?

Ans.—Not on the high ground; there was no soil there for it to do any good; it would dry up.

Int. 69.—Was there not, in the spring of the year, a regular growth of grass over these plains?

Ans.—Yes, such as it is; small, short, sour grass.

Re-examined by Mr. Beaman.

Int. 1.—How long have you lived in the United States?

Ans.—Seventeen years.

Int. 2.—What was your occupation before you came to this country?

Ans.—Game-keeper.

Int. 3.—Have you ever been on what is designated Muck Plain, on map marked B?

Ans.—I have been all over the whole plains, but I do not recollect ever having heard that part called Muck Plain.

Int. 4.—Referring to the prairies alluded to in cross-interrogatories 41 and 42, and in your answers to the same interrogatories, are the oaks any more abundant on those plains than on other parts of the Nisqually Plains?

Ans.—They are not more so there than on any other part.

Int. 5.—Whether or no there was any enclosed land within a mile of Fort Nisqually?

Ans.—There had been fences there that enclosed land, but there were none in my time?

Re-Cross-Examined by Judge Lander.

Int. 1.—Have you ever been one mile south of Fort Nisqually?

Ans.—I think I have been all around it.

Int. 2.—Look at the map marked B, now shown you, and on the enclosure marked Fort Farm, in a southeast and south direction from Fort Nisqually, and state whether you ever saw that enclosed ground or not.

Ans.—I saw that enclosed piece of ground, but I think it is more than a mile from the fort.

Int. 3.—What does it enclose; what you call high ground, or low ground, like the Steilacoom garden?

Ans.—I think it is both high and low ground.

Int. 4.—Are you certain that this enclosure is more than a mile from the fort?

Ans.—I think it is, to the best of my recollection.

Int. 5.—Was the enclosure in that shape when you carried the mail on that road?

Ans.—It was.

Re-examined by Mr. Beaman.

Int. 1.—How large a tract was the tract which you have spoken of as enclosed, more than a mile southeasterly of Fort Nisqually?

Ans.—I cannot state exactly how large it was.

Int. 2.—Was it cultivated by the people of the fort?

Ans.—It was.

Int. 3.—Was it more than fifty acres in area?

Ans.—I can't state; it is too long since I have been there.

Int. 4.—Whether or no there were remains of any fencing within a mile of the fort?

Ans.—They had, adjoining the fort, a pen to keep the horses in; I remember no other fences.

M. MOGK.

Sworn to and subscribed before me this ninth day of May, 1867.

CHARLES SERGEANT,
U. S. Commissioner.

UNITED STATES OF AMERICA, }
  Eastern District of Pennsylvania. }

I, Charles Sergeant, United States Commissioner, duly appointed and commissioned by the circuit court of the United States in and for the eastern district of Pennsylvania, do hereby certify that the foregoing deposition of Maximilian Mogk was taken and reduced to writing by L. C. Cleemann, my clerk, under my direction, and in my presence and in the presence of said witness, from his statements on the eighth and ninth days of May, 1867, at my office, No. 123 South Fifth street, Philadelphia, in pursuance of a verbal agreement made in my presence by C. C. Beaman, Esq., counsel for the United States, and Edward Lander, Esq., as counsel for the Puget's Sound Agricultural Company.

I further certify that to said witness, before his examination, I administered the following oath:

"You do swear that the evidence you are about to give in the matter of the claim of the Puget's Sound Agricultural Company against the United States shall be the truth, the whole truth, and nothing but the truth, so help you God."

I further certify that said foregoing deposition was carefully read to said witness, and then signed by him in my presence.

I do further certify that the paper hereto annexed, marked "B," is the one referred to in the testimony of Maximilian Mogk.

In testimony whereof I have hereunto set my hand and official seal, at my office in the city of Philadelphia, this ninth day of May, 1867.

[L. S.]

CHARLES SERGEANT,
United States Commissioner.

BRITISH AND AMERICAN JOINT COMMISSION

ON THE

HUDSON'S BAY AND PUGET'S SOUND AGRICULTURAL COMPANIES' CLAIMS.

———————

In the matter of the Claim of the Puget's Sound Agricultural Company against the United States.

Deposition of Mr. GEORGE W. LEE, witness produced on the part of the United States this 1st day of May, 1867, at Washington city, D. C. Mr. C. C. Beaman counsel of the United States, and Mr. Edward Lander counsel of the Puget's Sound Agricultural Company.

TESTIMONY OF GEORGE W. LEE.

Int. 1.—What is your name, residence, and occupation?

Ans.—My name is George W. Lee; my residence is Washington city, D. C. I am in the Quartermaster General's Office of the War Department.

Int. 2.—Have you ever lived in Washington Territory?

Ans.—I have. I went there in January, 1853; I left there in 1858, the latter part of May or early in June. My home, properly speaking, was at Steilacoom, Pierce county. When I first went on the Sound I was engaged in lumber business, getting piles and square timber for the San Francisco market. I was in this lumber business until about the middle or latter part of 1854. I then engaged in the newspaper business at Steilacoom, and remained at that, with few exceptions, until I left there in May or June, 1858.

Int. 3.—Are you acquainted with the post of the Puget's Sound Agricultural Company at Nisqually?

Ans.—Yes, I am.

20 P

Int. 4.—Will you describe it as you first saw it, and any changes that subsequently took place?

Ans.—It was an ordinary stockade, with some warehouses inside. The building in which Dr. Tolmie was living when I first went there was in very bad order, but he continued to improve it. The first time I saw it was early in 1853. There was a long warehouse on the beach, where they put goods over-night at the landing. There was a small place where a watchman lived, a servant of the Company; he was blind, I think; his name was James Scarf. The buildings were most of them of hewed logs. The building in which Dr. Tolmie lived was a frame building, of sawed lumber, as far as my memory serves me.

Int. 5.—What was the value of the Company's post at Nisqually?

Ans.—If you talk about the intrinsic value of the buildings, I should not think it would amount to any great sum. I should say the principal value was as a trading-post or business-stand. A few thousand dollars would put up such buildings.

Int. 6.—Was there any cultivated land around the post?

Ans.—There was a patch there, where they used to raise stuff for those that lived at the post—not more than an acre and a half or two acres.

Int. 7.—Were there any indications of other lands having been cultivated at a previous time?

Ans.—Yes, there were indications of land having been cultivated there.

Int. 8.—How would that appear?

Ans.—The old furrows, and other indications familiar to one who had been acquainted with cultivated land, showed [that] other lands had been cultivated.

Int. 9.—What was the character of this land that appeared to have been cultivated?

Ans.—It appeared to have been worn out. It was not what I would call enclosed; there were rails lying about it.

Int. 10.—Whether or not this land was covered with sorrel?

Ans.—The whole country through there was sorrel, as a general thing.

Int. 11.—Whether or no you are acquainted with a tract of land extending along the shores of Puget's Sound, from the Nisqually river on the one side to the Puyallup on the other, and back to the Coast range of mountains; and, if so, what is its character?

Ans.—I have ridden over the greater portion of it. Along on the Nisqually and Puyallup bottoms is an excellent quality of agricultural land, but liable to overflow, and covered with heavy timber. There are a few fern prairies among the fir timber—what they call patches of fern prairie. That is the character of the land skirting around the shores of the Sound and the base of the mountains. In the central portion it was sandy, gravelly prairies, with an occasional little lake and small patches of timber. The general character might be called prairie land.

Int. 12.—What was the general character of the prairie land?

Ans.—Very poor land.

Int. 13.—Whether or no it was capable of being permanently enriched by manure?

Ans.—Not, as far as my observation went.

Int. 14.—State why not.

Ans.—It was very heavily gravelled; in ploughing it up you would turn up nothing but gravel in most places. It would not hold manure; no base, nothing for the manure to mix with; what you would call leachy ground; manure would run right through.

Int. 15.—What was the value of this prairie land?

Ans.—Some of it wasn't worth anything. In damp places, where there was a little vegetable matter, you might raise fifteen or twenty bushels of grain to the acre; and that for not more than one or two crops. These damp places bore a very small proportion to the whole of the land. I would not waste my time in attempting to cultivate it for agricultural purposes. A few parties have taken up claims there, but, after spending some time, in many instances abandoned their claims.

Int. 16.—Did you have any occasion to notice the abundance of the oak timber on this land?

Ans.—Yes. The oak timber was not what I should call oak timber for commercial purposes. The character of the oak was scrubby and inferior; here and there an isolated tree. There were a good many oak bushes, scrubs.

Int. 17.—What did you estimate to have been the number of oak trees on the tract you have described per acre?

Ans.—It would not average a good oak tree to the acre, in my opinion.

Int. 18.—Whether or no there were any cattle roaming on these plains?

Ans.—Yes, I have seen cattle roaming there.

Int. 19.—Were they branded?

Ans.—I never noticed brands on them.

Int. 20.—What was the character of these cattle?

Ans.—The same kind of cattle we have in California—Spanish; what you call California wild cattle.

Int. 21.—Whether or no Dr. Tolmie or any officers of the Puget's Sound Agricultural Company shipped cattle from Steilacoom?

Ans.—I have seen them ship cattle from the Nisqually landing. I have seen several loads go down the Sound.

Int. 22.—What do you know of the character of the winter of 1852–3?

Ans.—The winter was very severe on the whole coast.

Int. 23.—Do you know anything of the destruction of cattle that winter?

Ans.—I know a good many cattle starved on the coast, from exposure to weather and scarcity of food.

Int. 24.—Do you know anything of the scarcity of provisions that winter?

Ans.—Provisions were very scarce; flour sold at $45 and $50 a barrel that winter. Most of the flour there came from San Francisco.

Int. 25.—Whether or no you are acquainted with the claim of William B. Bolton, on Puget's Sound, near Steilacoom?

Ans.—Yes, sir. It is between three and four miles from Steilacoom.

Int. 26.—What is the character of this claim?

Ans.—It is what they call a fir-timber-claim right on the shores of the Sound.

Int. 27.—What do you know of Bolton's business?

Ans.—He was ship-carpenter. He used to repair any little damage done to vessels, and he got out piles and square timber.

Int. 28.—Whether or no you know of any three acres of ground on Bolton's claim, or on the tract of land described in "Interrogatory 11," on which four hundred oak trees suitable for shipping could have been cut?

Ans.—There is no such place on Bolton's claim or on Puget's Sound, and very few such places in the world, in my opinion. By trees, I mean such as are fit for saw logs.

Int. 29.—Describe the mouth of the Steilacoom creek.

Ans.—It is not a navigable stream. No harbor there; no more than any other portion of the Sound. I can wade across the mouth of it in low-water; a loaded canoe could not get up it at low-water.

Int. 30.—What do you know of any mills on Steilacoom creek?

Ans.—There were two mills there; one was Chambers's and the other Bird's. Chambers's mill was the one nearest to the Sound; Bird's was about a mile above it. Chambers's was a saw-mill, afterwards, I think, turned into a grist-mill. The upper mill was a grist-mill, with a saw-mill attached. There were no other mills on this stream. There was not water enough to run both mills regularly. Chambers complained that the mill above him took the water from him. There was not water enough in the summer to run more than one of the mills regularly. The water was very low in the summer.

Int. 31.—What do you know of any mills on the Segwalitchew?

Ans.—There was a mill owned by Balch and Webber—a saw-mill. That did not amount to much.

Int. 32.—Did you ever visit the garden of the military post at Steilacoom?

Ans.—Yes, several times. It was a very nice place; a little wet; enriched by the manure hauled there from the station; a good deal of labor expended on it. It was kept in very good order.

Int. 33.—Whether or no you ever knew beef and mutton to be sold by Dr. Tolmie or his servants?

Ans.—Yes; I have bought both from him myself. He used to send a cart into Steilacoom with them.

Int. 34.—Whether or no you ever knew Dr. Tolmie to ship sheep, or to sell them to breeders or other persons?

Ans.—I have known sheep to be shipped from there. I have known parties to come to Nisqually to buy sheep, and they took them off with them. I think, in one instance, the brig Cyrus took off a lot of sheep, somewhere down the coast.

Int. 35.—When did the Americans begin to settle in Pierce county?

Ans.—In the fall of 1853. The first immigration came by way of the Cascade mountains; the few who came previously either came from Oregon, overland, or by water from San Francisco.

Int. 36.—What was the population of Pierce county when you left it?

Ans.—Not more, I think, than about 500 white population.

Int. 37.—Did you ever know any sales of land in Pierce county?

Ans.—I did not hear of sales of land. I knew of men selling their houses and some town lots.

Cross-Examination.

Int. 1.—Has not your occupation been that of, and were you not brought up to, the profession of the printer?

Ans.—Yes; but had nothing to do with it after serving my time in 1848, until I went to Steilacoom and connected myself with the Puget's Sound Courier in 1854.

Int. 2.—In what business were you engaged from 1848 until you came to Washington Territory in 1853?

Ans.—I was engaged in mining and trading in San Francisco

and the interior of California. In 1851 I went to Port Orford, in Oregon, engaged in making a settlement there, and looking for timber there, with a view of going into the timber business there, or anything else that would turn up. Then I was back in California again mining and trading, and, after being at that, I made arrangements with parties in San Francisco to furnish them with piles and square timber, and that was what took me to Puget's Sound.

Int. 3.—Did you not, at any time between 1848 and 1853, work at your trade?

Ans.—Not more than six weeks in the whole time. I did not follow it as a business. I gave it up on account of my health.

Int. 4.—Did you not work as a compositor in a printing office at Steilacoom, from the latter part of the summer of 1854 until May or June, 1858?

Ans.—A portion of the time, I did.

Int. 5.—Were you not, during the times I have mentioned, engaged in setting type?

Ans.—Not all the time.

Int. 6.—How many times were you ever at the house or landing, upon the claim of Mr. Bolton?

Ans.—Fully half a dozen times, if not more.

Int. 7.—Did you go there by land or by water?

Ans.—I have been there by land and water both.

Int. 8.—How many times have you been there by land, and which way does the road run; what portion of it runs along the prairie; what portion is along the beach, and below the bluff; how do you approach the clearing of Mr. Bolton—by the road, by beach, or by prairie?

Ans.—I suppose I have been there by land twice. The road runs parallel with the Sound, on the ridge. The road is a sort of trail. There is no gravelly prairie along the road, not of any large extent. Never went on the beach at all. Mr. Bolton's house is near the beach; I went right down the hill to his house. There is a road starting from Fort Steilacoom that is a roundabout way; but, going from the town of Steilacoom, there is a trail.

Int. 9—Does not this road, for the last mile before reaching his house, go through the forest of fir timber?

Ans.—The whole trail is timber land, with here and there an open patch.

Int. 10.—Did you see oak trees on this last mile of land in the fir forest?

Ans.—None, that I noticed.

Int. 11.—Does not this belt of fir timber, bordering on the Sound, for a mile above and a mile below the clearing at Bolton's claim, extend at least one-half mile back from the Sound?

Ans.—Yes, it does.

Int. 12.—Have you ever been back of Bolton's clearing, so as to go through the fir woods bordering on the Sound to the other prairie?

Ans.—No; I have not been on the prairie from the direction of Bolton's house. I have been on the prairie supposed to lie back of Bolton's House, from the direction of Fort Steilacoom.

Int. 13.—How large a prairie is this?

Ans.—From the length of time since I have been there, I cannot say how large the prairie is.

Int. 14.—How far from the post at Steilacoom is this prairie that you speak of?

Ans.—A mile and a half or two miles.

Int. 15.—Do you not know that the Chambers mill, on Steilacoom creek, is at least a mile and a half lower down the stream than the mill you call Bird's mill, and that the fall in the stream between these two mills is at least ten feet?

Ans.—I have already answered about the distance. I cannot answer as to the fall.

Int. 16.—Was the land on the road leading to Soldier's Garden, for the whole distance, covered with sorrel?

Ans.—I did not minutely examine; as a general thing, it was there. The only places you would not strike the sorrel was when you got down near the lakes.

Int. 17.—Was there not, from the summer of 1855 to the summer of 1857, an Indian war going on in the country around the Sound, and especially in the country back of Steil-acoom ?

Ans.—Yes.

Int. 18.—At the time you arrived in Steilacoom, in January, 1853, was there any snow upon the ground ?

Ans.—I am not positive.

Int. 19.—Was there any snow there between the time you arrived and the spring ; and, if so, how much was there, and how long did it remain ?

Ans.—I don't remember any. The weather was severe, but snow rarely falls on the Sound ; but I have known snow to be eight or ten miles from Steilacoom when there was none on the Sound.

Int. 20.—Did you see, after your arrival at Steilacoom, in 1853, during that winter or spring, any snow in the country back of Steilacoom ?

Ans.—I saw it at a distance.

Int. 21.—At what distance did you see it, and when ?

Ans.—On the Cascade mountains, a range of mountains back of Steilacoom, and on the hills running down to the canal, (Hood's.)

Examination-in-Chief Resumed.

Int. 1.—State all that you know in regard to Mr. Bolton's claim—its extent, the quality of its timber, and the opportunity you have had for knowing this ?

Ans.—When I have stopped there the question of timber would naturally come out, and we would go out to look at it. The timber on his claim, what I saw of it, was very good piles, good timber claim. I should say, though not familiar with his lines ; that from what showed me, that he had half a mile fronting on the Sound. I never saw any oak timber of any great quantity, more than was at any other places.

Int. 2.—Whether or no you ever understood from him that his claim extended into the prairie ?

Ans.—I never did.

Int. 3.—State all you know in regard to the location of

Bird's mill as having interfered with the running of Chamber's mill.

(Objected to as having already been inquired into in the examination-in-chief, and no new matter being brought out in cross-examination.)

Ans.—I know that when Bird's mill was put in operation, Judge Chambers found fault. There was talk of litigation or ——— in reference to the matter, Chambers claiming that there was not water enough for both mills; that Bird's mill took the water from him. Several theories existed as to the loss of the water; generally thought the water went into the ground.

(Chamber's statements objected to.)

Cross-Examination Resumed.

Int. 1.—Do you know anything more about the loss of water than you know from Chambers's complaints, and did he complain to you?

Ans.—All I know was from Chambers's conversations with me.

G. W. LEE.

In the matter of the Claim of the Puget's Sound Agricultural Company against the United States.

Deposition of WILLIAM B. McMURTRIE, witness examined on behalf of the United States, at Washington city, D. C., this 2d day of May, 1867.

TESTIMONY OF WILLIAM B. McMURTRIE.

Int. 1.—State your name, residence, and occupation.

Ans.—William B. McMurtrie; hydrographic draughtsman, Coast Survey; Washington, D. C.

Int. 2.—Are you acquainted with Steilacoom creek, which empties into Puget's Sound?

Ans.—Yes; I have been in it several times.

Int. 3.—Look at this map, entitled "Reconnoissance of Steilacoom Harbor, Washington Territory," and state by whom, and under what circumstances, it was made?

Ans.—It was made by Lieutenant James Alden, United States Navy, Assistant Coast Survey, in 1856, for the purpose of navigation. This map or chart was drawn by myself, as draughtsman of the survey party.

Int. 4.—Will you describe this creek?

Ans.—This creek, owing to the bars at the entrance, cannot be entered at low-water, except by small boats—the mean rise and fall of tides being 9.2 feet; mean rise of spring tide is 11.1 feet. This is serpentine in its course; but when once a small vessel is across the bar, it might lie with safety.

Int. 5.—How large a vessel could enter Steilacoom creek?

Ans.—As to the water, at high tide, a vessel drawing nine or ten feet might enter, but, owing to the narrowness of the channel and its serpentine course, it would be difficult for a large vessel to lie inside. I have never heard of any vessel lying in the creek.

Cross-Examination.

Int. 1.—Could not, at high-water, a vessel drawing twelve feet be warped into the creek?

Ans.—At spring tides, extraordinary high water, such a vessel might be warped in.

WM. B. McMURTRIE.

In the matter of the Claim of the Puget's Sound Agricultural Company against the United States.

Deposition of EDWARD I. ALLEN, witness produced on the part of the United States, and examined by agreement between C. C. Beaman, counsel for the United States, and Edward Lander, counsel for the Puget's Sound Agricultural Company.

TESTIMONY OF EDWARD I. ALLEN.

Int. 1.—What is your name, residence, and occupation?

Ans.—Edward I. Allen; Pittsburg, Pennsylvania; Secretary and Treasurer of the Pacific and Atlantic Telegraph Company of the United States.

Int. 2.—Are you acquainted with Nisqually, a post of the Puget's Sound Agricultural Company?

Ans.—I have been there frequently, at different times from 1852 to 1855.

Int. 3.—Describe the fort and post.

Ans.—Stockaded fort, with court and buildings enclosed.

Int. 4·—What business were you engaged in, in the years 1852 and 1855?

Ans.—The greater portion of the time, I was building the military road from Fort Steilacoom to Fort Walla-Walla.

Int. 5.—State whether you know the cost of labor in the territory about Nisqually, from the years 1852 to 1855.

Ans.—As to Indian labor the price depended almost entirely upon the person hiring. A stranger would have to pay more for Indian labor than the employés of the Company paid them, or any persons who had their confidence. The only white labor I was acquainted with was wood-chopping. I employed some twenty or forty wood-choppers. I paid them $60 per month and found them in provisions.

Int. 6.—State what was the value of the Puget's Sound Agricultural Company's post and buildings at Nisqually.

Ans.—I should suppose the buildings and enclosures there would cost the Company, when built, $3,000 or $4,000. It is difficult to estimate the value of buildings when one's observation was not made with the purpose of forming an estimate of the cost; but I would suppose that the post could have been built, at the time I was there, at a cost not much greater than the amount stated. I understood labor to have been higher when I was there than it had previously been, or afterwards was.

Int. 7.—What do you know of the claim made, from 1852 to 1855, to any lands about the fort at Nisqually?

Ans.—I always understood, at that time, that they claimed ten square miles. That was the extent of their claim, as I understood it from the settlers.

(Understanding of the witness objected to as hearsay, and incompetent.)

Int. 8.—What was the character of the land at Nisqually, extending along the shores of Puget's Sound from the Nisqually river on the one side to the Puyallup river on the other, and back to the Coast [Cascade] range of mountains?

Ans.—The woodlands and prairie generally very poor; narrow strips of arable land along the streams; difficult to enclose sufficient arable land to make a moderate-sized farm, in a compact shape. The prairie land was generally gravelly, very leachy, and continued cultivation decreased the crop raised, as the gravel worked to the surface and the soil became almost entirely lost to view. The bulk of the lands lying about Fort Nisqually were remarkably poor, having a scant growth of sorrel, to the almost utter exclusion of anything else. Frequently passing over those lands in rainy weather, when the rain had been continuous for days, I never saw any mud on those lands, from the almost complete absence of any material of which it could be made.

Int. 9.—What would you estimate to be the average value per acre of the tract of land described in the previous question?

Ans.—For the prairie lands generally, I would consider 25 cents per acre a fair valuation. The arable land would be worth probably $1.50 per acre. I should think 50 cents per acre would be a fair valuation for the whole of the land.

Int. 10.—What number of oak trees per acre would you estimate to have been on the tract of land described in the 8th interrogatory, and now read to you?

Ans.—I doubt whether there would be 150,000 oak trees on said tract of land; I doubt whether there was an oak tree to an acre. There were [a] few clumps of oak trees near the fort, lying between the fort and the Sound; further back, towards the mountains they were exceedingly rare. Here and there an oak tree might be seen in the belts of woods separating the prairies, and near the alluvials marking the course of the streams, but the deciduous trees generally are cottonwood and alder.

Int. 11.—What would you estimate to have been the value of these oak trees?

Ans.—They were so few in number, I never heard it made a matter of calculation by men owning mills. Designing at one time to go into the milling business myself, and desirous of locating in the best locality for making money, and endeavoring to acquire full information about the timber, I never at any time took into consideration the possibility of getting any considerable amount of oak timber any where on the Sound, nor ever had any suggestion made to me as to the possibility of getting any considerable quantity of oak timber on the Sound by those whose advice I sought.

Int. 12.—State what you know in regard to any cattle on the plains about Nisqually?

Ans.—I know that there was [a] considerable quantity of cattle on the plains, some of which were claimed by the settlers, but the large bodies of which were said to belong to the Hudson's Bay Company. The smaller bodies belonging to the settlers were generally found in close proximity to their farms, to prevent their escaping into the larger herds. The larger herds, said to belong to the Hudson's Bay Company, occupied prairies more distant from the settled farms. They were in a wild state, and when slaughtered were shot by men on horseback. Some of the prairies where they pastured it was dangerous to cross afoot, and I have been repeatedly warned that it was even dangerous to attempt it on horseback, on account of the ferocity of some of the bulls.

(Mr. Lander objected to the last portion of this answer, as being hearsay, and incompetent.)

On one or two occasions, on passing through, I was satisfied the danger was not an imaginary one.

Int. 13.—Do you know anything in regard to the value of these cattle?

Ans.—While building the military road from Steilacoom to Walla-Walla, I accepted the proposition of Dr. Tolmie to choose from such herds as I might be able to hunt down and shoot, and pay therefor at $5.00 per head. I so shot a considerable number of cattle, and paid for them at that price.

Int. 14.—What do you know of any other parties being supplied by cattle from these same herds?

Ans.—Messrs. Weed and Hurd, from Olympia, who supplied the market at Olympia with fresh beef, procured their cattle from D^r. Tolmie.

Int. 15.—What was the character of the winter of 1852, in Washington Territory, and what do you know of its effect upon your own or any other cattle?

Ans.—It was very severe; there was about two feet of snow on the ground for a long time. Large quantities of cat-tle died, not being able, from the depth of snow, to get anything to eat. Very few cattle, except those that were very fat before the snow fell, or those which were specially cared for by the settlers and fed regularly, survived; and great numbers of the latter even perished, I suppose, for want of proper shelter. I had five oxen of my own, which I attended to with great regularity every day while the snow lasted; I succeeded, by doing so, in saving all but one. The farmer from whom I purchased my hay, not taking the special care of his cattle which I took of mine, lost a considerable number. Nearly all the cattle east of the Cascades died that winter. I knew several parties who had herds of cattle east of the Cascades, from whom I derived this information.

(The latter part of this answer, as to cattle dying east of the Cascade range of mountains, objected to by Mr. Lander as irrelevant, and that portion from information of others as hearsay and incompetent.)

Int. 16.—Whether or no you ever heard anything from the Indians in regard to the destruction of the cattle this winter.

(Mr. Lander objects to this question as incompetent and irrelevant.)

Ans.—Frequently seeing sculls and bones of cattle in the mountains, the Indians stated that they were the bones of cattle that had left the plains and gone towards the mountains for subsistence during the severe season, and they perished there. Most likely some of the bones found near the base of the mountains were those of cattle surreptitiously killed by the Indians for their own purposes. Coming down from the mountains at one time, I discovered a party of Indians gathered around the carcase of one of these cattle, which they acknowledged having taken without leave. I frequently saw fresh beef in the lodges of the Indians on the Puyallup, which I suppose was obtained in the same way.

(Mr. Lander objects to the statements derived from the Indians.)

Int. 17.—Did you ever know of any cattle or horses being killed by wild beasts?

Ans.—There were many cougars in that country; they were very dangerous and ferocious. At one time, in my camp in the mountains, one came into the camp in daylight, and seemed utterly fearless, evidently driven by hunger, and appeared determined to seize a quarter of beef that was in camp; and although there were many men in the camp, they had no firearms, and had it not been for a larger body of men coming into camp at that moment, it would undoubtedly have seized the beef. A few days previously to this incident the packer who brought the beef to me reported five or six mares disabled or killed, within the limits of the land spoken of above, by cougars, and the stallion saved himself by plunging into the lake.

Int. 18.—Do you know anything as to the value of the sheep owned by the Puget's Sound Agricultural Company?

Ans.—I know there was mutton supplied by Dr. Tolmie to Messrs. Weed and Hurd, of Olympia. I cannot say what price they paid for it. At one time, in coming from Steilacoom to Cowlitz river, a drove of sheep was driven over at the same time by some Hudson Bay employés. It was customary with them to kill and eat what sheep they needed on the route, and as their choice seemed to be, as far as I could judge, governed by no consideration but the fatness of the animal chosen, I inferred that the valuation of the sheep would be as the basis of mutton per pound.

Int. 19.—What was the number and the character of the horses owned by the Company at Nisqually?

Ans.—I can't say as to the number; they were similar to those generally seen about the Hudson's Bay Company's stations, Indian ponies, used for packing, bearing generally the marks of the services they had undergone.

Int. 20.—What do you know of the price and value of such horses?

Ans.—I can only judge of the price of these animals by the price at which I could have obtained better, because not so hardly used, animals of the same stock. The offer was made by Piu-piu-mox-mox to our farm at Fort Walla-Walla to sell any number of horses we might choose out of his herds at $13 per head, payable in blankets. It was my design to have purchased a herd of these horses, and driven them across the plains to the States. This point was about 225 miles from Fort Steilacoom, which is near Nisqually.

(Mr. Lander objects to this answer, so far as it states the price of horses at Walla-Walla, as irrelevant.)

Int. 21.—What would it have cost to have brought a hundred horses from Walla-Walla to Nisqually?

Ans.—Two hundred dollars would be a liberal estimate.

Int. 22.—In your answer to Interrogatory 12, you have spoken of cattle as said to belong to the Hudson's Bay Company, did you mean that these cattle belonged to the Hudson's Bay Company or the Puget's Sound Agricultural Company? In answer to this question, make a statement of the connection between the two Companies, as understood by you and by the American settlers around Nisqually.

(Mr. Lander objects to that portion of the question as relates to the understanding of the witness and the American settlers as incompetent.)

Ans.—The distinction you make between the Hudson's Bay Company and the Puget's Sound Agricultural Company is one not made by the American settlers in that vicinity, so far as my knowledge extends. In all matters relating to the two Companies named, there is but one title given—that of Hudson's Bay Company. I found this also the custom of the former employés of the Hudson's Bay Company. My own and the general impression was, the so-called Puget's Sound Agricul-

21 P

tural Company was an organization made ·by the officers of the Hudson's Bay Company, through which claims could be urged against the United States which could not have been urged through the Hudson's Bay Company.

(Mr. Lander objects to the statements of the former employés of the Hudson's Bay Company; the understanding of this witness—his and other people's convictions—objected to as incompetent and irrelevant.)

Int. 23.—What were the relations of the Companies to officers of the United States and citizens resident in the Territory?

Ans.—The relations generally, so far as my knowledge extended, were not friendly with the settlers. Among .the settlers there seemed to be a great deal of hard feeling against the Hudson's Bay Company. Among officers the reverse seemed to be the case.

Cross-Examination of Edward I. Allen.

Int. 1.—At what time did you leave Puget's Sound? Please to give the month and year.

Ans.—It was about February or March, 1855.

Int. 2.—At what time did you arrive on the Sound?

Ans.—I think, about the beginning of October, 1852.

Int. 3.—How much of that two years and three months were you at Olympia?

Ans.—About eighteen months, I judge.

Int. 4.—Did you not take a donation claim in the timber near Olympia, and reside upon and cultivate that claim until you left the Sound?

Ans.—No, sir.

Int. 5.—When did you abandon this claim, or sell or deliver possession of it to any other person? Give, if you can, the date of the abandonment or transfer.

Ans.—I never either abandoned or transferred any claim in Washington Territory.

Int. 6.—Did you not take up a donation claim near Olympia? If so, state how far it was from that place, and how far from the Nisqually Plains.

Ans.—Under the act which allowed purchase after two years' residence, I purchased a claim about two and a half miles from Olympia, and about eighteen or twenty miles from Nisqually.

Int. 7.—Did you not file a notification in the Land Office declaring your intention to reside upon and cultivate this tract of land which you say you purchased, and did you not, about two years after the date of this notification, file in the Land Office an affidavit stating, among other things, that you had resided upon and cultivated this tract of land for the period of your said notification?

Ans.—Yes, sir.

Int. 8.—Was the military road on which you say you worked on the route across the Natchess Pass of the Cascade mountains, and was not your time chiefly occupied, while working on that road, on what is called the mountain sections of the road?

Ans.—It was across the Natchess Pass. While I was occupied upon that road, I was occupied nearly all the time in the mountain sections, with the exception of occasional returns to my domicil on Puget's Sound, to attend to crops and other matters relating thereto.

Int. 9.—Was there not a plain trail, easily distinguishable, leading across the plains from the point where you entered the woods, bordering on the Puyallup, to the military post called Fort Steilacoom, and from there by Fort Nisqually to Olympia?

Ans.—There was a regular road, as I should call it, running as you have designated.

Int. 10.—Was not this the route usually travelled by you on your visits to your claim, from your work in the mountains, except when you might occasionally visit the town of Steilacoom or go through there on your way to Olympia?

Ans.—Very nearly the road pursued.

Int. 11.—Was there not a place called Montgomery's near the line of woods bordering on the Puyallup, by which you travelled on your way to and from your work on the mountains?

Ans.—I know of such a place; it was on the edge of the woods.

Int. 12.—Were not your rides across the plains generally in the summer season?

Ans.—Yes, sir.

Int. 13.—Is not the summer, as a general rule, in that section of the country almost entirely free from rains?

Ans.—Yes, sir.

Int. 14.—What lands on the Nisqually plains have you ever seen cultivated two years in succession? If you have seen any, state where it was, and on whose claim.

Ans.—Judging from the old enclosures, I think I saw land that had been cultivated two years near Fort Nisqually. There was also a point about two-thirds up that bore the marks of having been cultivated two years in succession.

Int. 15.—Are you prepared to say that this land which you speak of had not been in cultivation, so far as you know anything about it, for twenty years, as well as the two you speak of.

Ans.—I can only say that I think it would be like lunacy for any man to attempt to cultivate this land for any number of years without using such facilities for keeping up its fertility as are not usually within the reach of agriculturists.

Int. 16.—Have you ever cultivated any land upon these plains, or have you ever stopped to examine any that has been turned up by the plough?

Ans.—I never cultivated any of that land; but I have on several occasions examined it when turned up by the plough.

Int. 17.—State one of those occasions, and where it was, how long you were off your horse, and how much land you walked over.

Ans.—I stopped at the house of a man near Montgomery's, and also at another place probably a mile and a half farther down. I may have spent several hours at either place, though I cannot recall exactly how long the time was, or the quantity of ground I went over; I only remember the general impression left on my mind of the character of the soil.

Int. 18.—Did you see and notice the crops borne on these pieces of land you saw ploughed?

Ans.—I don't know that I ever saw any crop cut from those pieces of land, though I saw grain growing.

Int. 19.—Were you able to distinguish between the cattle of the Hudson's Bay Company and those of the settlers, when you saw cattle feeding on the plains?

Ans.—As a general rule, the Hudson's Bay cattle were in a wild state, while those of the settlers were not. I don't recall seeing any herds of cattle belonging to the settlers in that vicinity, and noticing the difference; that those cattle of the settlers that I noticed there were not numerous enough to be in herds, were generally work cattle.

Int. 20.—Did you ever see any herds of cattle in crossing the plains?

Ans.—Yes, sir.

Int. 21.—Do you know whether these were cattle of the Company, or cattle of the settlers?

Ans.—I could not say from my own knowledge.

Int. 22.—Is not what you said about the cattle on the plains, and the difference between the Company's and the settlers' cattle there, derived from what has been told you?

Ans.—No. I have heard the statement of that difference made probably a dozen times, and my own slight observation confirms the opinion generally expressed in relation to the difference between cattle domesticated and those running wild.

Int. 23.—Were you ever chased or surrounded by any band of cattle, or chased or attacked by any single animal on these plains?

Ans.—On some of the small prairies off the ordinary lines of travel, where I had been frequently warned that it was dangerous to pass through, passing through on one or two occasions, while I was never absolutely attacked, or pursued, or surrounded, there were such demonstrations made of attack that I considered it prudent to get out of the way before an attack was made.

Int. 24.—In speaking of the leave granted you by Dr. Tol-

mie to take cattle at $5 a head, was not this during the year
1853, and while you were working upon the road across the
mountains, sustained by the voluntary contributions of the
settlers and others on Puget's Sound?

Ans.—I think not. I think it was a proposition by Dr.
Tolmie to me, as a contractor to build the military road for
the Government of the United States. While building the
road by voluntary contributions from the citizens, I think I
got no beef on these conditions from Dr. Tolmie. I think
Dr. Tolmie contributed an amount in cash, in common with
other residents.

Int. 25.—Was this proposition of Dr. Tolmie you speak of
in answer to Interrogatory 13, made to you in person by Dr.
Tolmie?

Ans.—I think it was, but I am not positive of it; but I
think I have, among the other vouchers for building that
road, Dr. Tolmie's receipt for the cattle. I remember distinctly that he accepted my own statement of the number
killed in settlement.

Int. 26.—By whom were these cattle shot for you?

Ans.—By an employé of my own. I cannot recollect his
name, but I have at home a list of the names of all the employés affixed to a contract regulating their wages.

Int. 27.—Was not this contract entered into, and the
names of these employés signed to it, in the year 1854?

Ans.—I think it was in the spring of 1854.

Int. 28.—Are you certain that you received no beef from
Dr. Tolmie in the year 1853, under this agreement you
speak of?

Ans.—I think not, but I am not positive.

Int. 29.—Did you buy any horses for either of your expeditions?

Ans.—Not that I remember.

Int. 30.—What pack animals did you use in the summer
of 1853?

Ans.—Pack animals furnished by the commandant at Fort
Steilacoom.

Int. 31.—At what time were you at Fort Walla-Walla?

Ans.—In July, 1854, I think.

Int. 32.—Was the offer from Piu-piu-mox-mox made to you in July, 1854?

Ans.—No.

Int. 33.—Did Piu-piu-mox-mox ever make to you in person the offer mentioned in your answer to interrogatory 20; and if so, when was it, and how many were you to buy?

Ans.—No, sir; the offer was made to the firm of which I was a partner. The offer was made in 1854. Our purpose was to have purchased about five hundred.

Int. 34.—What firm do you mean in your answer, and in what business were you concerned?

Ans.—The firm of Allen & Ensign, working under a charter granted by the Territorial Legislature, in ferrying across the Columbia river at Walla-Walla.

Int. 35.—Do you know anything more of this offer by Piu-piu-mox-mox except by hearsay and report?

Ans.—I know it as a man knows the business transactions of the firm in which he is engaged, from the record of his books, or the statement of his partner in business. In this case I had no reason to doubt the statement made by my partner, and was preparing, in company with some others, to make a purchase of five hundred, and take them to the States.

Int. 36.—Were not the persons with whom you conversed about timber, and going into the milling business, generally resident at Olympia or the vicinity?

Ans.—No, sir; they were persons in different localities.

Int. 37.—Did you not propose to erect your mill, if you did build one, near Olympia?

Ans.—I was prepared to build it where I could find the most money-making locality, though I preferred Olympia, if it would have paid better than any other point.

Int. 38.—Was not the cutting of lumber upon the Sound at that time confined chiefly to the production of fir lumber?

Ans.—Yes, sir.

Int. 39.—In all the conversations had about the business in connection with lumber, was not the fir the only tree thought of, or mentioned.

Ans.—No, sir.

Int. 40.—What other tree was mentioned?

Ans.—Cedar.

Examination-in-Chief Resumed.

Int. 1.—Where was your residence in Washington Territory?

Ans.—During the whole time on my claim, about only on necessary business.

Int. 2.—From what time were you under contract to build the road from Fort Steilacoom to Fort Walla-Walla?

Ans.—The contract was signed, I think, in the winter of 1853; the work was commenced on it in the spring of 1854.

Int. 3.—How many cattle do you estimate that you received from Dr. Tolmie at $5 a head, after you began to work on this road in the spring of 1854?

Ans.—I can't remember exactly; I should judge between thirty and fifty.

Cross-Examination Resumed.

Int. 1.—Was the contract with Dr. Tolmie in writing?

Ans.—I am not certain; if it was, it is among my papers at home.

Int. 2.—Did you ever have any verbal contract with Dr. Tolmie on this subject?

Ans.—I don't distinctly remember, but my impression is that I had.

Int. 3.—Did the proposition come from you to Dr. Tolmie, or from Dr. Tolmie to you?

Ans.—My impression is that it was Dr. Tolmie's own proposition.

Int. 4.—Where did he make it to you?

Ans.—My impression is not distinct, but my impression is that the proposition was made to me by Dr. Tolmie, in a conversation in the fort.

Int. 5.—Will you now state that this proposition was not made to you in 1853, while you were working on the road under subscription, and that it was not made by Dr. Tolmie as a part of his gift to the road, and to enable you and those who were with you working to assist the emigration through, to live more cheaply while engaged in the work?

Ans.—I do not think these were the circumstances under which the proposition was made.

Int. 6.—Was any beef shot under this agreement in 1853?

Ans.—I don't remember any being made in 1853.

Int. 7.—Did you cause any beef to be shot on the plains in 1853?

Ans.—I don't remember having done so.

Int. 8.—Who brought the beef to you in the mountains in 1853?

Ans.—I don't remember getting beef in 1853.

Int. 9.—How many men did you have in your party in 1853?

Ans.—About thirty.

Int. 10.—On what did they live?

Ans.—On beans, pork, &c. I don't recall any beef in 1853.

Int. 11.—Did not Lieut. Arnold talk with you about obtaining beef from Dr. Tolmie?

Ans.—Yes, sir.

Int. 12.—Can you now state whether the proposition you speak of, or contract, was made with yourself or Lieut. Arnold?

Ans.—My impression is that it was with me, but I am not positive.

Int. 13.—Is not your recollection rather confused about the whole matter, between what was said to you by Lieut. Arnold, and what you think was said to you by Dr. Tolmie?

Ans.—I am positive that a conversation with Lieut. Arnold on that subject; distinctly recollect the conversation. Lieut. Arnold had no connection with the military road until after the work was accepted by Captain McClellan. This would confirm my impression that the contract with Dr. Tolmie for beef related to the time when I was a contractor for the Government under Lieut. Arnold.

The counsel for the United States reserves the right to annex to this deposition a certified copy of the receipt of Dr. Tolmie, alluded to in the witness' answer to cross-interrogatory 25, if this receipt shall hereafter be found and authenticated.

EDWARD JAY ALLEN.

Sworn and subscribed before me this twenty-ninth day of May, A. D. 1867.

N. CALLAN,
Notary Public.

In the matter of the Claim of the Puget's Sound Agricultural Company against the United States.

Deposition of GEORGE GIBBS, witness examined on behalf of the United States, at Washington city, this third day of May, 1867.

TESTIMONY OF GEORGE GIBBS.

Int. 1.—State your name, occupation, and residence.
Ans.—George Gibbs, Clerk to the Commissioner on the part of the United States on this Commission; residence at present in Washington city, D. C.
Int. 2.—What have been your duties as Clerk to the Commission?
Ans.—I have been in charge of the office, and, in addition to the usual clerical duties, have pointed out to the counsel for the United States persons whom I knew to be acquainted with the subject in controversy, informing him of the matters with which they were severally acquainted.
Int. 3.—Is your salary a fixed amount, and not at all contingent?
Ans.—It is a per diem allowance, fixed by law.
Int. 4.—Have you any pecuniary interest in the decision of the questions before the Commission?
Ans.—None whatever.

Int. 5.—Are you acquainted with the character of the tract of country in Washington Territory, lying on Puget's Sound, known as the Nisqually Plains?

Ans.—I am well acquainted with it. I first went there early in the spring of 1854, and lived there, with intervals of absence, for three years. During that time I traveled the plains on foot and horseback frequently, and in almost every direction.

Int. 6.—What was your occupation during these three years?

Ans.—I was in the employment of the United States during most of that time, either in making reconnoissances for military roads, or acting as interpreter, and other similar capacities at Fort Steilacoom. I also farmed to a certain extent in the neighborhood of the garrison. I assisted in a survey of a road from Fort Steilacoom across the Cascade mountains, by way of the Natchess pass, examining two routes for the same. I also surveyed a road from Steilacoom to the Cowlitz river, examining two separate routes for that purpose. Also, subsequently, I was in the employment of the Northwestern Boundary Survey, as geologist, and in that capacity examined and made a report on these plains, with other parts of the Territory.

Int. 7.—Will you please describe the general character of these plains?

Ans.—The Nisqually Plains, so called, embrace a tract of about 160,000 acres, lying between the Nisqually and Puyallup rivers, on the southeast and northwest, between Puget's Sound on the west, and the forest extending to the Cascade mountains on the east. Taken as a body, it may be described as a pretty level prairie, elevated from 200 to 300 feet above tide-water, and rising in low benches, as it recedes from the Sound. It is skirted by forest, both on the rivers and towards the Sound. It is interspersed with small lakes, belts of timber, swamps, and rocky eminences covered with fir timber, and is watered by several streams. The whole belongs to that formation which geologists call drift, and is composed of boulder stones and gravel, mixed with sand, and interstratified with beds of clay. The soil is merely superficial, except on the immediate waters of some of the streams, and in the swamps which filled the hollows formerly occupied by lakes.

Int. 8.—What is the general character of this soil?

Ans.—Except as mentioned, along the borders of the streams or in the neighborhood of water, it is dry and sterile. The only vegetation, excepting weeds and low bushes, is the grass known as bunch grass, which forms no sod, but grows in separate tufts. The soil is so porous that, after one or two crops, it leaches through, leaving only gravel on the surface, and is beside so thoroughly exhausted that it will produce nothing but the sorrel which the sheep have disseminated almost everywhere they have ranged.

Int. 9.—Whether or no you have had any particular knowledge of the value of these plains for agriculture?

Ans.—I had occasion, in the spring of 1854, to examine a considerable part of them, with a view to selecting a claim for myself, to which I was entitled under the donation act, giving me a right to 320 acres wherever I might select it. The nearest point to the town of Steilacoom which I could find fit for settlement, was situated about five miles from the water upon Steilacoom creek. At that time but one other plain, excepting that occupied by the garrison, had been taken between the Sound and the place I selected, and that was taken by Mr. Bird for a saw-mill. But few settlers were then on the plains, and those mostly discharged Hudson's Bay Company servants, or soldiers whose term of service had expired. I had then a wide selection. I took up a tract of 320 acres on this creek, laying it out in as irregular a form as the act permitted, in order to secure the best ground, taking in both sides of the creek, and including a small quantity of muck land. I found, after experimenting, that none except the last-mentioned could be cultivated with any profit. This made a very good garden patch. The best portion of the land in the swale I sowed in wheat. The first year it produced a very good crop, say from twenty-five to thirty bushels. The next year it did not pay for harvesting.

I also tried oats and rye, sowing the rye on the upland; it made very good stalks, but the heads did not fill. The oats I was obliged to cut before they were ripe, on account of the grasshoppers, which, during some years, are very destructive. Of potatoes and peas I got very fair crops; but, finding that the gravel rose to the surface wherever the ground was broken, and that I should ruin the whole place, I gave up all idea of cultivating it, and sowed a considerable part of it with mixed timothy and clover seed. These grasses grew pretty well in the swale, but while I was there had formed no sod. The same was pretty much the experience of my neighbors. I planted an orchard of some two hundred trees, chiefly apple and pear, but it did not come to anything. In very good situations these fruits may be cultivated, but not to much advantage. Indian corn, tomatoes, melons, squashes, and pumpkins, and in general those vegetables which suffer from early frosts, cannot be raised with success. Indian corn never ripens.

Int. 10.—Whether or no you ever built a house, or made any permanent improvements on your place?

(Mr. Lander objects to this question, as irrelevant.)

Ans.—I built a small house, consisting of two rooms, a kitchen, and a wood-shed, and also a barn, and put nearly a mile of fencing altogether on the place. The total cost was something over $1,000.

Int. 11.—What has been done with your claim since you left it in 1856?

Ans.—It was occupied, I think, for about a year by Mr. D. E. Lane, who had previously cultivated it for me. When he went to his own place, he left it in charge of another person to take care of for whatever he could get off of it. The place was for sale some time, and I finally disposed of it last spring for $450 in gold, or about $600 in currency, and was very glad to get rid of it.

(All the above testimony, in regard to the value of Mr. Gibbs' farm and the improvements thereon, objected to as irrelevant.)

Int. 12.—What do you know of the garden of the military post?

Ans.—The garrison had a garden four or five miles from the post, upon another branch of Steilacoom creek, a mile or so beyond my place. It consisted of a narrow strip of land in a swale upon this creek. It was naturally rich, black earth, with some gravel interspersed, and was kept manured to the highest degree with stable manure from the garrison. Here very fine crops of vegetables were raised, but the place was so exceptional in quality that an adjoining settler was constantly attempting to bring it within his claim, and it was consequently never left without some one upon it. The reason for taking this place was that no other like it could be found within any reasonable distance. The claim upon which the barracks themselves were situated had been worn out prior to its going there, and could not be claimed.

Int. 13.—What do you know of the character of the land immediately around Fort Nisqually, the post of the Puget's Sound Agricultural Company?

Ans.—Close to the fort there was a garden, on the creek, where the ground was very good, where some flowering plants as well as vegetables were cultivated. The most of the land from there over what is called the American Plain, on the map now before me, as far as Steilacoom barracks, however, was dry and incapable of cultivation. The neighborhood of the fort itself was little else than a bed of red sorrel, and that weed prevailed over much of the adjoining district, to the almost entire destruction of the grass. The immediate neighborhood of Fort Nisqually seemed to have been formerly cropped, but abandoned from its sterility.

Int. 14.—What do you estimate to be the value of the tract of land you have described as the Nisqually Plains?

Ans.—One-fifth of the amount I consider to be absolutely without value; for the remainder, taking the whole, I should be very sorry to give the minimum Government price.

Int. 15.—What part of these plains were taken up when you went there in 1854, and by whom, and under what act?

Ans.—In the spring of 1854, there were very few white

inhabitants on the plains. Those were mostly either discharged servants of the Company, or soldiers whose term of service had expired. These persons had selected the best situations not occupied by the Puget's Sound Company. Muck Plain, in particular, was occupied by a small colony of Hudson's Bay Company's employés, and other former British subjects. These employés nearly all declared their intention to become citizens of the United States, and avail themselves of the privileges of the donation act. On the Canadian Plain there were also some Frenchmen. On the two branches of the Steilacoom creek the Americans predominated. All, of course, held under the same act.

Int. 16.—Did you ever know any of this land to be preempted?

Ans.—Never.

Int. 17.—Did you ever know any of it to be sold?

Ans.—I remember of no sale excepting my own.

Int. 18.—What fractional part of this tract was settled on?

Ans.—In 1854 the amount was very limited. In the fall of that year a few emigrants came in over the mountains, and, I think, some others in the succeeding year. Of these, a number, after looking around, went elsewhere. I have known several claims to be abandoned after they had been taken up. I should think that, even as late as 1858, less than one-half of the plains were claimed by individuals, and much less than that enclosed. In fact, for grazing purposes, it would not pay to enclose them.

Int. 19.—How much of this tract was occupied by the Puget's Sound Agricultural Company?

Ans.—I know of but two farms which the Company held— one a short distance east of Fort Nisqually, the other, called Kithlow's Station, occupied as a sheep farm, and the residence of the chief shepherd. They had two or three more sheep stations, where the different classes of sheep were kept by servants. At this time they had apparently given up what is stated to have been once their practice of moving their sheep corrals from point to point, but now kept them at stations, and drove them out to pasture from thence.

Int. 20.—What would you estimate to be the number of oak trees on this tract, and what was the quality of the oak?

Ans.—It is impossible to average them by the acre, as they do not grow equally scattered, but are generally in clumps here and there, with considerable intervals entirely destitute of them. On my place of 320 acres, there were two clumps of from ten to a dozen each, and some scattering ones, in all not over three dozen, according to the best of my recollection. I should think this was a fair average of the whole. The quality was inferior, the boles were rarely long enough to saw into plank, and the wood brash. These trees were chiefly used for firewood. A few of them might have been used for farming purposes, as repairing carts, &c., and also for the knees of boats and scows. They had no market value, settlers usually helping themselves from the common lands.

Int. 21.—Describe Fort Nisqually.

Ans.—Fort Nisqually, like most of the other posts of the Company, consists of several buildings enclosed within a stockade of logs about twelve feet high, and pointed at the top. The stockade was defended by two bastions, at transverse angles. Within were a warehouse and several other buildings, used as stores, &c. These were in a very dilapidated condition, and had been of very inferior quality from the beginning. About 1854 or 1855, Dr. Tolmie, then the Chief Trader in charge, erected a new dwelling. There were several buildings outside of the enclosure, such as a dairy and some others of which I have no distinct recollection. On the beach, under the bluff, a warehouse of some size.

Int. 22.—What was the value of these buildings?

Ans.—With the exception of Dr. Tolmie's house, and whatever advantages might be derived from the stockade, I do not think that any valuation could have been put upon the post. Nobody would have purchased the other buildings unless for a nominal sum, and for a temporary use. As regards the warehouse, I cannot give any opinion. As to the other outside buildings, I have no recollection further than that there were such.

Int. 23.—Whether or not there were any cattle on the

Nisqually Plains from the year 1854 to 1857; and if so, what was their character?

Ans.—There were bands of cattle there belonging to the Puget's Sound Company and to citizens. The cattle belonging to the Company, without being "wild cattle," were very wild. They had sprung from a mixture of English cattle with the wild Spanish stock. This was measurably the case with the cattle belonging to citizens, but they had a greater proportion of domesticated American cattle. The Company's cattle were so wild that, in butchering them, they were driven up by men on horseback, and shot. During my time I never saw any herding or branding of these cattle, except perhaps in the case of cows and calves.

Int. 24.—Whether or not these cattle are still on the plains?

Ans.—I imagine very few, if any, as, before I left the Sound, I heard that the Company had transferred all their remaining sheep and cattle to Vancouver's Island.

(So much of the answer as professes to be founded on hearsay objected to.)

Int. 25.—What do you know of the removal of the cattle?

Ans.—I know that the Company, for a considerable time previous, had been in the habit of shipping large quantities of cattle on the hoof, as well as in beef, to Victoria, for the supply of the town and the British squadron, as I supposed. They also sold beef to the troops at Fort Steilacoom and to the neighboring settlements.

Int. 26.—What do you know of the value of these cattle?

Ans.—The value of the wild cattle was very small, as I know that Dr. Tolmie offered to myself and others, whom he could rely upon, the privilege of shooting cattle at $5 a head on certain conditions, of which, I think, one was that we should report to him as speedily as possible the place where the animal was killed, in order that he might get the hide, or forward it to him ourselves.

(Statements of Dr. Tolmie objected to.)

Int. 27.—What do you know of the character of the sheep, and how the Company disposed of them?

Ans.—The sheep were small, but of excellent quality. The

22 P

Company butchered them, and sold the mutton at the garrison and in the neighboring settlements. They never would sell any alive to persons living on the plains. The increase beyond what they butchered were therefore sent away. A large number were shipped to San Juan Island in December, 1853. Dr. Tolmie drove another large band into Oregon. Other bands were shipped to Vancouver's Island, and, if I mistake not, to California also.

Int. 28.—What do you know of any mills on Steilacoom creek?

Ans.—The first mill built on Steilacoom creek was a flour mill, erected about half a mile north of the garrison by Mr. Thomas M. Chambers. Afterwards a Mr. Bird built a saw mill a mile or a mile and a half above him.

Int. 29.—Was there water enough in the creek to run the two mills?

Ans.—As the fall of water in the creek was very considerable, the same water, although its volume was not great during the latter part of the summer and the autumn, could have been worked over several times, had it not been for the porous nature of the soil, which rendered it next to impossible to make a dam tight. So much was this the case, that much of the water from the dam of Bird's mill escaped and found its way a distance of three-quarters of a mile, to the head of a ravine emptying into the creek below Chambers' mill, from which the garrison was supplied." What was originally a spring became a heavy stream. Mr. Chambers several times complained to me of the injury, and spoke of commencing a suit against Bird.

(Mr. Chambers' statements objected to.)

Cross-Examination Resumed, May 4, 1867.

Int. 1.—At what time, giving the day and month as well as you can, did you begin your employment on the United States Boundary Commission?

Ans.—In July, 1857.

Int. 2.—Was not that Boundary Commission employed in ascertaining the boundary line between the United States and Great Britain, in the Straits of Fuca and the Gulf of Georgia, and the position of the 49th parallel between the western shore of the Continent and the Rocky Mountains?

Ans.—Yes, sir; the boundary survey was engaged on that business.

Int. 3.—What other duties on that Commission were you engaged in than those of a geologist? Were you not, among other things, engaged in making a vocabulary of the language of the Indians on the islands and mainland near the 49th parallel?

Ans.—Yes, sir, I was so engaged, though not officially.

Int. 4.—What period of time, previous to your engagement in the Boundary Commission, have you devoted to the study of the theory of geology?

Ans.—It is impossible to say at this time, as my studies have been pursued at intervals, as opportunity afforded. I had studied geology before I left the States, and I had been previously employed as geologist to Captain McClellan's expedition on the Pacific Railroad survey.

Int. 6.—Were you not admitted to the bar in the city of New York; and did you not continue in your profession as a lawyer there, and as a writer, until you went to Oregon, some time in 1849?

Ans.—I finished my law studies, and was admitted to the bar in the city of New York. Nominally I continued in my profession as a lawyer until I left for Oregon; but having very little taste for the profession, I passed much of my time in other pursuits.

Int. 7.—Were you not, shortly after your arrival in Oregon, made deputy collector of the port of Astoria, and did you not continue in that position until your employment in the expedition of the then Captain McClellan?

Ans.—I was employed as deputy clerk and inspector, which is the legal name of the office, acting as deputy collector during the year 1850, until the spring of 1851. In the spring of 1851, I served for some time as commissary to a commission appointed to treat with the Indians of the Willamette Valley; thence I went down to California, and accompanied an expedition from the bay of San Francisco through the Coast mountains, to Klamath river, and up that river to the Shaste valley. Returning to San Francisco, I prepared a map of that portion of the country passed over, and a general report on the same. I spent the next succeeding year in the northern mines of California. In the winter of 1852, about Christmas, I returned to Oregon and qualified as collector of the port, having been appointed to that office in the meantime. I held that office six months, and was removed on the change of administration. I then joined the expedition under the then Captain, since Major General McClellan.

Int. 8.—In your answer to Interrogatory 9, you stated that you took up your claim in the spring of 1854. At what time did you begin your actual residence upon it?

Ans.—I took the claim early in the spring of 1854. Some time elapsed, say from one to two months, before I moved on to it, as I had to put up a house, make some fencing, and other preliminary improvements.

Int. 9.—Do you think that you are as accurate in the statement that you took up this claim in the spring of 1854, and went on to it personally within two months, to live, as you are in the other statements made in the other parts of your deposition?

Ans.—I am positive.

Int. 10.—How long did you continue to reside personally on this claim?

Ans.—I consider that my personal residence on the claim continued during the whole time of my stay upon Puget's Sound, that is, until the summer of 1858. I have already referred, in my direct examination, to occasional and temporary absences. Thus, in the summer of 1854, I surveyed the road from Fort Steilacoom to the Cascades, returning to my house to make a map of the route. So, also, in subsequent seasons I was absent on other expeditions, but, during these absences I always had persons on the place to take care of it; and if, at any time previous to my leaving the Sound, I had been out of occupation, I should have returned to it as my home.

Int. 11.—How many days, weeks, or months did you reside on and occupy the claim you mention, from the first day you went to live upon it until the day you left to survey the road you mention?

Ans.—Really I do not recollect. I think that our party started about the first week in July.

Int. 12.—Did you not pass the winter of 1854–5 at the garrison of Fort Steilacoom, so called?

Ans.—No; I was in there from day to day, and usually passed Sunday and Sunday nights there, but I passed most of the time and usually slept at my own house.

Int. 13.—Did you personally live on the claim in the summer of 1855?

Ans.—Only a portion of the summer. I was employed by Lieut. Derby, topographical engineers, to survey the routes for a military road from Fort Steilacoom to Fort Vancouver, and was absent on that duty.

Int. 14.—Were you upon this place personally, to live upon it, during the fall of 1855, the winter of 1855 and 1856, or the spring, summer, and fall of 1856?

Ans.—I was on the place only for a very brief period in the fall of 1855. I then went over to Vancouver on business; returned, I think, in December. The Indian war had then broken out, and a family had come in from the Puyallup river and occupied my house. It was the same family that had previously taken care of it. I was employed at the garrison during the rest of the winter, making a topographical map of the country, and also acting as interpreter for the post. In the spring of 1856 I was again employed in the survey of a portion of the military road from Astoria to the Twallatin plains, in Oregon. I then returned to the Sound, and shortly afterwards went down to Fort Townshend, where I was employed as quartermaster and commissary clerk to the post. There I remained until the arrival of the Boundary Commission, about the beginning of July, 1856. Within that time, between the spring of 1854 and the summer of 1856, I actually and *bona fide* inhabited my house, according to a note-book which I kept at the time—ten months, at different intervals.

Int. 15.—Did you, after the family you mentioned, took up its residence in your house, when you found them in its occupation in December, 1855, until the spring of 1857, when you say, in answer to Interrogatory 5, your residence on the Nisqually plains ceased, ever pass one single night at the house upon your claim? If so, give as near as you can the date of it?

Ans.—I wish to make a correction in my answer to Interrogatory 5. When I mentioned having resided on the claim for three years from the spring of 1854, I was thinking the boundary survey first came out in 1857. I should have stated two years. In reply to the question, I think it probable that I never did pass a night there. The family remained until all danger arising out of the Indian war had passed over. Mr. D. E. Lane, who had charge of the house at all times in my absence, then put another person in his place, and returned to his own claim. Whenever I was in Steilacoom, however, I used to ride out there, give directions as to what I wanted done, and get my dinner.

Int. 16.—Did you ever pay into the Land Office any money on account of this claim?

Ans.—No; I took it as a donation claim, and proved it up as such.

Int. 17.—Did you not notify that your residence on your claim commenced on the 16th day of February, 1855?

Ans.—Very likely. I put in a second notification in 1855, on altering the boundaries of my claim, and, I presume, thought it necessary to redate the time of occupation.

Int. 18.—Was not this second notification made under oath, and can you not now be positive as to the time you then swore your occupation of, and residence upon, this claim commenced?

Ans.—When, in the spring of 1854, I took that claim I necessarily put in a notification, and made oath to the time at which my occupation commenced. Early in 1855, as I believe, I changed the boundaries of that claim, in order to make them correspond with the line of my next neighbor; of course I had to put in a second notification, and verify it by a second oath. As I had not previously occupied the whole of this tract, I may have assigned the date of my second notification as the beginning of my residence.

Int. 19.—Did you swear in the notification of 1855 that you took this donation claim on the 16th of January, 1855?

Ans.—That is more than I can tell you, without seeing the notification.

Int. 20.—Can you not now recollect a date so important as that, on which you took possession of a farm of 320 acres, and laid the foundation of any title you might have to the land?

Ans.—No, sir.

Int. 21.—Will you now swear that on the 16th day of February, 1855, you were upon what you call your land claim on the Nisqually plains, and did then commence your residence and occupation thereon?

Ans.—I will now swear that at that date, as and before and after, I actually resided upon that place. Whether I was upon that land that particular day, or at Steilacoom, or at Olympia, or travelling around the country generally, I cannot say.

Int. 22.—State when you do consider that your occupation of that land, as a donation claim, actually commenced—giving the date, as near as your recollection at the present time enables you to do.

Ans.—My occupation of the original claim, taken in the spring of 1854—which claim was quadrangular—dated from that spring. When, in the subsequent spring, I changed the lines, conformably to those of my neighbor, I included six angles on the form of the tract, and, in filing a notification of the new claim, I presume I dated the occupation of that from the date of resurvey.

Int. 23.—Did your occupation and residence upon the claim which you sold begin on the 16th of February, 1855?

Ans.—I have already stated that I know nothing about the date of the 16th of February, 1855.

Int. 24.—State, if you can, when you did commence the occupation of and residence upon that donation claim which you say in your examination-in-chief that you sold.

Ans.—For all the purposes pertinent to this Commission, as I conceive, I took that claim in the spring of 1854; as I did then in fact take a claim there embracing the greater part of the land which I afterwards occupied. So far as regards the business of the Land Office, however, my claim should have dated from the time of altering its original boundaries.

Int. 25.—When did you notify the United States, through the proper officers of its Land Office, that you had begun your occupation of, and residence upon, the precise tract of land which in your examination you have stated that you afterwards sold?

Ans.—I presume, some time in the spring of 1855.

Int. 26.—Can you not at the present time give this date with any more certainty?

Ans.—Not from memory. It is probable that among my papers I may find a copy of the notification, a parol proof.

Int. 27.—Have you not within the last two years renewed, under oath, the statement containing the exact date which you had before sworn to as the time when you commenced your occupation and residence upon the specified claim which you afterwards say you sold?

Ans.—I filed the final proof at the time that I sold the claim in the spring of last year, and I presume that that contained an oath showing the date of commencement of the occupation.

Cross-Examination resumed May 27, 1867.

Witness desires to make the following corrections in his answers to his direct and cross-examination:

At that time I had not looked over my notes, and, on since examining them, find that I was in error about the date of my employment on the Boundary Survey. It was in July, 1857, and not 1856, that I joined the Commission, and, instead of leaving the Sound in 1858, I did not start for the mountains until the summer of 1859.

In answer to Interrogatory 14, I find that it was in the fall, not in the spring, of 1856 that I was employed on the Astoria road, and in the winter of 1856–7 that I was at Fort Townshend.

In my answer to Cross-Interrogatory 15, I made a miscorrection of a previous answer, which was in itself correct, in regard to the same date of the boundary survey.

Int. 28.—What do you mean by final proof, and what, in substance, did you prove before the officers of the Land Office?

Ans.—Such proof of residence and occupation as is required by the act generally known as the Donation Act, in order to enable me to obtain a title for the land.

Int. 29.—Were your notifications and the final proof received by the Register and Receiver at the Land Office of the United States and placed on file without objection?

Ans.—The notification was received without objection, and put on file. With regard to the final proof, it was forwarded from here to my agent at Olympia, and as I have never heard of any objection, I presume it was received without any.

Int. 30.—Were not these officers aware of the fact that the donation claim, notified upon and proved up by you, was upon the land of the Puget's Sound Agricultural Company?

Ans.—I think it is probable they knew it was upon the land *claimed* by the Puget's Sound Agricultural Company; but, as that claim had never been acknowledged by the United States, and was not generally admitted to be a just or equitable one by its officers in Washington Territory, or the citizens there, to any further extent than its farms and enclosures, I presume they had no option in the matter.

Int. 31.—Have you not requested the gentleman taking down this deposition to underscore the word claimed, in your answer, for the purpose of having it italicised when that answer shall be printed?

Ans.—Yes; for the purpose of distinguishing between property and the claim to property.

Int. 32.—Do you think, as a witness in this cause, it is necessary for you to settle by your testimony the legal rights of one of the parties to this proceeding?

Ans.—When a question is put in such a form that its answer, without explanation, would involve an admission, I think it right to make one.

Int. 33.—Did the register and receiver of the Land Office

issue to you, or to your agent, a certificate of your right to the donation claim as to which you testify?

Ans.—I never received one. Whether my agent did, I do not know.

Int. 34.—Was not this claim taken within the boundaries of the lands called and known to you to be the lands of the Puget's Sound Agricultural Company?

Ans.—It was within the boundaries of the land which it pretended to claim.

Int. 35.—Was not this fact known to you at the time you took this claim?

Ans.—Perfectly.

Int. 36.—Were you not notified verbally that you were a trespasser on the lands of the Company?

Ans.—Yes; Dr. Tolmie told me one day, soon after I went there, in a good-humored sort of way, that I was squatting on his ground.

Int. 37.—Did you not see a published notification notifying all persons against taking up claims there, or trespassing on the lands of the Company?

Ans.—I don't remember seeing such printed notification.

Int. 38.—Locate by a cross, if you can, upon this map now shown to you, and which is in evidence, the situation of the land which you took up and sold.

Ans.—I have made a cross on map B, marked by me "G. G." in the corner, on the Winter Stream, so called, running into Steilacoom river, which I believe was the place.

Int. 39.—Did you not take Dr. Tolmie's statement to be a positive and certain notification to you that you were a trespasser on the Company's lands?

Ans.—I presume that Dr. Tolmie wished to save whatever rights he might have by such a notification.

Int. 40.—Do you not think that your acquaintance with the officers of the garrison, and your known connection with Government employ in the Territory, induced many, relying on your action, to take donation claims on the lands of the Company?

Ans.—I don't suppose that my action had any influence on anybody else; if it did, I did not know it.

Int. 41.—Were not your opinions with reference to the rights of the Company to these lands strong and decided, and did you not express them freely to all persons with whom you conversed on this subject?

Ans.—My opinions certainly were decided, and I had no hesitation in expressing them; but I never put them forward with a view to attracting settlers there.

Int. 42.—Was not your opinion often asked by settlers upon these lands and others thinking of settling, in reference to the rights of the Company in the premises?

Ans.—I really don't remember.

Int. 43.—How long after the spring of 1854 did you occupy the house built by you on your claim?

Ans.—Off and on during the winter of 1854 and 1855, and at times during the summer of 1855. I kept my furniture, books, &c., there for certainly a year longer, excepting some articles which I removed into the post when I was employed there. I, however, continued to visit the place, and put improvements on it, until I went on the Boundary Survey, and even occasionally after that.

Int. 44.—Who supplied you during the winter of 1854–'5 and the summer of 1855, with the beef used by you?

Ans.—I got it partly from Dr. Tolmie and partly from the commissary at the garrison.

Int. 45.—Was there never any beef brought to you at your house for sale by any person?

Ans.—None to my knowledge besides what Dr. Tolmie's men drove there to be killed on the post.

Int. 46.—Do you feel certain that you never purchased beef except from those you have mentioned, and that you never had any offered you for sale during the years mentioned by any person?

Ans.—I have no recollection on the subject other than what I have already stated.

Int. 47.—Do you know of any killing of cattle occurring near you while you lived on your own place?

Ans.—I don't remember of any cattle being killed in my neighborhood, and I never saw any cattle killed but what were killed by the Company's servants.

Int. 48.—State anything that has been told you by others concerning their killing the Company's cattle.

Ans.—I have no recollection of anybody having told me that they had killed the Company's cattle, and I don't think it likely that any one who had surreptitiously killed cattle would have selected me as the proper confidant on the subject. I recollect Dr. Tolmie writing me some time during the Indian war that the remains of the Company's cattle were in the woods back of the plains. As those woods were at that time haunted by Indians, I have no doubt that a large part of the losses of the Company in cattle was due to them. In fact, the Indians would have had no hesitation at any time, whether a war had existed or not, in killing cattle whenever they could do so with impunity. As the cattle naturally take to the woods in the heated weather, or when there is snow on the ground, opportunities were not wanting.

Int. 49.—Do we now understand you as giving it as your unbiassed opinion that the greater part of the loss of the company's cattle was caused by Indians?

Ans.—I do not say that the greater part of the loss was caused by Indians, but I do believe that a very considerable part was. That some of the settlers, including the discharged servants of the company, and even persons in their employ.ment, killed cattle I do not doubt. I think that another portion of loss was due to the wolves and cougars, with which the bottom lands of the rivers were infested, but that the major part of the cattle were lost at all I do not believe.

Int. 50.—Did any of the Indians ever confess to you that they killed the company's cattle?

Ans.—I never inquired of them.

Int. 51.—Is this opinion which you have so confidently expressed, an opinion which was formed by you at the time of your residence on the Nisqually Plains?

Ans.—Certainly it is.

Int. 52.—Is it not affected, and does it not depend upon the testimony already given in this case, and now in print, proofs of which you have, as secretary, read over and corrected?

Ans.—As one of the clerks it has been my duty to read over and correct the proofs of the testimony put in both by the claimants and the defence. I am not aware that my opinion has been altered by either.

Int. 53.—As you never saw any cattle killed, and never were told by any person, white or Indian, that they had killed any, do you think that your means of knowledge are sufficient to enable you to give a correct opinion upon this matter without the aid of reports not under oath or the sworn testimony in the case?

Ans.—My opinion was made up originally from common and universal report and belief in the country.

Int. 54.—Did the company ever refuse to sell you any sheep?

Ans.—I never wanted to buy any on the hoof, but I understood that that was the case.

Int. 55.—Was this understanding that you speak of anything more than a report that came to your ears?

Ans.—It was so stated by settlers living on the plains, who mentioned as a reason for their not keeping sheep that Dr. Tolmie was afraid of disputes arising as to ownership, and for that reason refused to sell.

Int. 56.—How do you know that the increase of the sheep kept by the company, beyond what they butchered, were sent away?

Ans.—That is an impression which I obtained, I cannot distinctly say now in what manner. I do not think there was any increase of the flocks on the plains during the time that I was there, and I know that large numbers were sent away. My belief is that the Company did not want to increase their stock there.

Int. 57.—Did you ever see a large number of sheep shipped to San Juan Island, or is that statement founded also on report?

Ans.—I saw the sheep themselves at San Juan Island, and was told by Mr. Griffin, the Hudson's Bay Company's agent in charge, that he had brought them down there about the date specified in my former answer.

Int. 58.—Did you see any bands of sheep shipped to Vancouver Island?

Ans.—I have seen them shipped on board the Hudson's Bay Company's steamer Otter, which I understood to be bound to the Hudson's Bay Company's post at Victoria.

Int. 59.—What year was this; what time of the year? Where was the Otter lying at the time? How were the sheep put on board? How many did you actually see taken on board yourself, and from whom did you understand that they were being taken to Vancouver's Island?

Ans.—In answer to these questions, having no interest in the matter at the time, I never charged my memory with these details. The Otter frequently plied between Victoria, Steilacoom, and Nisqually, and other ports of the Sound, and often carried cattle and sheep.

Int. 60.—How many times will you say that you saw sheep on board the Otter while at anchor, or at the wharf on Puget's Sound?

Ans.—For the reason above stated, I am unable to say how often. That I have seen her with sheep on board I am very confident.

Int. 61.—Do you, of your own personal knowledge, know of any sheep being shipped to California?

Ans.—With regard to sending sheep to California, I cannot say positively whether I know it from personal observation or report, but I believe there is no doubt but that they were so sent.

Int. 62.—Do you know anything more of the shipping of cattle to Victoria than that which you have already stated with reference to sheep?

Ans.—I have frequently seen cattle and beef in quantities

on steamers bound for Victoria, both the Otter and, I think, the Constitution. The latter also brought beef to the Boundary Commission at Camp Simiahmoo.

Int. 63.—How do you know that these cattle, thus shipped on the Otter and the Constitution, were the cattle of the Company, which they were removing, and were not the cattle of the settlers, or cattle brought from Oregon for the purposes of shipment?

Ans.—Just as I know that the beef I ate at Steilacoom was the beef of the Company, by common repute. I know, too, that the officers of the Hudson's Bay Company stocked their farms on Vancouver's Island with cattle brought from the plains.

Int. 64.—Is not this last statement made by you, with reference to stocking farms on Vancouver's Island, also from hearsay and report?

Ans.—Yes; but I think the report came from the officers of the Company themselves, in conversation on the subject of farming on the Islands. In addition to the answer to the previous question, I believe that Dr. Tolmie himself latterly purchased cattle from Oregon, or elsewhere, for sale.

Int. 65.—Is not this last statement made by you, in answer to previous questions, also founded on hearsay and report?

Ans.—Undoubtedly; almost everything one knows is from hearsay.

Int. 66'—Have you not stated that you have studied law? and, as a lawyer, do you not know that your evidence should be founded on personal knowledge, and not from hearsay or report?

Ans.—In a wide scope of inquiry like this, embracing events that occurred during a number of years, and embracing a great variety of subjects, it is not always possible to distinguish those things actually and personally seen from those we have heard at the time, and, being either undisputed or satisfactorily proved, have impressed themselves on one's mind as facts.

Int. 67.—You have spoken in reference to the shipment of cattle in answer to Interrogatory 25, and you have also spoken in reference to the value of those cattle in answer to Interrogatory 26, and you have also spoken of the shipments of cattle in answer to Cross-Interrogatory 62. In all these answers to these interrogatories, have you or have you not had reference to the cattle mentioned in Interrogatory 25?

Ans.—I don't know that they were the same individual cattle, nor do I know whether all the cattle shipped to Victoria and elsewhere were Spanish cattle, or whether parts of them were not American cattle. Those that were sent down there for stock, I presume, were American cattle or mixed.

Int. 68.—At what year did the Constitution begin to run between Puget's Sound and Vancouver Island?

Ans.—I do not remember. I think that Hunt and Scranton had the Constitution or some other vessel on the Sound in 1856.

Int. 69.—Was the beef brought to the Boundary Commission, at Camp Simiahmoo, from the cattle of the Company on the Nisqually Plains?

Ans.—I think so, but I am not positive on that point. The Company furnished the principal supplies of beef to the Sound.

Int. 70.—Was not this camp at Simiahmoo in the winter of 1858-9?

Ans.—The camp was established in the winter of 1857, and was maintained, I think, until some time in 1860.

Int. 71.—Is not all you know about the shipments of cattle on the Constitution derived from the fact that you saw cattle delivered from the Constitution at the camp at Simiahmoo?

Ans.—No. I don't think we ever had cattle delivered on the hoof at Simiahmoo while I was there. I have seen beef driven on board a steamer—I think the Constitution—once certainly at Steilacoom wharf, and I am very positive that they were for Vancouver Island, and belonged to the Company.

Int. 72.—How do you know that they belonged to the Company?

Ans.—I am almost equally positive that I saw the Company's servants with them.

Int. 73.—Of what breed were these cattle?

Ans.—I don't recollect.

Int. 74.—Are you not farmer enough to see and note the difference between what you farmers call American cattle, and those which you have spoken of in your deposition as "wild cattle?"

Ans.—Yes, I am farmer enough to distinguish between the two, but I have not charged my memory with the character of a band of cattle that I saw a number of years ago, and which I never expected to drive, to own, or to eat.

Int. 75.—State, as near as you can, the year in which this shipment took place.

Ans.—Among frequent shipments of cattle from the plains; I cannot remember when this took place.

Int. 76.—State as distinctly as you can, any other time that you can recollect when you saw cattle shipped upon the steamer you have spoken of from the wharf at Steilacoom.

Ans.—That is the only occasion I can remember with distinctness.

Int. 77.—State any time when you can distinctly recollect you saw cattle shipped on any other steamer from the wharf at Steilacoom.

Ans.—As I have said before, I do not distinctly recollect any particular occasions, but I know that I have seen cattle on steamers at various times, either at the wharf or on the Sound, and that I supposed they were the Company's cattle.

Int. 78.—Can you distinctly state that you ever saw any cattle on board the steamer Otter at the landing at Nisqually?

Ans.—I think I have; I am not positive, however, on the subject.

Int. 79.—How many neighbors did you have, near your place, who took up claims?

Ans.—I do not remember; I recollect counting fourteen or fifteen claims of from one-half to an entire section, extending up the two forks of Steilacoom creek towards Montgomery's, but I can't give the entire number of claims taken on that part of the plains.

Int. 80.—Was Murty Fahy a neighbor of yours; if so, how far was he from you?

Ans.—He joined me on the east.

23 P

Int. 81.—Was W. Dougherty a neighbor?

Ans.—No, I think he lived to the north-eastward.

Int. 82.—Were Theophilus Seal and A. J. Knecht neighbors; and if so, how far from you?

Ans.—Knecht I do not remember; Theophilus Seal lived, I think, a mile or two from my house, to the southward; he was killed in the beginning of the Indian war.

Int. 83.—Were J. M. Savage, A. Bird, John Rigny, Mr. Leckey, and Thomas Dean, neighbors of yours; and, if so, at what distance did they live from you?

Ans.—I remember Savage's name. I think his farm was further up the creek. The brothers Bird had a mill some three miles from me, on Steilacoom creek. Rigny's claim was, I think, over towards the Puyallup. I don't remember where Leckey's claim was. Dean was the principal Puget's Sound Company's shepherd, and lived southwardly about three miles from me.

Int. 84.—Did not these people whose names have been mentioned build houses, and put up fences, and cultivate the land on which they resided?

Ans.—To a greater or less extent they did. Dean occupied and cultivated a farm that belonged to the Company, and on the Company's account.

Int. 85.—What did the land which they thus enclosed produce?

Ans.—Small portions of it produced wheat, oats, potatoes, and other vegetables. The rest was almost entirely left open for grazing, or enclosed for that purpose.

Int. 86.—Did you see any sorrel inside of these inclosures?

Ans.—There was plenty of it inside of mine, and in fact everywhere where the sheep ranged. They carried it with them.

Int. 87.—In your fields, did the sorrel spring up before the ground was broken, or afterwards?

Ans.—The sorrel was there before I came. After putting up the fences the sheep were of course stopped.

Int. 88.—Does not the sorrel only grow in the ground which has been ploughed?

Ans.—No, sir. It is almost the only thing that will grow

hausted by ploughing that nothing but sorrel would grow on it.

Ans.—Very little else would grow on the farm where Fort Steilacoom was built; very little else around Fort Nisqually; and in various other places, called the American plain, between Nisqually and Fort Steilacoom, that had been used and afterwards abandoned.

Int. 91.—Can you say how many years these lands, which you say had been used and abandoned, had been cultivated and cropped before they were abandoned?

Ans.—No; because they were abandoned before I went there.

Int. 92.—Have you any knowledge other than mere report that sheep disseminated this sorrel, which you say grew on abandoned lands?

Ans.—It is universally admitted that sheep do distribute this seed; and Dr. Tolmie admitted to me that the Company were responsible for its introduction.

Int. 93.—Is it from that universal admission, or from your own personal experience, that you make the statement that the sheep have disseminated sorrel almost everywhere they have ranged?

Ans.—I have noticed that where sheep have been corralled, and the grass was most eaten out, that there was most sorrel.

Int. 94.—How can you tell where sheep have been corralled, and where they have not?

Ans.—By bare spots on the ground, and the remains of fences where they had been corralled, and from the information of persons who knew.

Int. 95.—Are you not farmer enough to know that sheep are corralled, as you call it, on poor land for the purpose of enriching it?

Ans.—Yes, I know that perfectly well; and yet, at the same time, if sheep have been eating sorrel they will drop the seed with their manure.

Int. 96.—Have you not seen at Olympia tomatoes, melons, squashes, and pumpkins raised upon the Sound?

Ans.—Yes, but not that I recollect raised on the plains, except pumpkins, which I have once seen there raised by Mr. Lane. Tomatoes might grow in sheltered spots, but I don't think that they ripen well; they are subject to be destroyed by late and early frosts.

Int. 97.—Do you know of any vegetable that will grow near Olympia that will not grow on the place you have called the Post Garden on the Nisqually Plains?

Ans.—In the first place I don't know that all the vegetables I saw at Olympia were grown there. In the second place, plants will grow in the sheltered yards of a town that will not grow in the open fields. The vegetables grown at the Post Garden were, I think, chiefly roots.

Int. 98.—Has not Mr. Keach an orchard of fruit-bearing apple trees within the boundaries of the Company's land, as shown by the map?

Ans.—I don't know.

Int. 99.—Are there not fruit-bearing apple trees near the Company's post at Nisqually?

Ans.—None that I know of.

Int. 100.—Did you personally attend to the care and cultivation of the orchard which you planted at your farm?

Ans.—Yes; I superintended the setting out of the trees personally, and in the subsequent year the pruning.

Int. 101.—Was this an experiment of your's to ascertain whether the apple tree would grow on the plains?

Ans.—The matter was at that time altogether an experiment. One of Mr. Llewellen's people had come over from the Willamette to set up a nursery there, and I purchased the trees from him and had them set out. I think there were very few, if any, fruit trees in bearing on the plains previously.

Int. 102.—Was not this man you mentioned engaged in the same business at the time you left the Sound?

country?

Ans.—I think a German had taken a claim on Wyatchew Lake.

Int. 104.—Were you not actuated in taking this donation claim as much by the pleasantness of the situation, the oak trees affording shade, the small stream running through the land, its proximity to your friends at the garrison, as to the quality of the soil and its agricultural advantages?

Ans.—I took that claim from a variety of motives. In the first place my motive for taking a claim on the plains at all was to be out of the woods, and not necessitated to make a clearing. Again, as giving room to move about in any direction and at all seasons of the year. The proximity to the garrison was also an inducement, not only on account of the society there, but because my employment in great part depended upon the military. The special inducement I had in taking that place was that after riding round and examining the neighborhood I could find no better one. I certainly thought that this would have proved more productive than it did.

Int. 105.—Did you not take this place, among other reasons, for the purpose of speculation, believing that in a few years that you could sell it for a price much more than it cost you?

Ans.—Yes; and got bit in the expectation.

Int. 106.—Do you not know that many American settlers on the plains came over the mountains in the fall of 1853 and took claims?

Ans.—There were some; I do not think there were many. Mr. Lane was one of them. He took a claim on, I think, Spootsilth Lake, but after building a house, and residing there one year, abandoned it, and went to the forks of the Puyallup river, outside of any land claimed by the Company.

Int. 107.—Did not more American settlers come over in the fall of 1853 than at any other time?

Ans.—I can't say; I was, during that fall, east of the

mountains, and did not reach Olympia until, I think, January 1st. What settlers came over had by that time dispersed. The road across the mountains was open only one year after 1853. A party, I think, under Colonel Allen, who had worked it the year previous, completed it so far as the means would allow, but it soon afterwards washed out and became impassable. Only a few emigrants arrived in the fall of 1854 by that route.

Int. 108.—Did not the land enclosed within your fences produce a better crop of grass than that outside the fences?

Ans.—Of course; because it was not so eaten down.

Int. 109.—Is not your personal and practical knowledge and experience of farming upon the Nisqually Plains, and of their agricultural and pastoral capacity, confined to the period which you spent on your place?

Ans.—No; whenever I was up at Steilacoom I used to ride out on the plains to see how things got on, and talk with my acquaintances.

Int. 110.—Does the talk with your acquaintances form any part of that knowledge of the agricultural and pastoral capacities of the plains which you have detailed in this examination?

Ans.—Their experience, added to what I saw myself, I presume did considerably; it at least confirmed my former views.

Int. 111.—Before you left the Sound, had any portions of the lands been enclosed for grazing purposes?

Ans.—Yes; for grazing purposes, and further to secure the donation claims of individuals.

Int. 112.—Have you not reduced to writing the statement of witnesses about to be examined in behalf of the United States in this case, and have you not given those notes to counsel of the United States?

Ans.—Yes, sir; on several occasions I have done so. There being a great many different points involved in the case, and neither of the examining counsel having been personally acquainted with the witnesses or the subjects within their knowledge, I have usually informed counsel of what points to examine upon. When the witness was present or speedily to be examined, I have usually done so verbally, or by a short memorandum in writing. In a few cases, where some time might elapse before examination, or I did not expect to be present, I have given fuller minutes to counsel.

Int. 113.—Have you not furnished counsel for the United States questions and also matters of inquiry to be propounded to witnesses that have been produced on behalf of the claimant in this case?

Ans.—Yes; as there were a great many matters within my knowledge which could not be within the knowledge of counsel.

Int. 114.—Have you not corresponded with persons residing on this side of the continent, as well as with others residing in Washington and Oregon Territories, with a view to elicit from them evidence or information by which the cause of the claimant might be weakened or defeated.

Ans.—Frequently, so far as I considered the justice or the rights of the United States dictated.

Int. 115.—Do you consider this part of your duties, as clerk of this Commission, paid by the United States, or is it the action of your own personal feeling in this matter?

Ans.—I do not consider it as at all incompatible with my duties as one of the clerks of the Commission; I have acted in the matter as I think a citizen of the United States possessing information valuable to the Government, and requested to furnish it by the counsel for the Government, should do, for the purpose of preventing imposition upon the United States. I neither consider it part of my duty, nor incompatible with my duty, officially.

Cross-Examination resumed, May 30, 1867.

Int. 116.—Have you not, without the request of counsel beforehand, made search for and found witnesses on behalf of the United States in this case, learned what they would testify to, and then informed the counsel of the names of the witnesses and the substance of their evidence?

Ans.—Yes.

Int. 117.—Have you not been diligent in this matter, and attended to it with zeal?

Ans.—Yes, sir.

Int. 118.—Is not this action of yours the product of a strong personal feeling on your part?

Ans.—I wish to state distinctly that I have no personal unkind feeling towards any officer or employé of the Hudson's Bay or Puget's Sound Agricultural Company, but, on the contrary, my relations with them have always been of the most agreeable kind; that I have received from many of them the most open hospitality and friendly assistance in the pursuit of my studies; that the only feeling with which I have been actuated in this case has been a strong conviction of the injustice and exorbitancy of these claims.

Int. 119.—Have you not often, and before the commencement of this proceeding, and while you resided upon Puget's Sound, openly expressed your opinion against any rights of the Puget's Sound Company to any land upon the Nisqually Plains?

Ans.—In regard to the claims of the Puget's Sound Agricultural Company, as set forth in their memorial, that is, the pretended claim to the whole of the open country between the Nisqually and the Puyallup rivers, Puget's Sound and the mountains, I have often and openly expressed my opinion as against their right, when the subject has arisen in conversation, or my opinion has been asked by those interested. I have always looked upon the Puget's Sound Agricultural Company as an illegitimate child of the Hudson's Bay Company, and that the object in forming the association was to accomplish indirectly what the Hudson's Bay Company could not accomplish directly. In my opinion, before the treaty of 1846, the Company had no legal existence, except as among the partners thereto. It was simply an association of squatters upon the public lands of the United States, and acknowledged to be a Company only in that treaty, whereby the right of the United States to the territories on the Pacific, north of the 49th parallel, was given up to Great Britain. As to the question whether certain farms situated within the area of this claim have not by the terms of that treaty been granted to this supposititious Company, I have had doubts, which I have expressed.

Int. 120.—Do you not believe that you have freely expressed this opinion, or opinions in substance like it, in the presence of settlers, or persons thinking of settling upon the Nisqually plains?

Ans.—I think it is more than likely that I did, but not with any view of inducing them to settle there; and, for that matter, my opinions were shared by all the officers of the Government, and every other American who looked into the question, and, any way, my opinion would have had no more influence than the opinion of any one else, not being in any way official.

Int. 121.—Do you mean to include in the term officers of the Government, both the civil and military?

Ans.—Both, so far as I ever heard them express their opinion.

Int. 122.—Did you not often hear these opinions expressed by these officers in the presence of persons who were citizens of the country or intending to become so?

Ans.—I have no recollection on the subject.

Int. 123.—Is it not your impression that these opinions were freely expressed without reference to who might be within hearing?

Ans.—Very probably. The topic was one of general interest in the country. It was one not only of great importance to the Government of the United States, but came home to every man's door. I do not think there was any motive, therefore, either in promulgating or concealing those opinions.

Int. 124.—Did you remain in employment at Fort Townshend until you joined the Boundary Commission?

Ans.—No; I think I was at Steilacoom after leaving Fort Townshend, before I went to Victoria—before joining the Commission. On this point, however, I will not be positive.

Int. 125.—Did you go into Camp Simiahmoo after joining the Commission?

Ans.—Yes.

Int. 126.—How far is Fort Townshend from Fort Steilacoom, and what is the communication?

Ans.—About eighty miles. The communication is by water.

Int. 127.—Where was the camp of Simiahmoo situated, what distance from Steilacoom, and what was the communication?

Ans.—The camp of Simiahmoo was on Simiahmoo Bay, near the forty-ninth parallel. The distance from Steilacoom was, by travelled route, about one hundred and forty-five miles. The communication was also by water.

Int. 128.—Where is Astoria situated, and how far from Steilacoom?

Ans.—Astoria is in the State of Oregon, and not far from the mouth of the Columbia river, distant from Steilacoom, by the travelled route, by way of the Cowlitz river, about one hundred and fifty miles.

GEORGE GIBBS.

WASHINGTON, *May* 30, 1867.

In the matter of the Claim of the Puget's Sound Agricultural Company against the United States.

Direct Examination of Mr. George Gibbs resumed this 17th *day day of August,* 1867.

Int. 1.—Please to state whether you desire to make any further explanation in reference to the matters of Cross-Interrogatories, Nos. 17 to 25, inclusive, on the subject of your land claim on the Nisqually Plains; and, if so, proceed to make the same.

Ans.—Yes, sir, I do. On looking over my papers I have found a rough draft of the second notification to which I have heretofore referred as giving the revised boundaries of my claim, and by that rough draft of an affidavit, signed by myself, I find that I had resided upon and cultivated that part of the public land in Washington Territory particularly described in the annexed notification to the Register and Receiver of said Territory, continuously, from the 17th day of May, 1854, to the 16th day of February, 1865, at which date the said affidavit was subscribed and sworn to before the Register of said Territory.

Int. 2.—Have you or not refreshed your memory by inspection of that original draft?

Ans.—I have.

Int. 3.—Please to state whether or not, having so refreshed your memory, you are able to state the facts from recollection in the terms in which you stated them in response to Interrogatory No. 1, above.

Ans.—I am.

Cross-Examination.

Int. 1.—At the time of your cross-examination on the 26th day of May, 1867, had you any recollection whatever of this draft of an affidavit signed by you which you have this day produced?

Ans.—I had a distinct recollection, as I stated in my deposition on that or some subsequent day, of having filed a second notification somewhat changing the boundaries of my claim in order to accommodate them with those of my neighbors. I had a vague impression at the time that it was necessary for me to renew and post-date the time of my taking that claim, and that I might therefore have done so. I find, on reference to this renewed notification, that the date of the original claim was preserved.

Int. 2.—On what day did you swear to your notification of the taking of your donation claim?

Ans.—I made one notification, accompanied by an oath, of my taking a claim in the spring of 1854, as I believe, and at or about the date expressed in the affidavit to which I have referred. When, in the subsequent spring of 1855, I altered the lines to make them conform to those of my neighbors, I made the new affidavit with simply those changes, which were immaterial, my residence and occupation of the whole claim having been just as full and complete as if the limits had been correctly described in the first place.

Int. 3.—On what day did you swear to that second or new affidavit that you have spoken of in your last answer?

Ans.—As I believe, on the 16th day of February, 1855.

Int. 4.—Are you now positive that you made this affidavit on the 16th day of February, 1855?

Ans.—I suppose so, from the fact that the draft is so dated.

Int. 5.—Have you any recollection of the officer before whom your affidavit was made, and the name of that officer?

Ans.—None, except I presume, as of course, that it was made before the proper officer.

Int. 6.—Do you know who was present at the time you took the oath?

Ans.—I do not, excepting that Charles H. Mason, Secretary of the Territory, and I think at that time Acting Governor, and Richard Arnold, a Lieutenant in the Army of the United States, now Captain and Brevet Brigadier General, were attesting witnesses to the facts that they knew me personally and knew that I had resided upon that claim and cultivated the same continuously between the date I had stated I took it and the date of that affidavit; and I presume they were present when I made the affidavit, as they probably made theirs at the same time.

Int. 7.—Do you know anything more of the date on which you swore to your second notification on your donation claim, and as to who were present at the taking of the oath, than what you have learned by the inspection of this unsworn-to notification, which I now hold, and which you have mentioned and referred to in your answer-in-chief of this day?

Ans.—No; I should not have recollected the details set forth in that paper. I recollect distinctly taking the claim and filing a notification thereof in the spring of 1854, and I also recollect correcting the lines and filing a new notification subsequently; the date of that notification I should not have remembered without reference to the memorandum draft already described, nor, but for that, should I even have remembered that Mr. Mason and Lieutenant Arnold were the attesting witness until this paper recalled the fact to my memory.

Int. 8.—As this memorandum draft is merely signed and dated, but not sworn to, do you now feel certain that affidavits corresponding to the drafts in this memorandum were actually sworn to by yourself and C. H. Mason and Richard Arnold, on the 16th day of February, 1855?

Ans.—I do.

Int. 9.—Before what officer were those affidavits made?

Ans.—I do not remember; but by refreshing my memory by inspection of the draft I presume before the Register of the Land Office.

Int. 10.—Who was Register at that time?

Ans.—I do not remember.

Int. 11.—Do you remember whether the oath was taken in the office of the Register or in that of C. H. Mason?

Ans.—No, I don't.

Int. 12.—Did the Register of the Land Office furnish the printed form or blank on which this memorandum of notification and affidavit has been drawn up?

Ans.—I don't remember.

GEORGE GIBBS.

DISTRICT OF COLUMBIA, }
  County of Washington. }

I, Nicholas Callan, a notary public in and for the county and district aforesaid, do hereby certify that the foregoing depositions, hereto attached, of George W. Lee, William B. McMurtrie, and George Gibbs, witnesses produced by and on behalf of the United States, as also the cross-examination of Edward J. Allen, a witness previously examined in chief before Samuel H. Huntington, clerk of the Court of Claims, in the matter of the Claim of the Puget's Sound Agricultural Company against the same, now pending before the British and American Joint Commission for the final adjustment thereof, were taken and reduced to writing in the said city of Wash-

ington, under my direction, by a person agreed upon by Charles
C. Beaman, jr., Esq., attorney for the United States, and Edward Lander, Esq., attorney for said Company, according to
the dates appended to the several depositions when they were
respectively signed. I further certify that to each of said witnesses, before his examination, I administered the following
oath:

"You swear that the evidence you shall give in the matter
of the Claims of the Puget's Sound Agricultural Company
against the United States of America shall be the truth, the
whole truth, and nothing but the truth: so help you God."

And that, after the same was reduced to writing, the deposition of each witness was carefully read to and then signed
by him in the presence of the counsel for claimants and defendants. I further certify that the map enclosed, and marked
"A. W. W. B.," is the one referred to in the examination of
the said W. B. McMurtrie.

In testimony whereof I have hereunto set my hand and
[SEAL.] official seal this 24th day of August, 1867.

N. CALLAN,
Notary Public.

---

*In the matter of the Claim of the Puget's Sound Agricultural
Company against the United States.*

Deposition of *George Suckley, M. D.*, of the city of New York,
duly sworn and examined in the said city, by virtue of an
agreement between Charles C. Beaman, jr., agent and
attorney for the United States of America, and Edward
Lander, agent and attorney for the Puget's Sound Agricultural Company, before me, W. H. Gardner, a notary
public of the State of New York, duly commissioned and
sworn, on the part of the United States.

TESTIMONY OF GEORGE SUCKLEY, M. D.
Witness recalled.

Int. 1.—In your answer to Interrogatory 11, in your previous cross-examination, you say "It is my belief and conviction that twelve miles square of the Puget's Sound land claimed by the Company is naturally of greater agricultural value than a tract of land of the same size in Duchess county, New York." Please explain more fully what you meant by that answer.

(The re-examination of this witness in relation to his answer to a cross-interrogatory in his former examination, which was closed more than fourteen months ago, objected to.)

Ans.—I did not mean Duchess county as it now is, in its improved state, since it has been cultivated by white people; but I meant by saying "naturally" that, in the condition of the sections, compared as they existed prior to cultivation, I would prefer the land on the said claim. My answer had no reference to increase in value caused by improvements of civilized man.

GEORGE SUCKLEY.

STATE OF NEW YORK, }
City and County of New York. }

I, W. H. Gardner, a notary in and for the State of New York, duly commissioned and sworn, do hereby certify that the foregoing deposition of George Suckley was taken and reduced to writing by me, in the presence of said witness, from his statements, on this twenty-third day of July, 1867, at No. 103 St. Mark's Place, in the city of New York, in pursuance of a verbal agreement made between Chas. C. Beaman, jr., Esq., as counsel for the United States, and Edward Lander, Esq., counsel for the Puget's Sound Agricultural Company. I further certify that, to said witness, before his examination, I administered the following oath:

"You do swear, in the presence of the ever-living God, that the answers to be given by you to the interrogatories and cross-interrogatories to be propounded to you by me in the matter of the Claim of the Puget's Sound Agricultural Company against the United States, shall be the truth, the whole truth, and nothing but the truth."

I further certify that the said deposition was by me carefully read to said witness and then signed by him in my presence.

In testimony whereof I have hereunto set my hand
[SEAL.]   and affixed my official seal this twenty-third day of
July, in the year, 1867.

W. H. GARDNER,
Notary Public.